CONTROVERSY
AND
COALITION:

The New
Feminist
Movement

SOCIAL MOVEMENTS PAST & PRESENT

Irwin T. Sanders,
Editor

CONTROVERSY
AND
COALITION:

The New
Feminist
Movement

Myra Marx Ferree

Beth B. Hess

Twayne Publishers • Boston

Controversy and Coalition:
The New Feminist Movement

Myra Marx Ferree
Beth B. Hess

Copyright © 1985 by G. K. Hall & Company

All Rights Reserved
Published by Twayne Publishers
A Division of G. K. Hall & Company
A publishing subsidiary of ITT
70 Lincoln Street, Boston, Massachusetts 02111

Printed on permanent/durable
acid-free paper and bound in
the United States of America

First Printing

This book was designed by
Marne B. Sultz and typeset in
Century Oldstyle by Compset, Inc.

**Library of Congress Cataloging in
Publication Data**

Ferree, Myra Marx.
Controversy and coalition.

Bibliography: p. 201
Includes index.
1. Feminism — United States. I. Hess, Beth B.,
1928– . II. Sanders, Irwin, Taylor, 1909–
III. Title.
HQ1426.F475 1985 305.4′2′0973 84-22421
ISBN 0-8057-9707-6
ISBN 0-8057-9713-0 (pbk.)

CONTENTS

ABOUT THE AUTHORS

Myra Marx Ferree, associate professor of sociology at the University of Connecticut, has been interested in the New Feminist Movement since she was an undergraduate and read Millet's *Sexual Politics*. Her Ph.D. dissertation (Harvard, 1976) was on working-class women's perceptions of and reaction to feminism. Some of the results of that study were published as articles in *Psychology Today, Social Problems, Sex Roles,* and the *Sociological Quarterly*. She has also done research on housework and housewives, on sex-role attitudes among Cuban immigrant women, and on class differences in women's attitudes toward paid work and housework. Professor Ferree's current interests include research on the feminist movement in West Germany and German studies of the daily work life and orientations of working-class women, on the objective and subjective status as breadwinner of employed married women in the United States, and on women's paid employment and quality of life in India. She is chair-elect of the Section on Sex and Gender of the American Sociological Association.

Beth B. Hess is professor of sociology at County College of Morris, Randolph, New Jersey. A graduate of Radcliffe College and Rutgers University, she has published books and articles on social gerontology, the sociology of age, friendship, and older women. Professor Hess is a Fellow of the Gerontological Society of America, and is currently an officer of the Eastern Sociological Society, the Society for the Study of Social Problems, and Sociologists for Women in Society. Her most recent publications include the second edition of *Sociology* (with E. Markson and P. Stein); the third edition of *Growing Old in America* (edited with E. Markson); and *Women and the Family: Two Decades of Change* (edited with M. B. Sussman).

INTRODUCTION

Although this volume is one of a series on social movements, we have taken as our topic a much broader and deeper phenomenon: the new feminism. It is, in fact, impossible to write of the organized feminist movement without placing it in the context of many diverse strands of feeling and action. In one sense, these underlying currents are "the movement," of which organized feminism is only one highly visible element. This diversity is our central theme. Throughout the book, we shall speak of multiple feminisms: movements with a common conviction that the present social system does not recognize the value of women or act to promote women's good.

Oversimplification characterizes much of what has been written about the contemporary women's movement, both in the professional and popular press. In large part, this stems from the need to make order out of the seeming chaos of movement ideas and actions. In part, also, there has been a real failure to appreciate either the value of diversity or the capacity of movement organizations to absorb conflict. And, lastly, there is always the tendency of observers to impose their meaning on events rather than to attempt to understand from the point of view of diverse participants.

Although we have been participants as well as observers over the past decade and a half, we also cannot claim to have captured all facets of the new feminism, or even to have interpreted correctly those aspects described in this book. But our own backgrounds and experiences with feminism are very different, and in coming to appreciate each other's perspective, we feel that we have come to understand the diversity of feminism in new ways. Our goal is to present each form of contemporary feminism in its own terms and in relation to the whole in a way that incorporates both an insider's and outsider's perspective.

We are also attempting a fresh look at the status of American women and of feminist thought, actions, and organizations in the more than sixty years after the passage of the suffrage amendment. In this we benefit from two decades of feminist scholarship, itself an outgrowth of the trends we describe. Many long-accepted assumptions can be shown to rest on superficial impressions repeated so often that they become a kind of "truth." A revisionist view of the new feminism does not require a wholesale disregard of previous research; rather, we shall highlight previously overlooked aspects of women's experience in society and in the movement, and integrate these into the more conventional scenario.

One crucial point, all too often overlooked, is that feminism has a long and diverse history. In dealing with the New Feminist Movement, that is, with American feminism after suffrage, and the organizational forms it has taken in recent years, we are tackling a broad subject, but one that is only part of an even larger historical phenomenon. Eleanor Flexner's classic study, *Century of Struggle* (1959), provides an introduction to the first and second waves of feminist thought and action that preceded the current movement. It is important to remember, as we consider the goals and struggles of the third wave of American feminists, that women were not simply *given* an education or the right to vote, but that earlier feminists struggled, at great personal cost, against political repression and social ridicule, to gain each victory. The conditions that so many women take for granted today were the hard-won fruits of decades of sacrifice and activism. Nor were the earlier feminists able to gain all they sought; many of their goals remain issues for the new feminists: reproductive freedom, genuine equality in male-female relationships, changes in the occupational structure and the workplace, and socially recognized personhood. These are not new goals. By looking at the New Feminist Movement, we are concentrating at relatively new attempts to articulate and achieve some comparatively old goals.

Several stylistic devices deserve comment. As feminists, we are generally more comfortable using the pronoun "we" to refer both to feminists and to women as a group. This usage, however, led to continued awkwardness in the text. Making we-they distinctions among different types of feminists and different subgroups of women seemed antithetical to our goal of presenting the ideas and actions of each group in their own terms, yet we could not honestly claim membership in all of these groups. We reluctantly decided that it would be wisest to use "they" consistently, reserving "we" for reference to ourselves as authors.

Secondly, to distinguish the two threads of our topic we use the word *feminism* to refer to changes in consciousness and *movement* to denote organizational activity. Clearly, there are many women and men who share a new perception of gender-based oppression and opportunity, but who have not taken part in organized efforts for change because they have not had the time or occasion to do so. There are probably also some movement members whose participation in a specific movement organization is based on immediate self-interest more than on their consciousness and commitment to the feminist cause. And then there are those many individuals who have benefitted from the changes wrought by the movement, yet who are quick to declare, "I'm not a feminist, but . . . ," disavowing any relationship to the organized movement, but identifying to a greater or lesser extent with its goals. In some way, all these persons are part of our story—as are those who have fueled a powerful countermovement backlash. For there can be no doubt that the New Feminist Movement represents the most broad-based critique of traditional social arrangements, from the interpersonal to the institutional, of any contemporary social movement. This challenge has been developing over the past two hundred years in the United States and Western Europe, and has now spread throughout the world (Mies and Jayawardena, 1981; Carr, 1984). Already, there have been many legal and administrative changes affecting public and private life, and even if these were to be repealed tomorrow, the greater changes that have taken place within individual and social consciousness could not be so easily erased.

In sum, feminism and the movement are here to stay, in all their apparent confusion and multiplicity of forms. And this is why it is important that its recent development be described, that its ideology and goals be understood, that its tensions and triumphs be recognized, and that its many strands be evaluated as both distinct "submovements" and as necessary components of the broad coalition that composes the New Feminist Movement.

Eleanor Roosevelt, second from left, with close friends, including Marion Dickerman, the first woman to run for elective office in New York State. From the 1920s to the 1960s Eleanor Roosevelt was at the center of a network of women activists in and out of government. Fittingly, in 1960 John F. Kennedy appointed her to chair the Commission on the Status of Women, from which one part of the New Feminist Movement would emerge. *Photograph courtesy of the F.D.R. Library.*

CHAPTER ONE

Setting the Stage

Where Did All the Feminists Go?

This is the question often posed by those who examine the history of American women following the passage of the Suffrage Amendment in 1920. A powerful coalition of women's groups had been forged in the early decades of this century to press for the right to vote, yet by 1924 little remained of a nationally organized women's movement. The common wisdom is that only a shared focus on the amendment held such a diverse collection of groups together, so that once suffrage was gained, few other issues or interests linked women across regional, class, age, and cultural divisions. Leaders of the suffrage movement never generated a broadly feminist consciousness among its various constituents, and failed to attack the roots of women's inferior status in all areas of social life, particularly in the family. For whatever reasons—sheer diversity or lack of ideological depth, or a naive belief that the crucial battle had been won—an organized movement for women's equality ceased to be a visible political or cultural force throughout the next four decades.

Yet we must distinguish its organizational form from the deeper impulses that constitute a "social movement." As defined by McCarthy and Zald (1977), "social movements" consist of opinions and beliefs in favor of changing the structure of a society and its system of allocating scarce rewards. "Social movement organizations" are the formal structures designed to achieve the goals of the movement. In this sense, feminists and feminism did not fade away even in the 1920s. Rather, many individual women pursued

1

feminist goals in nonorganizational activities and nonfeminist organizations. During these decades (1920–60), major demographic and social trends led to the emergence of a new feminist consciousness rooted in the everyday experiences of American women. Thus, suffrage was only the culmination of one phase in the history of twentieth-century feminism, a corner that was turned—an ending, but also the beginning of a new period of feminist development.

Employment Trends

Labor force participation. One of the most significant and startling trends of the past forty years is the increased participation of women in work outside the home. In 1920, women composed 20 percent of the civilian labor force, compared to almost 45 percent today. Similarly, about one fourth of all women were in the labor force in 1920, a figure that had also doubled by 1980. While the sheer magnitude of this increase is impressive, changes in composition of the female work force may be even more significant. In the 1920s, 77 percent of women workers were young and single, mostly from immigrant and poor families, although many young middle-class women were also entering the labor force. Typically, these women left work when they married. Black women, however, were an exception; in 1920, 43 percent of black females age sixteen and over were employed, whether married or not, most often as domestic servants, replacing live-in white immigrant "girls" in middle- and upper-class homes (Katzman 1978). Unmarried young white women, in turn, flocked to jobs in the newly expanding worlds of office work and retail sales, in which they saw an opportunity to gain an independence and status their mothers had never known.

In contrast, among women in the labor force today, 60 percent are married, 15 percent are widowed and divorced, and only 25 percent are single. Moreover, over 48 percent of mothers with children under the age of five are in the labor force, as are over 41 percent of women with infants under a year old (Bureau of the Census, 1983e). Indeed, the most rapid increase in labor force participation today is among women of childbearing years, unlike the pattern of the period 1940–60 when the increase was largely due to the reentry of women who had left work for child raising and only returned in middle age for "second careers" (Blau 1979). Between 1960 and 1980, however, the expansion of the female labor force involved women under age forty-five. This pattern can be characterized as "limited departure" rather than "reentry," as mothers interrupted employment for increasingly shorter periods of child raising, or simply shifted to part-time work. Despite such changes, the great majority of women's jobs are still in the office and retail sectors.

Nonetheless, a female labor force composed of married women, many of whom are middle-aged and middle class, is something very different from one populated by young nonmarried women. In proposing a "sociotechnological theory of the Women's Movement," Huber (1977) claims that "only after married women entered the labor force on a long-term basis did the Woman's Movement develop into a force that could not be reversed" (371). If prestige and power come from control of the exchange of goods outside the household, Huber suggests that married women can use these resources more effectively than the nonmarried "working girls" of half a century ago.

It would be an oversimplification, however, to think of women's labor force participation as a consistent long-term (secular) trend. During the Great Depression (1928–39), for example, married women in white-collar jobs were thought to take jobs from married men; thus, for example, the many rules against hiring married women as schoolteachers. Yet, most of the jobs held by women, even white-collar ones, did not appeal to men, and employers were content to pay the lower wages that women tolerated (Milkman 1979). Scharf (1980) notes that while women did not withdraw from the labor force in large numbers during the Depression, they were limited in the type of employment available, and tended to lower their aspirations accordingly. The only acceptable reason for their working was economic necessity, leading to a denial of individualistic goals or need for personal fulfillment (thus also reducing the possibility of a feminist consciousness emerging from the workplace). The Depression years can best be interpreted as a period of retrenchment—in terms of promotions, aspirations, and moving into male-dominated occupations—rather than of withdrawal from the workplace.

The Great Depression ended with American involvement in World War II and the subsequent absence of young male workers. At the same time, the demand for labor in defense industries rose dramatically, and women were encouraged to do their "patriotic duty" by temporarily replacing "their men" on the production line (Rupp 1979). As a result, married women's participation rates increased by almost 50 percent between 1940 and 1944, with most new entrants being older (35 +) married women. As seen in Table 1.1, married women's share of the female labor force rose from 36.4 percent in 1940 to 45.7 percent in 1944, while that of single women declined.

Employers and unions considered this situation a temporary wartime necessity; the concept that there was "men's work" and "women's work" remained intact, regardless of how often contradicted in actual experience

Table 1.1.
Marital Status of Women in the Civilian Labor Force: 1940–81

Year	Total (1,000)	Percent Distribution, Female Labor Force			Female Labor Force as Percent of Female Population				
		Single	Married	Widowed or divorced	Total	Single	Married, total	Married, husband present	Widowed or divorced
1940	13,840	48.5	36.4	15.1	27.4	48.1	16.7	14.7	32.0
1944	18,449	40.9	45.7	13.4	35.0	58.6	25.6	21.7	35.7
1947	16,323	37.9	46.2	15.9	29.8	51.2	21.4	20.0	34.6
1950	17,795	31.6	52.1	16.3	31.4	50.5	24.8	23.8	36.0
1955	20,154	25.2	58.7	16.0	33.5	46.4	29.4	27.7	36.0
1960	22,516	24.0	59.9	16.1	34.8	44.1	31.7	30.5	37.1
1965	25,952	22.8	62.2	15.0	36.7	40.5	35.7	34.7	35.7
1968	28,778	22.1	63.4	14.6	40.7	51.3	39.1	38.3	35.8
1969	29,898	21.7	63.9	14.4	41.6	51.2	40.4	39.6	35.8
1970	31,233	22.3	63.4	14.3	42.6	53.0	41.4	40.8	36.2
1971	31,778	22.7	63.0	14.2	42.5	52.8	41.4	40.8	35.7
1972	33,132	22.8	62.9	14.3	43.7	55.0	42.2	41.5	37.2
1973	34,195	22.9	62.8	14.2	44.2	55.9	42.8	42.2	36.7
1974	35,708	23.4	62.2	14.4	45.3	57.4	43.8	43.1	37.8
1975	36,981	23.2	62.3	14.5	46.0	57.0	45.1	44.4	37.7
1976	38,399	24.2	61.6	14.3	46.8	59.2	45.8	45.1	37.3
1977	40,053	24.2	61.0	14.8	48.0	59.2	47.2	46.6	39.0
1978	41,747	25.1	59.8	15.1	49.2	60.7	48.1	47.5	39.9
1979	43,844	25.8	59.5	14.8	50.8	62.9	49.9	49.3	40.0
1980	44,934	25.0	59.7	15.3	51.1	61.5	50.7	50.1	41.0
1981	46,415	25.0	59.3	15.6	52.0	62.3	51.7	51.0	41.9

Source: U.S. Bureau of the Census 1983b, 383.

(Milkman 1982). At the start of the war, most women workers accepted this definition of their labor, but by war's end they had become increasingly attached to their work roles. A survey by the Women's Bureau in 1945 found that over 75 percent of women workers indicated that they would prefer to stay on rather than hand over their jobs to returning men (Chafe 1977). But without a feminist movement to support them, the women could not resist the pressure to leave the labor force, much less challenge either job segregation or the ideological underpinnings of gender distinctions in the workplace (Milkman 1982). Not all went quietly, however. Unionized women auto workers in Detroit protested militantly, but union leaders were not prepared to help women keep their jobs or to fight against the sexual division of labor (Gabin 1982).

The ideology of this period was perfectly expressed in a best-selling book, *Modern Woman: The Lost Sex* (Lundberg and Farnham 1947), which claimed that the idea of an "independent woman is a contradiction in terms" because it violates the laws of nature (Chafe 1977). Not only were there few cultural supports for working women, but many material ones were also withdrawn; for example, federally funded day care was phased out by 1946. Nonetheless, large numbers of women remained in the labor force, even as they bore and raised an unusually large cohort of offspring. Thus, by the 1960s, a generation of young women from intact middle-class homes had grown up with the experience of a working mother (Berkin 1979).

But we must not exaggerate the work experience of American women even during the war years. As Table 1.1 shows, even at the height of the war—1944—only 35 percent of the female population fourteen years and older was employed. This proportion dips to under one in three by 1947, but increases steadily from that point on.

Nor did women forsake the workplace altogether during the 1950s for the benefits of home and hearth. To the contrary, the percentage of wife-mothers in the labor force rose steadily. This trend is hardly surprising, since the number of children born during the Great Depression and reaching adulthood in the postwar period was not sufficient to meet the labor force demands of the 1950s. There were jobs enough for men in those fields defined as "men's work," leaving the world of "women's work" open to married women who supplemented family income to meet expanding consumer needs (Ryan 1979).

Public reaction, as always, was ambivalent: on the one hand, there was the need for the kinds of paid work typically done by women; on the other, the strong belief that family care is a woman's most important responsibility (Kessler-Harris 1976; Ryan 1979). Employed wives and mothers are simultaneously accepted and condemned, a contradiction that leads many women to define their work as an extension of family obligation, and others to challenge the idea that work is of secondary significance to women.

Neither disapproval nor lack of opportunity for advancement stemmed the flow of women into the labor force, as jobs opened up in offices, stores, educational institutions, and health care facilities. The expansion of women's education reinforced this trend. The mainstays of white female employment before the 1920s (and of black female employment until the 1960s)—factory, domestic, and farm work—have largely been replaced by occupations that require formal education but still pay poorly.

Women in higher education.   For the past one hundred years, the proportions of boys and girls enrolled in elementary and secondary schools has been roughly similar. In higher education, however, more men than women have enrolled and many more stayed through graduation. Only in 1980 did the number of women entering colleges and universities exceed that of men, suggesting that increasing numbers will also enter graduate schools. But the trend toward higher education for women has not followed a simple unilinear pattern, as shown in Table 1.2.

In 1920, twice as many men as women received bachelor's or master's degrees, and five times more earned doctorates. Of course, in 1920 undergraduate education was an elite undertaking; less than 8 percent of the "college-aged" population actually went to college, compared with over 40 percent today. A college-educated woman in 1920 was thus aware of being a member of a small privileged group. She was also more likely than noncollege women to remain unmarried and to pursue a career, one reason why parents often opposed women's education—they wanted a "normal" daughter.

By 1970, four women received bachelor's and master's degrees for every five men, but the ratio for doctorates remained fewer than one in six (U.S. Bureau of the Census 1975, 385–86). After World War II, higher education became increasingly available to the mass public, as the number and size of colleges and universities expanded to accommodate the wave of veterans offered a subsidized education by a grateful nation. The influx of veterans initially tilted enrollments in favor of men, but also "normalized" going to college. Sending a daughter to college became a logical extension of parents' aspirations to middle-class status, but going on to graduate school implied more career commitment than was proper for women. Nonetheless, many women proceeded to obtain professional degrees, although it is only in the last few years that women's share of doctorates reached even one in three (U.S. Bureau of the Census 1981, 165).

Table 1.2.
Women in Higher Education: 1900–81

Year	Women as Percentage of Undergraduates	Women with Bachelor (or First Professional Degree)	Women as Percent of Doctorates	Women as Percentage of Full-time Faculty
1900	35	19	6	20
1920	47	34	15	26
1940	40	41	13	28
1960	36	35	10	22
1970	41	41	13	25
1975	45	43	21	24
1981	50	48	31	26

Adapted from: Graham 1978, 766; U.S. Bureau of the Census 1983b, 166; and U.S. Dept. of Education, 1982, Table 98.

Perhaps because of rising educational levels, career aspirations among women did not decline between the 1920s and 1960s, as so often thought (Stricker 1979). Women's interest in medicine, law, business, and college teaching remained high, but there were many barriers to their participation, including opposition from male-dominated professional gatekeepers and the extraordinary difficulties of combining a career and family. Feminists in the postsuffrage years were unable to change the social structure that forced women to choose between children and a profession. Thus, the few middle-class women who succeeded in high status careers in the early decades of this century typically remained unmarried or without children, stranded on the shore of social change rather than at the edge of an incoming tide, and sometimes disappointed that other women failed to follow them.

Although the proportion of women physicians, attorneys, professors, and business executives remained low between 1930 and 1970, the absolute number of women entering professions actually increased throughout this period. Increasingly, also, professional women were married rather than single; when they left the labor force it was because of institutional requirements or the absence of encouragement and support (particularly from husbands), rather than in response to the irresistible appeal of family life. Many remained but were caught in positions of little mobility or prestige. Stricker (1979) concludes that "domesticity had not conquered the minds of American women, even in the 1950s. . . . What was missing through all these years was not a base of discontent or significant numbers of career women, but a feminist movement to interpret these discontents as collective phenomena, rooted in fundamentally inegalitarian social and economic struc-

tures" (490). As long as each woman thought herself an exception or suf-
fered alone, the guilt of being "unnatural," the dominant ideology—or
"feminine mystique" (Friedan 1963)—remained unchallenged.

Higher education and labor force participation were essential but not sufficient conditions for the emergence of a feminist movement. The experience of women in the workplace, earning their own money, making new
friends, and expanding their skills, but also encountering prejudice, discrimination, humiliation, harassment, and outright hostility, helped produce the
two fundamental prerequisites for a new feminist movement. On the one
hand, paid employment and unpaid volunteer work provided women with
resources—skills, friendship networks, money, professional contacts, and
experiences that would help in organizational development. Typing and run-
ning a mimeograph machine, for example, are skills that are trivialized and
underpaid in the business world, but invaluable assets to the fledgling
organizer.

On the other hand, the negative experiences of exclusion, devaluation,
and grudging acceptance in the labor force and higher education, produced
what sociologists call "marginality"—being partly in and partly out, simultaneously accepted and rejected, at the edge or margin of an institution or
society in general. Marginality produces stress but also permits creativity,
including criticism of existing arrangements. Such marginality for women
provided the opportunity to build the ideological base of the new feminism.
A sense that the taken-for-granted world is neither legitimate nor inevitable
is the psychological precondition, just as a resource base is the social precondition, for forming an organized movement for change.

The Postmaterialist Ethic

Women's experience of marginality may have also been increased by important changes in the socialization of the young. Under the influence of
child-centered psychologies in the postwar period, parents became increasingly aware, often to the point of anxiety, of the effects of their child-rearing
practices. Beginning with middle-class parents and gradually filtering down,
child rearing was marked by intense concern with the development of each
child, greater permissiveness, an emphasis on self-control and mastery, and
willingness to listen to "experts" (Bronfenbrenner 1958). While most of this
expert advice (e.g., Spock 1945) prescribed different ways of handling female and male offspring, the basic trend was toward greater equality (egalitarianism) in parent-child relationships, between parents, and among their
children. In the middle-class family, where the timing and number of off-

spring were apt to be planned, daughters were now likely to receive the same amount of parental attention as sons, and were expected to do well in school, develop self-esteem, and go to college. To be sure, achievement after graduation was to be in the area of raising a family and providing emotional support to one's husband, but socialization to self-assurance and productivity cannot be so easily limited.

By the 1960s, young women who valued and were prepared for achievement were faced with a cultural climate that questioned the importance of striving for material success. The new culture, sometimes called "postmaterialist" (Inglehart 1977; Yankelovich 1981), criticized the existing occupational morality based on the "Protestant Ethic" described by Max Weber (1904–5/1958). In this industrial ethic, virtue was demonstrated by sacrifice, gratification was deferred (sometimes into the next generation), accumulation was honored, and salvation was ensured by hard work. In the eighteenth and nineteenth centuries, the new industrial workforce had to be trained out of the rhythms of agricultural and craft production and into the highly regulated patterns of time clocks, fixed shifts, and steadily increasing production quotas. The "materialist" world view thus achieved reduced an individual's identity to an occupational role and encouraged frantic effort to earn enough to accumulate ever more material possessions.

Such an approach to life appeared to satisfy the typical workers of the boom years following World War II, working class and middle class alike, who were considerably better off materially than their parents had been. For their children, however, who could take material comforts for granted, the ideology of materialism seemed hollow. In opposition to what they perceived as the narrowness and "uptightness" of their parents' lives, they rejected accumulation and status-climbing as the primary measures of success.

If happiness could not be found in work itself or in possessions, it must lie in other aspects of life: in personal relationships, in social concerns, in political involvement—that is, in "the community," with "community" understood in the emotional sense, and communities as places where people live (rather than only work). In short, the entire nonwork world that had been seen as the "special sphere" of women was rediscovered, particularly by men, even as the world of paid employment became increasingly attractive and accessible to women. As older women, once confined to home and community, viewed careers and achievement uncritically as new opportunities, young women shared the ambivalence of young men toward materialism and individual success.

Postmaterialist values, rejecting competition in the workplace and wasteful consumption in the home, can most easily be adopted by people who already possess a secure material base: education, affluence, and leisure for reflection. The rejection of materialism also poses a fundamental challenge to another aspect of modern life, the rule of "experts" in all spheres of life. The word that emerged to express this challenge was "liberation," defined as the freedom to do "one's own thing," to develop one's abilities, and to be released from artificial restraints on expression. Once in the air, however, the concept of liberation could not be limited to the personal freedom of affluent college youth. All forms of arbitrary restraint are called into question—not only those of social class, but of race and gender as well. The political challenge facing women became not only to open the system, but to transform it.

Family Trends

Sex and marriage.   No less than the 1960s, the 1920s were a decade of profound change in sexual mores and family relationships. Victorian morality gave way to unprecedented liberties for "flaming youth": sexual freedom, the ability of unmarrieds to live away from home, less constricting clothes to symbolize this newfound casualness, and, most enticing for young middle-class women, the chance to work at a "glamor job" in an office or shop. The new morality that had been an elite life-style in the early years of the century became a mass phenomenon after World War I. In the excitement of breaking old taboos, few young women were aware of the grime behind the glitter: the dead-end nature of their jobs and their increasing vulnerability to sexual exploitation. They saw neither the need nor necessity for political organizing on behalf of women's rights since they saw themselves as already occupationally and sexually liberated.

At the same time, ideals of family life were being transformed, from an authoritarian pattern to one emphasizing companionship and romantic love. In essence, family life was made increasingly attractive to young women who ultimately became disillusioned with their newfound freedoms and jobs. As a career actually offered less than it once seemed to promise, particularly in terms of income and mobility, having a family may have seemed more attractive than before, especially since the women who came into adulthood after World War I could expect a different type of family life than that of their mothers.

Not only was mate selection freed from parental control and marital relationships made more egalitarian, but couples increasingly exercised choice over the number and spacing of their offspring. During the Great Depression, birth rates fell dramatically, without the inexpensive and effective legal contraceptive devices available today. Disillusion with this new sort of "partnership" family as it operates in reality (with women always the "junior partner") took some time to emerge, but emerge it did. By 1947, Farnham and Lundberg were blaming women for their discontent and exhorting them to try harder to be happy.

In contrast to the "sexual revolution" of the decade following World War I, particularly the freedom enjoyed by young women, the Great Depression brought a renewed emphasis on sexual control, largely in the interests of reducing family size. During World War II, sexual abstinence was one of those "sacrifices to the war effort" expected of women whose husbands were in the armed forces, although the same demands were rarely made of men. In general, then, the years between 1930 and 1945 were marked by a relatively puritanical view of sexuality. Yet the companionate ideal of marriage was also based upon a mutuality of sexual fulfillment, at least implicitly recognizing the sexual interests of women but only within marriage. The American perception of sexuality had shifted from an activity whose justification is the creation of new life to one that is pleasurable in its own right: from an emphasis on procreation to that of recreation. Gone, or going, were some of the emotional inhibitions that constrained female sexuality in the past. The 1960s would most resemble the 1920s in terms of closing the gap between male and female sexual behaviors, although a "double standard" of evaluation remains.

It is important to distinguish between sexual freedom and gender equality. In many ways, the new permissiveness toward sexual activity renders women more vulnerable to exploitation than in the past; without genuine equality in the other spheres of social life, she cannot excrcise freedom of choice in her sexual relationships. Thus, sexuality has become a major feminist issue.

Fertility.   Control over fertility is as important as labor force participation in the liberation of women. Most obviously, being freed from a constant cycle of pregnancy and breast feeding has clear health and energy benefits; having fewer offspring reduces the time required to raise a family; but, most importantly, being able to exercise choice in this most intimate area enhances a sense of power over one's own life.

With the exception of the years between 1947 and 1963, the long-term trend in our society has been toward lower birth rates (number of children per 1,000 population) and fertility (average number of children to women in the childbearing years). In part, lowered fertility reflects the high probability that each infant will survive birth and childhood, so that a woman need bear only as many offspring as desired. In the past, high rates of infant mortality meant that a woman might give birth to seven or eight children in the hope that three or four would live to adulthood. Declining birth rates are also characteristic of modern industrial societies in general; as people move off the land to towns and cities, the economic value of children changes from an asset to a financial burden.

There is also a strong link between a woman's employment expectations and her fertility behavior, although the direction of cause and effect probably runs both ways. That is, women are able to enter the labor force because they have few children, and a commitment to work reduces both the desire and need to have many children. Clearly, married women who work outside the home, especially those oriented toward careers, do have fewer offspring than the nonemployed. Variations in fertility are also associated with educational attainment: the higher the level of education, the fewer the offspring, and we have already documented the expanding educational horizons of women currently in their childbearing years. Fertility declines may also reflect the absence of strong social support for mothers.

Recent data on fertility expectations (Bureau of the Census 1984) indicate that the birth rate will remain at today's historically low levels. Most women aged eighteen to thirty-four expect to have one or two children, few anticipate large families, and almost 11 percent expect to remain childfree. These women will have completed childbearing while still relatively young, and for all but the first four to five years will share child-care responsibilities with the schools. Since the typical American mother can now look forward to a life expectancy of close to eighty years, it is clear that childbearing and child rearing will absorb only a fraction of that lifetime. These demographic realities have forced many women to think about "what to do with the rest of my life," increasing the likelihood that they will enter the labor force or assume heavier voluntary association responsibilities. Either way, they will develop a sense of self outside the traditional roles of wife-mother and encounter the mixed acceptance/rejection of marginality.

Women with few child-care obligations and those working outside the home (whether for pay or not) are "structurally available" for social movement recruitment, simply by virtue of not being isolated within the home. Nonemployed women with few offspring will also have time and energy to devote to movement activities, while those who are both employed and mothers have a doubly marginal position that enables them to take a critical stance toward both employment and motherhood as social institutions.

Housewives and housework. What of the women who heeded the call to renounce work outside the home in favor of devoting themselves to the "labor of love" within the household? The 1950s are generally perceived as an era of domestic bliss in the United States, in which the fertility rate almost doubled that of the Depression years. The newly built suburbs drew millions of middle-class families from the cities; husbands, as members of the small birth cohorts of the Depression years, experienced unprecedented opportunities for upward mobility with the dramatic expansion of white-collar jobs (Oppenheimer 1982). Wives found themselves isolated in these new communities, continually encouraged by the media to reach ever-higher levels of consumership and cleanliness. In these circumstances the majority of suburban women devoted themselves to caring for their achieving husbands and their three or four offspring.

Despite the introduction of "labor-saving" devices such as freezers, clothes washers and dryers, and dishwashing machines, there was little change in the time spent on homemaking tasks between the 1920s and 1960s—nonemployed homemakers spent an average of 51 hours a week in 1924, and 55 hours four decades later (Vanek 1974). The time once spent in food preparation is now used to shop for it; and the laundry that middle-class households once sent out is now done by wives in the home (Strasser 1982).

At the same time, many tasks once performed within the household have been given to experts outside the home: most notably, the education of children, food preparation, and a variety of social services to family members. As Ryan (1979) puts it, as this type of work left the home, so finally did the women themselves, to perform outside what they had done inside: school teaching, nursing, social work, and food preparation and handling.

During this period, also, child-care tasks expanded, not so much as a function of more children but of greater parental investment in the well-being of their offspring. Child care became a more socioemotional task, as the middle-class family attempted to transmit a general level of school-tested competence, thus emphasizing the educational role of the mother, while the working-class family attempted to defend against breakup and downward mobility, thus casting the mother in the moral role of stabilizer (Ryan 1981).

For those who steadfastly remained in the home, true happiness often proved elusive. Ultimately, as we know from events of the 1960s, a creeping sense of isolation in a daytime ghetto, of exclusion from the "real world" of power and prestige, led to vague feelings of discontent. Obliged to perform tasks once done by servants but now upgraded and mechanized, the suburban woman became a housewife in a more complete way than ever before. Many women began to perceive the restrictions of their lives, but until the emergence of the new feminism they lacked a frame of reference in which to interpret their discontent.

We must also remember that not all segments of the population shared in the prosperity of the 1950s. Many studies of working-class families and communities in the 1950s found that interests and activities remained sharply divided by sex, in contrast to the new norm of "togetherness" that characterized middle-class family life. But as primary consumers of family advice columns in newspapers and magazines, women of all classes developed new expectations of partnership and mutuality that men did not share (Komarovsky 1962; Rubin 1977; Berger 1968). The desire to change their husbands and restructure their marriages on more companionate lines makes many working-class women receptive to feminism.

Black families in the 1950s were at the bottom of the economic ladder, intentionally excluded from the opportunities and general prosperity of the postwar period. As with other women of the working class, black women combined paid employment with housework, family support, and autonomy strivings, but found little recognition or support for their double burden—from either their husbands or the wider society. Unlike their white working-class counterparts, black women remained largely confined to domestic labor, in their paid as well as their unpaid work. Although it is often assumed that the ultimate ambition of black women is to become a fulltime housewife, dependent upon a stable wage-earning husband, in fact their daily struggle for survival and the many varieties of discrimination they encountered (including social reforms that focused primarily on the black male ego and opportunities have brought many black women into the embrace of the new feminism.

Women without husbands. Poverty is a powerful predictor of family instability and breakdown through desertion, divorce, and separation. Although divorce today is not uncommon at any social class level, there is more of it among the poor. One of the latent consequences of the companionate marriage ideal is that there are few compelling reasons to remain in a relationship that fails to provide affection or is clearly destructive. Thus, modern marriage systems are also characterized by high rates of divorce. Today, the probability of a newly formed marriage remaining intact for thirty years or more is roughly 50 percent. As most divorced people remarry, at any given moment the great majority of American adults are in a marriage relationship. But, for a number of years many women will be heads of single-parent households.

Most divorced women must earn enough to care for themselves and their offspring. In 1981, fewer than half of the 59 percent of divorced women who were awarded child support payments received the full amount due, and only about two fifths of the 15 percent awarded alimony were paid in full (U.S. Bureau of the Census 1983). Overall, payments from ex-husbands account for only 20 to 25 percent of the total income of these women. Since 1975, there have been over one million divorces each year, forcing large numbers of women with children onto welfare or into the labor force, typically in low-skill, low-pay employment. In both their family and work lives, then, millions of American women will have experienced the less beneficial aspects of being female.

Black women are particularly likely to be raising children without the financial or emotional support of a husband. Because women's wages are typically too low to support dependents without assistance, and because black women's wages are especially low, black women supporting children have had to develop ways of sharing income and child care. Families composed of several generations of female kin are one alternative that not only makes financial survival possible, but encourages female solidarity and an appreciation for both paid work and housework as essential contributions to family well-being, a combination that can become a powerful impetus to feminism. Both black and white women raising children without the support of a husband tend also to appreciate the importance of female independence and self-sufficiency, as well as family cooperation and solidarity that goes beyond the limits of the conventional nuclear family.

Another group of potential recruits to feminism are the growing numbers of "displaced homemakers"—older women who through divorce or widowhood have been left without financial support. Their children are too old to qualify them for family welfare programs, yet they themselves are too young to receive Social Security benefits. Thrust into the labor market with few skills, and subject to the general cultural devaluation of older women, many have been attracted to self-help groups and organizations concerned with their special needs. These women have been victimized by the double standards of both aging and gender, but they also lack many of the resources needed to fight actively for change.

These various changes in the institution of marriage and family life—in sexual mores, marriage ideals, fertility, and marital stability—constitute the reality of the lives of most women. As with the trends in employment and education described earlier in this chapter, changes both empowered women and confronted them with new obstacles. The home was no refuge.

The period between 1920 and 1960 was thus a very different environment from that which nurtured the earlier phase of American feminism. The historian William Chafe (1972, 1977) suggests that the earlier movement failed to survive because "the day-to-day structure of most women's lives reinforced the existing distribution of sex roles. . . . The real problem was a social milieu which proved inhospitable to more far-reaching change" (1977:119). The New Feminist Movement, on the other hand, has grown out of prevailing social trends and is thus grounded in the actual experiences of women—at work and at home—that have reinforced the perceptions both of inequality and unfairness, *and* of change and new opportunities. The earlier movement went as far as the challenge to male supremacy could go at that historical moment. It required four decades of basic social change to create the conditions for the emergence of the third wave. Moreover, the early twentieth-century movement itself contributed to the rise of its daughter movement (Giele 1984).

Political Trends

The coalition after suffrage. Having achieved their primary goal of bringing women into the political process, at least at the level of the right to vote, the various partners in the suffrage movement went their separate ways. The coalition could not have held together much longer in any event, given the deep cultural and ideological divisions within its ranks. Some suffragists saw the movement as an opportunity to extend a basic American right to deserving segments of the female population. Angry that "drunken male immigrant layabouts" could vote while educated ladies could not, theirs was a longstanding elitist position, marked by explicit racism and anti-immigrant sentiment.

Other suffragists perceived the vote as a means of influencing legislation to protect the less fortunate, particularly impoverished and exploited immigrant and black girls and women, a longstanding anti-elitist position that united women across lines of social class (Tax 1981). Such alliances had been successful in organizing women workers and in providing community and neighborhood supports for housewives and mothers in the years before suffrage. These activists wanted newly enfranchised women to use their votes to transform society, to protect the weak (most often women and children), and to increase social equality—goals that were considered generally progressive and humane rather than distinctly feminist.

Only a minority of movement "radicals" viewed the vote as the first step toward full equality for all women. They were not very successful in promoting this vision among other members of the coalition, or in enlisting the support of the new generation of young women coming of age in the Roaring Twenties with its promise of sexual freedom, so often confused with liberation from gender role restrictions. The more the radicals insisted on the importance of organizing women to fight for their own special interests, the more they were ridiculed as "old fashioned" (Hacker 1951).

As a result, with the exception of Alice Paul's National Women's Party (NWP), few women's organizations in the decades between 1920 and 1960 embraced explicitly feminist goals, and even the NWP had only one plank in its platform—passage of the Equal Rights Amendment. Rather, women's concerns were folded into the programs of many different organizations and groups. Many women shifted their attention to other social movements: for example, temperance, with its aim of restoring family security among the working class; settlement houses, concerned with improving the lot of the poor and immigrant population; birth control and family planning; or union organizing (then illegal) for better working conditions among all wage-earners.

In addition, there were formal organizations such as the National Federation of Business and Professional Women's Clubs (BPW), the League of Women Voters (LWV) and the American Association of University Women (AAUW), whose members were very much aware of issues relating to the health and welfare of women and children, and who could be counted on to exert political pressure over particular pieces of legislation. And there were many such pieces of legislation over the next few decades for which the support of women's groups was essential: child protection laws, workplace safety rules, consumer rights, and public health programs.

Still, it was difficult to pinpoint a "women's vote" in the same sense that politicians spoke of other voting blocs such as farmers, Catholics, Jews, or Southerners. Indeed, women's voting rates remained lower than men's throughout the next five decades, most likely as a lingering effect of domestic values among those born before World War I. Women also failed to rally around female candidates. On issues that did not have an obvious "women's" component, voters—both male and female—were influenced by their many other social identities: race, religion, ethnicity, region of the country, rural/urban residence, and the like. Other than having achieved the right to vote, the legal status of women changed little throughout this period.

Yet, it can also be argued that women needed experience in organizations they themselves controlled before they could gain the assurance and skills required to compete in male-dominated institutions (Freedman 1979). In this view, the Women's Christian Temperance Union, League of Women Voters, the National Federation of Business and Professional Women's Clubs, and the like served the crucial function of bringing women together and heightening their consciousness of being female and relatively powerless. Far from being a diversion, participation in exclusively female organizations was an essential precondition of the new feminism, illustrating the value of maintaining a "woman's culture" through separate institutions (Freedman 1979). Many feminists today see such a culture as an important source of support and esteem, while also encouraging women to move onto the larger political scene.

Women in electoral politics.   Moving into the world of politics has been a slow process for women. Between 1920 and 1970, few women ran for office, and even fewer were elected. On rare occasions, a widow entered Congress "over the dead body" of her husband, selected by a state governor to fill her husband's remaining term of office. Although the few women who filled a "widow's term" were typically politically active and able women, it was not expected that they would subsequently be nominated in their own right. This pattern was broken by Margaret Chase Smith of Maine who not only completed her husband's term but was reelected four times to the House of Representatives before serving four additional six-year terms in the Senate. Later, both Maureen Neuberger of Oregon and Lindy Boggs of Louisiana were nominated and elected to Congress at the conclusion of their widow's term. Smith was the only woman senator throughout her two decades of office, and after she died, there were no others until 1978. At this writing, there are two women senators out of 100 and nineteen women among the 435 members of the House of Representatives.

The first woman governor also entered over her husband's body (he was impeached in 1917): "Ma" Ferguson of Texas, who served two terms in the 1920s. It was not until 1974 that a nonwidowed woman (Ella Grasso of Connecticut) was elected governor on her own political record, and even then she faced hostility, as in the campaign slogan "Connecticut Needs a Governor not a Governess."

Up to the 1970s, most women interested in politics were found in the lower ranks of campaign organizations—the envelope-stuffers and stamp-lickers without whom many a male candidate could not have won. Politically active women were able to make careers out of party organizational work, but unlike men of similar experience, they lacked an independent constituency to give them leverage within the party, and were rarely supported for elective office. After suffrage, both the Republican and Democrat parties established state and national female cochairmanships of the party organization. Despite their titles and responsibilities, these women had little independent power; male party leaders chose loyal subordinates, not competitors.

Other highly political feminists who remained active after suffrage found a home in the National Woman's Party, the International League for Peace and

Freedom, or the many union and socialist organizations of the 1930s, and in nonelective government offices. In general, however, political women faced the same dilemma as those interested in careers or higher education: the spirit was there but the support system was lacking. There was little encouragement in the culture or the social structure, or even in their interpersonal networks, for combining marriage, child rearing, and demanding responsibilities outside the home.

Yet many did remain in the political arena, although the 1920s offered little in the way of opportunity or recognition. The possibility of political power and influence came a decade later, with Franklin Roosevelt and the New Deal. By this time, many activist women had won a degree of recognition within the Democratic party and the labor movement—not leadership roles, but reputations for hard work and dedication. Some, such as Mary Anderson, head of the Women's Bureau of the Department of Labor, had been in place during previous administrations, but the New Deal brought increased responsibility to her department. Others, such as Frances Perkins, entered the Roosevelt cabinet at the top (as Secretary of Labor from 1933 to 1945), and still others moved into decision-making jobs at lower levels of the bureaucracy. While many of these women had received their political training in the suffrage movement, they entered government not as feminists first but social activists for many causes. In advancing the goals of their departments and bureaus—largely charged with social welfare programs—they also protected and extended the rights of women. The historian Susan Ware (1981) describes the network of personal and professional interests that bound together twenty-cight high-ranking women in the New Deal. These women were able to work together out of an overriding commitment to the cause of improved health, security, and welfare for all Americans. They wished to become role models of competence and dedication for other women, yet at no time did they openly confront the basic sources of discrimination against women or attack the ideals of patriarchy. The influence they exercised in the 1930s gradually declined as the New Deal itself drew back from major program initiatives, and as the war in Europe absorbed Roosevelt's attention.

It took another two decades for women's political influence once more to reach the level of the early days of the New Deal. With the exception of Margaret Chase Smith and Eleanor Roosevelt, few women's voices—much less, staunchly feminist ones—reached the public. Nonetheless, an important precedent had been set: women could handle the rigors of public office; administer a cabinet department; and represent a politically powerful constituency. Eleanor Roosevelt became an internationally recognized symbol of America's humanitarian concerns, most especially where the well-being of women and children was at stake. Because of her high symbolic value, she was selected by President John F. Kennedy to chair a special commission on the status of women in the United States that he had promised to create during his successful 1960 campaign.

By this time, several dozen talented women had risen to positions of influence in both the Democratic and Republican parties, but it was the Kennedy staff that most clearly saw the potential appeal of women's issues. Emphasizing the traditional association of the Democratic party with social welfare programs most beneficial to women, and also embracing the newer demands for equal treatment, the Kennedy campaign brought women's rights back into the political forum.

By 1960, there were many female—and feminist—bureaucrats who had worked their way up the system from the days of Roosevelt and Truman. They constituted a critical mass in the "woodwork" of the administration in Washington and various state capitals. Relatively invisible, but capable and well-connected, these women entered government in administrative posts largely concerned with health, education, and welfare programs. Having mastered the tasks of managing programs and dealing with legislatures, they were now in positions of influence, and available for recruitment to the new feminism. In chapter 3 we shall see just how crucial to the movement these women would soon be.

Conclusions

Thus the stage is set for the emergence of the powerful social movements of the 1960s. The four decades under review in this chapter were characterized by numerous shifts in values, attitudes, and beliefs concerning the proper roles of men and women in the workplace and in the home. Changes in access to crucial opportunities and resources gave women greater control than in the past over their productive and reproductive labor. The old structures of thought and behavior could scarcely accommodate these changes. Traditional assumptions of inferiority and subordination were undermined, but as we will see in the next chapter, these changes needed to be analyzed and interpreted to create a social movement that would directly challenge male authority and power.

It is the function of a movement organization to provide such a frame of reference—an ideology that gives meaning and shape to these everyday experiences, and an agenda for action to bring about desired change and to mobilize a resource base (potential members, funds, access to media, and so forth). This organization is linked to an external environment; that is, there will be historical moments in which certain actions are likely to be more (or less) successful, and historical conditions under which changes can endure or be turned back. Each of these elements seemed to fall into place in the early 1960s. All that was needed was the script, the set of ideas that could initiate action and structure events. The ideas, ideals, and ideology of the New Feminist Movement are the subject of the next chapter.

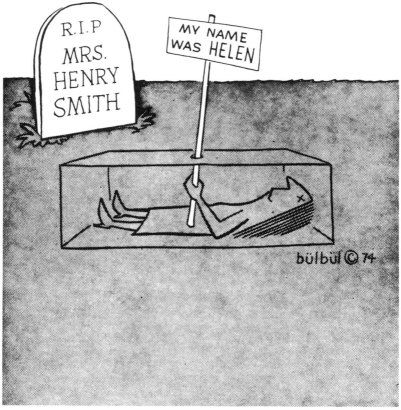

This cartoon expresses resistance to one way in which our society strips women of their identity. The discontent felt by women remained a private issue until feminist theorists forged these concerns into a coherent public issue. *Cartoon courtesy of Bulbul.*

CHAPTER TWO

Ideas, Ideals, and Ideology

If there is anything on which students of social movements agree, it is that a series of social, economic, and even cultural changes, no matter how dramatic, does not by itself give rise to a social movement. The considerable changes in the status and opportunities of American women described in the previous chapter were nonetheless important. They produced the conditions that made it difficult, if not impossible, to sustain a women's movement after suffrage, but at the same time created conditions that by the 1960s made it impossible to ignore women's second-class status. But social movements, which are organized efforts to change social arrangements, are different from broad currents of social change that take place without anyone's direction or efforts.

In this chapter we discuss the general problem of bringing a social movement into existence, the ideas by which people define the kind of change worth striving for, and the strategies adopted for accomplishing these changes. These ideological elements, in conjunction with available resources, generate the organizational forms that permit people to act collectively.

The Basis of Social Movements

Social movements do not emerge only because there is a problem in society. Problems always exist, but only certain conditions are protested and not even these at all times. It is obvious, for example, that American women faced a great many barriers in the 1930s and 1950s but did not then organize to fight for their rights. What does it take to construct a social movement that is a credible representative of the demands and aspirations of a group?

Grievances.   One way to explain the relative lack of protest of bad situations is to assume that many people are not bothered by terrible conditions. That is, people become reconciled to poverty and protest only when they suffer further impoverishment; again, women may become accustomed to the idea that their husbands will beat them and so get angry only when the assaults increase. This line of reasoning explains protest as a result of changes in "grievance level": if people are not complaining, then they must not be unhappy. The idea that women who join the women's movement are more unhappy than other women and that women who do not join are satisfied with their situation is an example of this type of thinking. Actually, many people in extremely miserable conditions will never join any social movement because their situation seems so hopeless or they have no energy left from the struggle for survival. Moreover, many people are joiners rather than leaders and will only be activated if there is an appropriate movement for them to join.

Relative Deprivation.   Although grievances alone cannot explain why protest emerges when it does, the translation of objective problems into subjectively experienced grievances is an important factor. Social comparison can help to establish a sense of what is fair or unfair, and to make people angry rather than simply unhappy. Problems often become protestable grievances when individuals see themselves as members of a group that is not doing well relative to some comparison group (Runciman 1966; Vanneman and Pettigrew 1972). Freeman argues that middle-class women in the 1960s became candidates for a protest movement as the gap in education between women and men closed, while differences in "qualitative and quantitative occupational rewards" widened, so that women saw themselves as relatively disadvantaged (1975, 31–32).

Perceived Cost.   Another explanation focuses on the expected costs and benefits of change. A generalized sense of trust supports social order by creating the perception that the government works for the long-run good of all (Gamson 1968; Paige 1971). When the government or the social system is seen as legitimate, people tend to interpret problems as individual failings or as unfortunate side effects of necessary policies (Kluegel and Smith 1982; Pettigrew 1979); in either case the individual is not entitled to anger. By eroding this generalized trust, the other social movements of the 1960s made change seem more acceptable. However, even in times of change, participation in a social movement involves risks. People with grievances may not protest because of perceived costs—a broken marriage, a lost job, the ridicule of friends. Women demanding change on behalf of women risk the relationships with men that ensure certain privileges, and perhaps even their survival. Repression effectively increases the costs of involvement with a social movement. Yet once a social movement appears successful, other kinds of change seem more probable and less risky. Thus the naive assumption in early women's liberation articles that "The [New Left] Revolution" was just around the corner (e.g., Dunbar 1970) made feminist participation seem easier and more rewarding.

Group Consciousness. Another factor is the development of identification with the group, particularly by the relatively privileged who have the resources to spare for protest activities. Such identification is difficult. Describing women's lack of "minority group consciousness" in the 1940s, Hacker (1951) noted that, unlike blacks and other minority groups, women were not socially segregated, but tied to men who provided protection and a limited amount of power. In addition, women competed with other women but rarely directly with men and, like all oppressed groups, were encouraged to identify with the oppressor. As Jo Freeman, a founding member of Chicago Women's Liberation, describes herself in premovement days: "[I was] one of many girls who had internalized an individualistic version of what Betty Friedan was to call the 'three-sex theory': there's men, there's women and there's me. Thus it was quite possible for me to share the socially accepted prejudices against women without ever drawing the appropriate conclusions about my own inferiority" (1975, viii). Others have noted that identification with "a group called women" is necessary for feminism. This group consciousness can arise from movement involvement as well as precede it when movement ideas provide a framework for reinterpreting one's own experiences (Cassell 1977; Gurin 1982).

Thus, to explain the reemergence of feminism in the 1960s we must look beyond personal motives to assess the actual social environment and opportunities for change. Instead of thinking of the New Feminist Movement as an aggregation of individuals with personal problems, we need to look at feminism as a genuinely *social* phenomenon, as women in the 1960s became convinced that it was worth their while to take risks, to share their resources, and to act collectively.

Organization. Social movement theorists have often noted the extreme difficulties in organizing collective action. Some believe that collective action is only worthwhile under certain relatively rare conditions, but that people realistically perceive and grasp these opportunities (Olson 1968;

McCarthy and Zald 1977). Others suggest that while such opportunities are minimally necessary, not all such moments are seized: people are not always aware of their chances or able to organize quickly or effectively (Gamson 1975; Tilly 1978). This perspective on social movements is called "mobilization theory," because it assumes that, while most people have grievances, social movements arise only when groups succeed in mobilizing their resources for action.

Two types of resources are required for a social movement: the specific skills and material objects needed for effective action, but also an ideology, or way of explaining reality that makes sense to potential participants and justifies their involvement. The ideology must support identification with the group (which is probably prior to feelings of grievance) and perceptions of opportunities for change (which is prior to taking advantage of them).

Concrete resources are important, of course, but ideas identify these resources and provide strategies for their use. Even in favorable circumstances, a social movement will not emerge until specific individuals actually mobilize resources available to the group, by persuading people to contribute time or money (or whatever) and by developing an organizational format for allocating this time, money, etc. Leadership—as innovative action, not hierarchical command—is therefore the first and most crucial resource for a movement. But such innovative actions have to attract followers, who come only when resources and ideology are put together in an appealing fashion. For example, it is not enough to distribute thousands of flyers, their message also must make sense to those who read them. Otherwise, rather than a social movement, one gets a massive litter problem. But active participation often takes a bit of a "push" as well as the "pull" of value congruence. The push could be the invitation or encouragement of people one knows, or even just a visible opportunity to participate, such as a local demonstration.

The combination of ideology and resources required for movement growth is central to the concept of the "co-optable social network" (Pinard 1968, Freeman 1973). A social network consists of persons already linked by some shared interest; co-optable means that this interest provides a preexisting basis for sympathy and understanding among network members, so the messages of the emerging movement are likely to be regarded favorably. The network itself is also a concrete resource that the movement uses for its own purposes. Networks can be formal organizations (e.g., the YWCA), other social movements (e.g., the New Left), or simply an informal set of links between people (e.g., the office grapevine). In short, people who are already organized, formally or informally, are easier to recruit into active participation in social movements than are isolated individuals, but the lines of communication are effective only for messages that can be seen as appropriate. Resources and ideology work together—or not at all.

In the previous chapter, we outlined the problems and possibilities that confronted women in the 1960s. Not only did women at this time have certain very real grievances in the areas of work, sexuality, and family life, but opportunities for change were also present. Women now had more objective resources in education, income, and time than were available earlier during the Depression, the war, and the baby boom. New ideas about intimacy, equality, and achievement had created an audience to which the feminist message could appeal.

In the next sections, we examine the ideological framework of the movement, the traditions it utilized, and the contributions of creative leadership in some major writers and thinkers who shaped the language and ideas of contemporary feminism.

The Ideological Framework of Feminism

To understand the feminist critique and agenda for change, it is first necessary to define the concept of "feminism." Because of the diversity of feminist groups and feminist issues, confusion over the meaning of the term is common. No person or group in or outside the women's movement, including ourselves, is in a position to offer an authoritative definition, but there are elements that, taken together, characterize a feminist worldview.

Feminist principles. The first and most basic claim of feminism is that women are a special category of people with certain characteristics in common, whether due to biology (e.g., the ability to give birth) or experience (e.g., the responsibility for feeding and nurturing children), whether fixed (e.g., being mothers) or historically and culturally variable (e.g., being housewives).

The second premise is that only women should define what is feminine. It is for women to say what women are like, what women want, what women enjoy, what women can do. This means both that each individual woman must be the judge of what is right for her, and that women can, by pooling experiences and sharing insights, arrive at a collective understanding of what it is to be a woman.

The third basic principle of feminism is a recognition of and dissatisfaction with living in a "man's world," where men define a "good" woman as one who meets their expectations, who serves and pleases them, who follows the rules they have created. Feminists are acutely aware that men have the power, but not the right, to do this.

Consequently, the fourth basic claim that feminism makes is for radical (root) change: to dismantle this "man's world," end men's unjust power, and claim for women what is rightfully theirs. For feminists, the crucial question in seeking change is what is good for women. In this view, making the world meet women's needs is not a means to some other goal, such as peace, socialism, or individual freedom, but an end in itself. Although placed fourth, in some ways this claim is the most essential characteristic of the feminist perspective. Many women accept the first three premises, but do not go on from there to imagine the possibility of a different world. They say, "It's a man's world . . . boys will be boys . . . what else could you expect from a man . . . women's work is never done . . ."; this is how it has always been and women will have to make the best of it. In contrast, feminism rejects the idea that women's subordination is natural and inevitable, the price paid for being born female. Change is possible, but it will not come without struggle; therefore, women must take control of their own destiny.

Despite agreement on these fundamental principles, there is great diversity in ideas for realizing social change, stemming from the different ideological roots from which feminism has grown.

The historical roots of feminism. Although the 1960s mark the emergence of a second major American feminist movement, feminism itself is much older. Even though there have always been individual women who struggled to define themselves on their own terms, feminism as a system of ideas with widespread appeal dates from the mid-eighteenth century, when the industrial revolution had dissolved traditional social relationships and vastly accelerated the pace of change. Alongside the social changes produced by industrial capitalism—which encouraged invention and the accumulation of wealth—the issue of women's place became a topic of concern. In the flux of changing institutional patterns and values, new possibilities for personal freedom and individual achievement emerged that would have to be either opened or closed to women; they could not be ignored. For middle-class men, it was a matter of balancing their own freedom from traditional authority against the potential loss of their power over women. For working-class men, the extreme poverty of early capitalism seemed the result rather than the cause of women's growing independence. For both, a "place" had to be found for women that would not challenge male control. As men debated what women's place and women's nature should be, early feminists such as Mary Wollstonecraft asserted their right to determine this for themselves, not in terms of what would please men, but on the basis of what was good for women.

Many of the beliefs about women's nature and role in society that are called "traditional" are thus in actuality no older than feminist ideas; both developed a few centuries ago. But it was the men's definitions that prevailed and were subsequently transformed into actual social relationships (e.g., the devotion of women's energies to full-time mothering of a limited number of children), and that have acquired a taken-for-granted quality that makes them extremely difficult to challenge. Moreover, the status quo is now perceived as representing some timeless "traditional" view of women, rather than as the outcome of a history of struggle in which feminists also won some battles. The idea of women as more moral than men, for example, was seen as shockingly feminist before the nineteenth century. Coeducation is another battle feminists won, although it remains a hollow victory when boys are given support that their female classmates do not receive.

Three feminist traditions.   Three intellectual traditions have nourished feminism, each imparting its own particular character and learnings. Olive Banks (1981) speaks of these as the three "faces" of feminism, each pointing in a different direction. These three traditions—moral reform, liberalism, and socialism—share certain concerns but also diverge in ways that greatly affect feminist thinking.

Moral reform.   Moral reformers often draw their conclusions from religious premises, such as a belief that social justice is God's work. The moral reform tradition of advocacy for the oppressed and for world peace is a particularly strong element in reform Judaism, liberal Christianity, and certain deist religions such as Unitarianism and Quakerism. Moral reformers have a strong sense of identification with the poor, an aversion to violence (hence the commitment to nonviolent direct action), and a vision of human relationships that affirm the dignity and value of each person and of the social and economic arrangements that would make such interpersonal relationships possible. This tradition influenced feminists to stress the link between the personal and the political, as integrity requires attention to how one acts in "little things" as well as in major decisions. Moreover, moral reformers condemn economic relationships that distort and corrupt our yearnings for human affection and self-realization.

In the nineteenth century, moral reform feminists fought against slavery and prostitution ("white slavery"), as well as the double standard in sexual relations. They tried to establish temperance in the use of alcohol and to provide social supports for immigrants. Most of these goals would improve the status of women (who were then, as now, overrepresented among the most poor and exploited) as well as express the moral values that reformers thought women possessed in greater measure than did men. The moral reform tradition can be seen in contemporary feminist concern with nonexploitative sexuality, in the demand for consistency in personal and political life, in the outrage over male violence, in the belief that women are "natural" pacifists, and in the efforts to provide support and protection to women who are victims of physical abuse and/or economic exploitation.

Liberalism. The liberal tradition of individualism and equal rights is based on the Enlightenment belief in the power of reason and personal development, as well as on the ideals of the French and American revolutions. Liberals see individuals as shaped by their experiences, particularly by their formal and informal education, which should develop each person's particular talents and prepare her/him for responsible citizenship. Liberals tend not to see a conflict between the good of each individual and that of the community as a whole. Classical liberalism affirms merit based on individual achievement (rather than status ascribed by birth), equality of rights as citizens (rather than a distinction between rulers and subjects), a social order based on contract (rather than divine law) and a minimum of social restraint on individual action (rather than a prescribed set of social obligations).

Not all liberals intended these principles to be applied to everyone; the "Founding Fathers" consciously excluded both women and blacks, appealing to "natural subordination" to deny women the right to vote, to be educated, to enter into contracts, to support themselves, or to live independently. Arguing that there were no fundamental differences in the nature of women and men that would legitimate this exclusion, liberal feminists—whether Mary Wollstonecraft in the eighteenth century or Betty Friedan in the twentieth—have stressed the importance for women of being, in Virginia Woolf's words, "independent of mind and of means." The liberal tradition can be seen in the contemporary feminist emphasis on woman's need for her own income, on access to any and all occupations and to the responsibilities and privileges of citizenship, on the right to control her own body, and on the importance of education.

Socialism. The socialist tradition includes Marx and Engels but has an even longer history. Although Marxists distinguish their "scientific socialism" from "utopian" socialism, this distinction has more to do with the means of achieving socialism than with their vision of socialist society. Socialist principles affirm a society based on mutual support and the recognition of human needs, on collective decision making and pooled resources, and on the value of work as a human activity. Socialism condemns the distortion of human values created by the profit motive and individual competition, and the resulting exploitation. Socialists believe that greed and competition must be actively restrained for a caring community to emerge. In the caring community, many of the functions of the traditional family would be assumed by society as a whole—physical care of children, the elderly, and the ill; economic support for those unable to work; decisions about the allocation of labor, etc.—and the traditional family would disappear because it would have become unnecessary.

For most socialists the end of the family would be equivalent to the liberation of women, but many nonfeminist socialists assume that the entry of women into the paid labor force and the establishment of a socialist government lead automatically to the disappearance of the family. Socialist feminists not only question this assumption but argue that the socialist community could assume not only the positive functions of families but also their exploitative aspects, especially male domination. Socialist feminists point out that in practice socialists have often chosen to strengthen both the nuclear family and male authority within it. The socialist tradition in feminism is particularly evident in attempts to develop communal alternatives to the nuclear family, in efforts to eliminate inhumane working conditions and to establish work control over the processes of production, and in the emphasis on egalitarianism and collective decision making.

To summarize, feminism is not a single point of view but a set of principles for interpreting the status of women and demanding change. The particular nature of the interpretation and demands depends on the broader ideological perspective from which the world is seen. The three traditions of moral reform, liberalism, and socialism have historically provided such frameworks, so individuals and organizations that share these traditions will be part of cooptable networks for the reemergence and growth of feminism. The feminism generated in each tradition will have its own distinctive characteristics but will also share concerns with other feminists as well as with nonfeminists of the same tradition.

The race analogy.   American feminism has long been associated with efforts to end racism and the oppression of black people, efforts that have had their roots in all three of the traditions described above. Among the earliest active feminists were Frances Wright and the Grimké sisters. Fanny Wright (1795–1852) campaigned for free public education for both boys and girls, for an end to slavery, and for the establishment of racially integrated communities. She was a socialist who predated Marx and, like many of the socialists of her time, she attempted to demonstrate her principles by establishing a "utopian" interracial community called Nashoba in Tennessee in 1825. The commune lasted only four years, but Wright continued to the end of her life to give well-attended lectures on the virtues of education, the corruption of slavery, and the dignity of the working class.

Sarah (1792–1873) and Angelina (1805–79) Grimké were antislavery activists in the moral reform tradition who fought for women's right to participate directly in the abolition movement and not merely as fund-raisers for projects carried out by men. The Grimké sisters gave public lectures against slavery and for the right of women even to give public lectures. The link between feminism and black rights in the liberal tradition had been apparent even before the abolition movement. When Abigail Adams wrote to her husband, John, to "remember the ladies" in the new Declaration of Independence since "all men would be tyrants if they could," he wrote back that "I cannot but laugh. We have been told that our Struggle has loosened the bands of Government every where . . . that Indians slighted their Guardians and Negroes grew insolent to their Masters. But your letter was the first intimation that another tribe more numerous and powerfull than all the rest were grown discontented" (quoted in Rossi 1973, 11).

Black women, like Sojourner Truth (1795–1883) and Ida B. Wells (1862–1931), also fought actively on both fronts. Sojourner Truth was an ex-slave and active public speaker for abolition who also made impassioned and effective speeches for women's rights. She reminded both movements that they were ignoring black women for whom both race and sex were real oppressions. Wells was a journalist whose primary cause was the abolition of lynching. Since black men were often lynched on the pretext of a supposed sexual assault on "white womanhood," she not only worked to organize black women, but also to mobilize white women's organizations to reject this vicious form of sexual politics (Davis 1981). Both Wells and Truth felt that the rights of women and blacks were inseparable in practice as well as in theory. Sojourner Truth made the connection clear in a speech in 1867 that could as easily have been delivered in 1967:

There is a great stir about colored men getting their rights, but not a word about colored women; and if colored men get their rights and not colored women theirs, you see the colored men will be masters over the women, and it will be just as bad as it was before. So I am for keeping the thing going while things are stirring; because if we wait again till it is still, it will take a great while to get it going again. (quoted in Stimpson 1971, 636)

As a result not merely of these beginnings but of the ongoing association of women's rights with black rights both in principle and in practice, American feminists tend to perceive women as a minority group.

The analogy of sex and race, common to all three major traditions, can be both helpful and troubling. It is helpful when it clarifies the extent to which disabilities facing both women and blacks arise from their previous common status as property rather than persons, or when it illustrates the common stereotypes that are developed for subordinated people: neither intelligent nor ambitious, but childish and unreliable; happy with monotonous work and hard labor, but in need of "protection" in their nonwork lives. This analogy, prevalent in the nineteenth-century feminist movement, was reexamined in Gunnar Myrdal's famous study of racism, *An American Dilemma,* published in 1944 and widely read by black rights activists in the 1950s and 1960s. The appendix, entitled "A Parallel with the Negro Problem," gave a shock of recognition to many women students and civil rights workers. Feminists coined the term "sexism," on the model of racism, to describe a condition based on more than stereotyping and prejudice, an exclusion built into the very institutional framework of our society.

The link between sexism and racism becomes somewhat problematic when it is asserted that the processes of exploitation and liberation will necessarily be the same for both groups. One of the earliest claims made by women who were rediscovering feminism was that women were "the niggers of the world," that is, that they were exploited in just the same fashion as blacks, but even more pervasively (Willis 1970, 56). Similarities were exaggerated to make a polemical point:

Black people fell under two patterns of dominance and subservience which emerged under slavery, and which are analogous to patterns of male-female relationships in industrial societies. One pattern is the paternalistic one (house servants, livery men, entertainers, etc.). The second pattern is the exploitative pattern of the fieldhands. Among females today, housewives and women on welfare are subject to the paternalistic pattern. The exploitative pattern rules the lives of more than a third of the population of females (those who work for wages including paid domestic work). (Dunbar 1970, 485)

The analogy "male is to female as white is to black" encouraged feminists to stress that women would have to organize separately from men. Marge Piercy, for example, argued: "We are oppressed, and we will achieve our liberation by fighting for it the same as any other oppressed group. . . . I once thought all that was necessary was to make men understand that they would achieve their own liberation, too, by joining in the struggle for women's liberation; but it has come to seem a little too much like the chickens trying to educate the chicken farmer. I think of myself as a house nigger who is a slow learner besides" (1970, 429).

Integration raised the danger of co-optation, of receiving too many advantages from the "master" to risk demanding change, so that even relationships with men that women found rewarding were seen as undesirable. Concepts such as imperialism and colonialism that describe the relations between countries were first extended to encompass "Third World people" within "first world" countries (e. g., racial minorities in the United States) and then by analogy to women, so that some feminists spoke of male control of women's bodies as "colonization." In this framework the solution is independence for women as a group rather than as discrete individuals. But this analogy hardly helps to clarify what collective independence would mean.

Separatism also builds on the minority group analogy in more positive ways, by acknowledging the value of a separate culture, first, as a source of social support for individuals whose own worth can be affirmed there as nowhere else in society and, second, as a practical contribution to resistance. Social movements depend heavily on the co-optable networks and group consciousness that a subculture can provide. Black churches, colleges, and communities contributed significantly to the black protest movement; to what extent could women find or create similar resources? The danger in self-segregation as a strategy for change is that such isolation from the powerful can actually decrease access to resources and perpetuate powerlessness.

The minority group analogy is positively misleading, moreover, in its implication that women and blacks are distinct groups, ignoring black women entirely, that is, assuming that "all the women are white, all the blacks are men" (Hull, Scott, and Smith 1982) and that these "minority groups" are in competition with each other. In fact, black men, black women, and white women have each been taken advantage of in different ways, and thus now occupy different social and economic positions. Little is gained by comparing these positions and trying to decide who is worst off. As Stimpson notes: "Behind the competition for the unpleasant title of Most Oppressed Group in America lay a serious moral and political question. If history, which is so miserly about justice, is to help only one of several suffering groups, what standards can we possibly use to choose that group?" (1971, 638).

Effective coalitions can replace invidious distinctions only by recognizing "common differences" (Joseph and Lewis 1981). Race and sex are both used to oppress people, but they are differently institutionalized forms of inequality. White women can secure certain privileges within the system but also pay for them with personal subservience; black men are given license to exercise male privileges but only within the confines of the black community, and at great cost to black women; black women have more independence from the patriarchal family, but are subject to extreme economic exploitation and poverty.

Parallels between racism and sexism, therefore, must always be treated with caution. In some respects, the nature of oppression is illuminated; in other respects, essential differences are obscured. For contemporary feminists, however, this analogy was a steppingstone to their own increasingly sophisticated analyses of "woman's place."

Feminist Issues and Authors

For the generation of women who came of age in the 1940s and 1950s feminism as an intellectual tradition was virtually invisible. The few authors who raised feminist concerns in those years went unread until they were rediscovered in the 1960s. The popular wisdom was expressed in Freudianism and functionalism, two approaches to social behavior that assumed gender differences were given by nature even while advising men and women to make constant efforts to adjust and conform to "nature." These beliefs were among the first targets of feminist critics, who claimed that the social sciences were being used not to understand reality but to construct it, and thus to control individual behavior (Friedan 1963; Weisstein 1968; Millett 1970). As a consequence, the nature of sex differences in reality and in ideology became a crucial issue in the development of feminist theory

Sex role stereotyping and the limitation of human potential. The recognition that many of the observed differences between men and women were created and maintained by arbitrary beliefs and social arrangements was greatly helped by the republication in 1963 of Margaret Mead's classic study of preliterate societies in which the "natural" roles of each sex were reversed or obscured (1935). Yet, regardless of ascribed temperament or division of labor, women's roles were everywhere subordinate and more limited than those of men. The different evaluation of male and female roles was explored in *The Second Sex* (1957) by Simone de Beauvoir, a French existentialist and socialist. She showed that women are not treated as the subjects of their own experiences, but are instead described as objects of men's wishes and anxieties. Although existentialists see self-awareness and conscious action as crucial to genuinely human existence, de Beauvoir noted that women were assumed to lack these capacities. Further, women's position in society undermines their chances of coming to awareness, as women are cast in the role of "the Other," less able to experience themselves as full human beings than as persons different from, and existing in relation to, male humanity.

Perhaps the single most influential critique of women's position in contemporary society was Betty Friedan's ten-year follow-up study of her Smith

College graduating class, *The Feminine Mystique* (1963). Friedan documented a widespread unhappiness which she called "the problem that had no name." Unwilling to blame this unhappiness on a woman's "failure to adjust" to life as a housewife, Friedan argued that the problem lay, first, with the nature of housework as a full-time occupation for women who had been trained to be able to do more, and second, with the culture that presented housework as the only acceptable career for "normal" women.

Friedan analyzed the role of the mass media in promoting the belief that the only happy woman was the housewife—women who worked outside the home always came to a bad end. She noted that training women to be appropriate mates for achieving men had been accepted as the goal of higher education for women. By teaching conformity rather than encouraging women to develop their own potential, colleges had failed their female students. *The Feminine Mystique* also contained an indictment of the American infatuation with Freudian psychology and of therapists who cultivated anxiety in women by equating their impulses to achieve with "masculinity striving," bad mothering, and sexual maladjustment. Friedan argued that women would not only be happier but be less possessive and stifling mothers, as well as more relaxed and satisfied sexual partners, if they had real careers that challenged their abilities and developed their potential.

Friedan's book clearly struck a responsive chord in the American public. Not only did it become an immediate best-seller, but all the major women's magazines published excerpts and responses. Friedan herself became a familiar figure on the lecture circuit and a focus of public controversy. Her indictment of housework as an inadequate lifetime career for educated and capable women was often distorted by the media into an attack on housewives as stupid or incompetent, a clear contradiction of Friedan's basic point: that the fault lay in the system and not in individual women. Many women who read the book felt that for the first time there was someone who understood what they were going through. But Friedan's solutions—to go back to school, make a career commitment, look for an appropriately demanding job—did not go beyond challenging women to take themselves seriously. Once women themselves rejected the "feminine mystique," other, more basic, problems began to be recognized.

Because feminist thinking has grown and developed enormously since 1963, it is now possible to recognize some of the limitations of Friedan's analysis. One issue she never raised, for example, was the question of why women alone should be held responsible for housework and child care. Friedan argues only that women should be allowed *additional* spheres of activity for self-development. Nor were issues of class or race considered; it was simply assumed that any woman who wanted could get a decent education and pursue a fulfilling career. Since there have never been enough high status jobs to go around, the hard question of how the workplace could be restructured to make fulfilling work possible for all who want it must also be addressed. Friedan thought the "problem that had no name" was limited to college-educated, middle-class women but twenty years later it is possible to see that it is actually more widespread. Even women with little formal education find that raising a few children is not a lifetime occupation, and that the isolation of full-time child care can be oppressive. Finally, Friedan's discussion of female sexuality suggested that women were not "achieving" orgasm as often as they "should," but assumed that more of the same—heterosexual, monogamous, genitally focused intercourse—was a satisfactory goal, an assumption that feminists increasingly questioned.

Power and sexuality: The longest war. Unlike their nineteenth-century counterparts, women in the 1960s believed that they were entitled to sexual satisfaction and to a fulfilling sexual life, but it had become clear that most women, regardless of their level of sexual activity, were not satisfied with their sexual experiences. Under the influence of Freudian psychology, they had interpreted their dissatisfaction as a personal failing: they had sexual "hang-ups" or refused to "accept their femininity." In a group context, however, such individual problems could be recognized as collective in nature and as a legitimate grievance. These realizations were brought to widespread attention with the publication of Kate Millett's *Sexual Politics* (1970).

Written at the height of the Vietnam War (1969–70), *Sexual Politics* drew an analogy between contemporary American culture and that of "primitive" societies characterized by a "men's house" and initiation rituals for boys coming to manhood. In both the penis is viewed as a weapon, and masculinity equated with killing, violence, and militarism. This was encouraged by "bonding" with other men, and by rejecting and despising everything "feminine" in themselves or others. As Millett presents it, patriarchy (the rule of men) is a universal form of social organization related to all that is violent and abusive in society, but most particularly to violence against women, as exemplified in the act of rape. Millett presented rape not as an expression of sexual desire, but of "aggression, hatred, contempt and the desire to break or violate personality" and argued that "masculine hostility (psychological or physical) in specifically sexual contexts" functions "to provide a means of control over a subordinate group" (44–47).

Thus, international politics and interpersonal relations show the same underlying dynamic—men trying to prove their "masculinity." Inherent in this process is hatred and contempt not only for all women but for "unmanly" men; homosexuals are patriarchy's "failures." In Millett's own view, homosexuality could better be seen as rebellion against a system that demands brutality from men and a desire to suffer from women. Millett showed that misogyny (the hatred of women) and approval of sexual violence are common themes in contemporary American fiction. She established a framework for seeing that "the personal is political," so that even women's experiences in bed are part of a pattern of male power. While the link between sex and violence is frequently denounced as deviant, it is actually a central part of our society's view of ordinary sexuality and gender, a view that defines women not merely as objects, but as "sex objects" and gives men status based on their "conquests" of women.

Other feminists were also examining the realities of women's sexual experience in patriarchal culture. Ann Koedt (1970) refuted the accepted Freudian view that "mature," passive women had a deeper and better ("vaginal") orgasm, and showed that "frigidity" was more a product of passivity and ignorance than of "poor adjustment" to the female role. The prevalence of rape and the way in which the victim is punished were examined in detail by Brownmiller (1975) and Russell (1975), whose analysis suggested that rapists were "normal" in that they were acting out a culturally approved pattern rather than a personal psychological disturbance. Heterosexual relationships under patriarchy were presented as fundamentally exploitative, unsatisfying, and potentially dangerous for women—and patriarchy seemed a virtually universal principle of social organization. Clearly, the "sexual revolution" of the 1960s, as manifested in the increased availability of pornography and in the assumption that buying a woman dinner entitles a man to sex, made women more, not less, vulnerable to sexual exploitation.

Feminists insist that mutually satisfying sexuality requires relationships of equality, where both partners can freely express their desires (Shulman 1980; Diamond 1980). But as long as women are socially and economically unequal and dependent on the support of men, how can women be free to enter into or reject sexual relationships? As Shulman put the problem: "The heart of our sexual dissatisfaction with men was that without power women were forced to sell [sex] or forgo it, and we were still powerless" (1980, 620). For some women the search for egalitarian and mutually satisfying sexual relationships led to adoption of a lesbian identity; a few argued for celibacy; and many tried to restructure their heterosexual relationships to eliminate the effects of social inequality.

The Lesbian Alternative.   The choice of a lesbian identity was based not only on a view of male sexuality as invariably violent and woman-hating

(Dworkin 1974), but also on the positive value given to female sexuality and female identity. Such a positive evaluation is difficult to achieve in a society characterized by a male definition of sexuality that tends "to lump the female and sex together as if the whole burden of the onus and stigma it attaches to sex were the fault of the female alone" (Millett 1970, 51). To value both the female body and oneself as a woman and person is clearly related to the ability to love oneself and to love other women, whether in a platonic or a sexual sense. Advocates of the lesbian alternative present this as part of a continuum of female solidarity, with the most highly "woman-identified woman" expressing her commitment in a physically loving relationship (Rich 1980).

Some feminists took this concept to the extreme of claiming that "feminism is the theory, lesbianism the practice," as if any relationship with a man were at best hypocritical and at worst self-destructive, thus defining a lesbian as a better feminist than a hetero- or bisexual woman. Most feminists, however, refused to reduce politics to sexuality, even while continuing to see sexuality as part of political reality (Shulman 1980). As we will see in later chapters, the role of lesbians and lesbianism in the New Feminist Movement remains a lively issue, but the idea that a woman could break free from the constraints of patriarchy by changing sexual partners, or sexual orientation, or even by forgoing sex altogether, is now widely acknowledged to be simplistic. Concentrating on sexuality as a source of identity and a means of self-expression, Millett and others found some common themes but too quickly jumped to the conclusion that these were universal. For example, the evidence for women's "essential" pacifism is just as mixed as the evidence for women's "natural passivity." Although Millett herself argued that male violence and hostility toward women were products of culture rather than of the "nature" of men, her emphasis on the universality of patriarchy led others to conclude that male aggression was somehow innate, and that women were therefore morally superior (e.g., Daly 1978). This claim was central to the moral reform tradition of feminism in previous generations, but now as then, by emphasizing innate qualities, it limits the potential for change. Moreover, those who propose an essential difference in nature between men and women too often stereotype and dehumanize "the Other." It is possible, however, that the real radicalism of a feminist revolution will arise from its refusal to dehumanize anyone, even those men who have hated and physically abused women.

Motherhood and autonomy. While Millett offered an introduction to a feminist analysis of power and sexuality, Shulamith Firestone took the first step in reexamining the old Freudian argument that "biology is destiny." In *The Dialectic of Sex* (1970), she combined Freudian with Marxist analysis. Suggesting that Freud was basically correct that women envied men, she argued that it was not the penis itself but the social power that goes with it that is the object of envy. Because a mother's position in the family remains subordinate, the psychological dynamics continue to unfold as Freud described them. The Marxist argument that there was a material basis for relationships of exploitation and oppression led her to locate the subordinate position of mothers in the biological necessity for women to give birth. In other words, rather than seeing patriarchy as based on attitudes and ideas alone, she sought the roots of men's social power in concrete facts, especially in the facts of reproduction. Because she did not see any way for mothers to avoid subordination, she concluded that the only way for women to be free was to renounce motherhood. *The Dialectic of Sex* ends with a vision of the future in which childbearing would be taken over by technology; not only test-tube conception but gestation as well. Although most readers, including most feminists, found Firestone's conclusions distasteful, they were prodded to think about how women could be mothers without being oppressed by the experience.

Freedom for mothers, the emerging feminist analysis argued, will exist only when women can freely choose to have children or not (Petchesky 1980). Compulsory motherhood, whether due to the absence of birth control or of any other meaningful life's work, is not acceptable. A woman's right to make that decision herself, unimpeded by government policy or by social pressure for *or* against childbearing is crucial to the freedom of all women. As feminists noted, even the experience of giving birth had become an exercise in powerlessness, as male doctors and hospital administrators assumed control over the birth process. Mothers themselves had little to say about the timing, the setting, or the techniques of childbirth (Rothman 1982). In addition to control over the decision to give birth, therefore, women need to repossess the entire process through such choices as home births, midwives, limited anesthesia, and active participation of self and other family members in the birth. The developing feminist analysis of mothering as a source of power taken from and turned against women has generated both controversy and constructive strategies for change (Rossi 1977; Rich 1976; Ruddick 1980).

The distinction between motherhood as the biological experience of giving birth and mothering as the social experience of caring for small children is a crucial element in feminist analysis. As a biological experience, the critical problem is increasing women's control over motherhood; as a social role, the issue of control is combined with the issue of sharing child care with men.

Some theorists (Chodorow 1978; Dinnerstein 1976) propose that children raised exclusively by women will develop psychological traits (such as the desire to mother in women, and hostility to women in men) that inevitably reproduce the gender-based differences in personality and behavior that are evident in present society. From this point of view, the continued oppression of women rests on the material base of the division of labor in child rearing rather than on either simple prejudice or "natural" differences between the sexes. Some feminists argue that men are and will continue to be largely excluded from intense involvement in child care because the structure of the economy penalizes child rearing so severely—few families can afford the total or partial loss of a "man-sized" paycheck. Thus, to change the division of child rearing labor in any significant way will necessitate substantial changes in the structure of other types of work.

Most feminists agree on the need to relieve mothers of some of the burden of child rearing by provision of child care outside the home; many also argue that increased participation by fathers is equally essential to women's freedom. Additionally, some are beginning to question whether the view of children as a burden and impediment to women's autonomy does justice to the meaning of children in women's lives; if women were not forced to give up so much when they have children, perhaps the role of child care in teaching adults spontaneity and generosity would be more valued. Others note that psychodynamic theories assume that most children will be living in the same households as their biological parents, or at the very least, in nuclear families, yet the question of shared parenting could involve a larger and perhaps more voluntary family.

Theoretical diversity in the new feminist movement today. At this time there are some interpretations of feminist principles that seem to cluster together and other ideas on which feminists frequently disagree. One controversial question concerns the limits of individualism, both as means and as end of social change. Is the whole purpose of feminism to produce free and unfettered individuals or to create a new form of community? Is feminism to be realized through individual transformation (and consequent sociopolitical change) or through a sociopolitical struggle that creates the conditions for individual transformation? All social movements are points of intersection between personal and social change, but the tension between the individual and the social dimensions seems especially pronounced in the New Feminist Movement.

Indeed, present-day feminists combine personal and social change in virtually all possible ways in developing an agenda for the movement. If we look at both the *means* (personal transformation or sociopolitical change) and the *ends* (an individual freed from social restraint or a new and stronger community) of social change advocated by feminists, the following typology emerges:

Figure 2.1.
Varieties of Modern Feminism

		MEANS	
		Personal Transformation	*Sociopolitical Change*
	Free Individuals	Career	Liberal
ENDS			
	New Communities	Radical	Socialist

The particular terms used in this table describe different emphases and are not necessarily in opposition. An individual feminist may move from one orientation to another as the conditions of her life change; or she may seek a balance between certain types. The point of this typology is that these differences do not reflect a tension between better or worse feminists, but between different styles and strategies, each of which may be appropriate for certain situations or at certain times.

Career feminism emphasizes the need for individual women to take their lives into their own hands and dare to be what they can become, to fight back if men try to stop or limit them, and to help other women. For many, this orientation centers on women's right to any sort of job in society, even those that have been traditionally defined as male. If women stick together and refuse to let men dictate to them, they will discover that they have the power to accomplish their goals. But first, women must discover their own potential and learn to act assertively. Creating support networks and achieving personal goals are key ideas in this approach.

Radical feminists also emphasize the power that women already have in themselves and the need for mental transformation that would free women to act powerfully. This power, however, is not to be used to enter and achieve in the male world, but rather to reject that world completely. Women's ties to one another are crucial, not as a defense or a lever to power, but as a source of joy in themselves. Women who define and care for themselves create a community that does not need men to function or to be important. While this leaves the "rest" of the world under male control, a radical feminist community provides an image of female freedom and possibility that is healing and transforming for women. By offering women an alternative to male control, radical feminists plant a seed of doubt about the naturalness or inevitability of current social patterns, and encourage resistance to these arrangements. Lesbian feminism and cultural feminism are two variations on this vision.

Liberal feminism is most typically expressed in demands for social and political change that would eliminate the unjust advantages of men and guarantee equal rights. Throughout its long history, liberal feminism has stressed the importance and the autonomy of the individual. In contrast to the traditional liberal's exclusion of women, the liberal feminist claims that women and men are equally entitled to be treated as individual people. Unlike career feminists, liberal feminists see social policy as an important force in establishing access to economic opportunity and civil rights. The Equal Rights Amendment is one measure crucial to liberal feminists, who also stress changing the division of labor in the household, eliminating stereotypes in education, and increasing personal choice in childbearing and child rearing.

Socialist feminism focuses on the importance of changing the basic structural arrangements of society, a goal shared with liberal feminists. Socialist feminists, however, consider the liberal concept of isolated individuals with abstract rights and choices a harmful myth that perpetuates inequalities. In contrast, both men and women are seen as social beings, imbedded in a network of concrete social and economic relationships. Capitalist relationships force people to compete with each other in order to survive, restricting and distorting human nature, both male and female. Socialists seek an end to these competitive relationships, and to the exploitation of the weak by the strong. In contrast to traditional socialists, socialist feminists see patriarchy as another force that distorts and limits human possibilities. They argue that all social structures permitting one group (men, capitalists, whites) to control and benefit from another (women, workers, blacks) must be eliminated. Despite controversies about which form of exploitation, if any, is more fundamental than the rest, socialist feminists share a vision of a new community that, as a community, recognizes and develops the human potential of every person.

Given this diversity of perspectives in the movement, the variety of traditions that have contributed to its growth, and the broad range of issues that have been raised, it is not surprising that the New Feminist Movement has no one central spokesperson or organization. In the next chapter we will look at the initial resources and organizational dynamics that sparked the emergence of this diverse movement.

The Miss America Pageant protest of 1968 gave rise to the image of feminists as "bra burners." In fact, no undergarments were burned but bras, girdles, curlers, makeup, and spiked heels were put into a "freedom trashcan" to symbolize rejection of cultural ideals of femininity that confine and distort women's bodies. *Photograph by Miriam Bokser.*

CHAPTER THREE

Reemergence of a Feminist Movement, 1963–70

In the preceding chapters we have traced the demographic and ideological foundations upon which a social movement could be established. By the early 1960s there were hundreds of thousands of women "structurally available" for recruitment; that is, they had actually experienced discrimination and recognized the gap between their talents, skills, and expectations on the one hand, and the reality of their position in the home, schools, and workplace, on the other. Ideas about the causes of their lower status became personally relevant, and authors who addressed this issue found—finally—a ready readership. But resources and ideas must be mobilized in order to create a social movement organization. In this chapter we describe the reemergence of an organized feminist movement and follow its early history, beginning with the link between feminism and civil rights activism in the 1950s and 1960s.

Feminism and the Civil Rights Movements

The history of the New Feminist Movement is intricately interwoven with that of the other dominant social movement of our times—the civil rights movement (Blumberg 1984). In this respect, contemporary feminism resembles the earlier movement for women's rights that was linked to the cause of abolishing slavery in the United States (Giele 1984). The abolition and civil rights movement provided models of moral protest and effective change that inspired women to seek full equality for themselves. In addition, in both eras the active involvement of black and white women prepared them for their later activism on behalf of feminist goals.

From their work in the civil rights movement, women acquired a number of valuable resources. First and most important was a sense of personal power, of taking on a difficult task and making things happen. Secondly, women became skilled in organizing people and events, and in using effective tactics for implementing change and manipulating the media: civil disobedience, mass demonstrations, passive resistance, community organizing, law suits, and the mimeograph machine and press release. They also learned another crucial lesson: that if they were to pursue feminist goals, it would have to be in a movement of their own. This realization came slowly, to many different groups of women as they participated in the other social movement of the 1960s.

The civil rights movement began in the mid-1950s with a series of acts of civil disobedience: a tired working woman refusing to move to the back of the bus; black students sitting-in at a department store lunch counter; and a host of other public challenges to both the formal (legal) and informal (customary) structures of segregation in the American South. The publicity generated by these actions and by the violent reaction of local officials transformed the movement into a moral cause—a matter of justice. This appeal to religious values had an immediate impact on some Southern white Protestants, especially those younger women who recognized the inherent conflict between Southern culture and the ideals of Christianity.

The white women who joined the crusade for civil rights in the late 1950s were primarily from the South and its deeply religious traditions (Evans 1979). In rejecting the role of "Southern lady," they were free to develop a new sense of self based on their abiding commitment to moral reform and their personal experiences in the civil rights movement. The strong hardworking black women engaged in community organizing were role models for them—an ideal of womanhood very different from their own tradition. It was not long before these women recognized a link between racism and sexism.

As women began to articulate their own concerns within the civil rights movement, they met the argument that women's needs are less pressing than those of blacks, and some were willing to put aside feminist goals so as not to divert attention from what they saw as the greater struggle. As with many women in the earlier abolition movement, they believed that social movements were competing rather than complementary agents of change. The historical reality is that diverse social movements have had a mutually reinforcing effect, leading to eras of remarkable change along a variety of social fronts, while periods of repression and rigidity are inhospitable to any social movement, regardless of the issue or constituency. Thus, social movement activists typically have more to gain than to lose from the existence of other movements for change. But for male activists, threatened by women's demands for sharing leadership and setting priorities, the advantages of cooperation were obscured by the challenge to their authority.

Women's own cause would not be deferred forever. In both the abolition and civil rights movements, the experience of women gradually reinforced their anger at male indifference to their cause. Who should be expected to be more sympathetic to feminist goals than those who recognized injustice in a racial context? Yet some of the same men who spoke so eloquently of freedom and justice openly showed their contempt for women, sharing the attitudes and beliefs about women typical of most men of their era. Women were sexual conquests, supportive workers behind the scenes, effective organizers on a local level; only in these secondary roles were they welcome in the cause. When women questioned their limited power within the movement, and ultimately in the society, they were ridiculed, abused, and excluded.

The tension between the black rights movement and the emergent women's movement was not merely a matter of competition for resources or of internal power struggles, but also reflected a conflict in goals. Much of the male leadership in the black movement, and virtually all of their white male sympathizers, believed that the costs of racism were borne primarily by black men, "emasculated" by their lack of economic power. They claimed that without the power that comes from earnings, black men "lost" control over their families, and without the ability to dominate their wives and children they lose their self-respect. The ideal that men should be sole providers for their families was accepted uncritically, so that poverty was seen as a blow to the male ego, the only ego that counted. As forcefully stated by Grier and Cobbs (1968), "the essence of the male animal is to strut."

In this view, female-centered families were equated with female power or matriarchy and considered psychologically damaging (particularly to male children) as well as socially destructive (Moynihan 1965). Black women who did not subordinate themselves to their "natural" superiors were accused of being "castrating," further contributing to the inability of black men to become stable breadwinners. The relative strength and independence of black women was considered less an asset to the black community than a symptom, if not the cause, of its distress. As long as leaders in the civil rights movement accepted the norm of male authority in the family and community as the ideal toward which they were striving, women's challenges to that authority would create a fundamental conflict.

Thus, while the civil rights movements offered a model of analysis and organizing experience for women who became active in the New Feminist Movement, there were areas of potential discord between the two movements. As before the Civil War, decades of protest and growing public support for the principle of equal rights under law created a climate of opinion in which the feminist message appeared less exotic or unreasonable than it might have if the women's movement had been the first to surface. But male authority, in both theory and practice, in the black rights movement was in direct contradiction to feminist goals.

Organizational Styles of the New Feminism

As we have noted, there is no single entity that can be labeled "the" New Feminist Movement. Rather, several different organizational forms and theoretical emphases developed out of divergent sets of experience. The New Feminist Movement is a loosely linked collection of formal organizations, occupational caucuses, friendship circles, collectives, and interest groups. Nonetheless, it is possible to identify historical moments when important elements in this mix emerged as self-conscious units, committed to social change on behalf of women.

It is first necessary to distinguish two major strands in the early development of the New Feminist Movement. Some analysts (e.g., Carden 1974; Cassell 1977) use the terms "women's rights" and "women's liberation" to refer to these different types of groups. *Women's rights* groups were those formal, structured organizations established to pursue equality through legislation, the courts, and lobbying; that is, to fight a political battle on political turf. *Women's liberation* groups were the relatively informal, loosely structured networks of women in the community, struggling for feminist goals outside of the conventional political system, through consciousness-raising (CR) and support groups, self-help projects, media-directed actions, and efforts to construct more egalitarian relationships in their personal lives.

Other students of the movement, following Freeman (1973, 1975) prefer to speak of "two branches," an older one and a younger one, that differ in age, structure, and style. Both branches, claims Freeman (1975), were concerned with rights and liberation, and the distinction between them is not simply that of reform versus revolution. Rather, each branch emerged from a unique set of historical circumstances involving a particular age group of women. In the period between 1963 and 1973 younger and older women faced different problems and developed different ways of dealing with them. Within each age group, a branch of feminism developed independently of the other branch, recruiting members from the co-optable networks available to it. Only in the early 1970s, as the mass media brought awareness of feminism to persons outside these specific networks, did the two branches begin to develop overlapping memberships and complementary strategies.

It is, therefore, more accurate to refer to "strands" rather than branches, since branches grow apart and remain separate, while strands typically intertwine to produce a particular fabric. Following the distinction proposed by Rothschild-Whitt (1979), we shall speak of a "bureaucratic strand" and a "collective strand" of feminism taking shape in the period 1963–70. As these strands emerged in the mid-1960s, two different organizational modes developed, reflecting the history and needs of their members.

Bureaucratic and collectivist modes of organization.

The terms bureaucratic and collectivist describe more than variation in organizational structure; there are also marked differences in recruitment, activities, and the actualization of values. Most fundamentally, bureaucratic organizations are concerned with achieving concrete goals, while for collectivist organizations the means are as important, if not more so, than the ends of action. The consequences of this basic differences can be seen in Table 3.1.

The bureaucratic organization, in terms of Max Weber's (1922) ideal type, is characterized by a formal division of labor, written rules, universal standards of performance, hierarchical offices, impersonal relationships, technical expertise, and individualistic achievement norms. In contrast, the ideal type of collectivist organization is a community of like-minded persons, with minimal division of labor, rules, or differential rewards. Interaction among staff is wholistic, personalized, informal, and designed to achieve consensus. The types of collectivist organizations studied by Rothschild-Whitt, for example, included a "free" school, a law collective, a food cooperative, a storefront health clinic, and an alternative newspaper—precisely the type of experimental institution characteristic of the youth culture of the 1960s.

It is not difficult to see that bureaucratic or "individualist" organizations would appeal to women who have already achieved some personal success within that type of organization. They know how the game is played and are confident of their ability to make such systems work. In addition, their time is limited by family and work obligations, so that engaging in collectivist activities or in day-long consensus-seeking meetings would seem an intolerable

Table 3.1.

Comparison of Two Ideal Types of Organization*

	Bureaucratic	*Collectivist*
1. **Authority**	Resides in individuals by virtue of the offices they hold. Hierarchical structure. Compliance to fixed rules	Resides in collectivity as a whole, although may be temporarily delegated. Compliance to consensus fluid and subject to negotiation.
2. **Rules**	Fixed and impartial.	Ad hoc, situational.
3. **Social Control**	Supervision, formal sanctions.	Personalized appeals, and shared values.
4. **Social Relations**	Impersonal, role based, segmented, instrumental.	Communal, wholistic, personal, expressive.
5. **Recruitment and Advancement**	On basis of skill, specialized training, and formal certification. Employment as career, with advancement by seniority or achievement.	Network contacts, values, personality factors. Career and advancement not meaningful. No hierarchy of positions.
6. **Incentives**	Money and power.	Solidarity and value realization.
7. **Social Stratification**	Differential rewards by office; inequality.	Egalitarian; limited differentials in rewards.
8. **Differentiation**	High degree of division of labor. Difference between mental and manual work, and between administrative and performance tasks. Specialization of function, segmental roles. Ideal of specialist, expert.	Minimal division of labor. Administration combined with performance tasks. Generalization of jobs and functions. Wholistic roles Ideal of amateur, jack-of-all-trades.

Adapted from Rothschild-Whitt 1979, 519.

waste of time. While members of collectivist organizations take pride in "doing the right thing" (i.e., actualizing values), the bureaucratic mode is designed for "effectiveness" (i.e., realizing goals). For this reason, bureaucratic organizations attract women confronting specific obstacles and seeking concrete changes. The bureaucratic mode also separates work from other activities, to the benefit of women already balancing a multitude of competing demands.

Collectivist organizations, on the other hand, appealed to the antiauthoritarian principles of youthful veterans of the 1960s community organizing campaigns and student resistance movements. The job rotation characteristic of such groups also provided skill training in various fields. The time-consuming decision-making process meant that only those without demanding family and career commitments could fully participate. Value realization and solidarity were especially compelling incentives to people with weak family ties but strong moral commitments. Friendship and peer relationships in general were more crucial to younger than to older women. The communal, expressive, egalitarian nature of collectivist work organizations required a degree of personal attention and nurturance that most older women could not afford. Thus it was that feminists of the 1960s arrived at their organizational niches from two very different histories and traditions. In the remainder of this chapter we shall describe the development of these two strands of feminist activism.

The Bureaucratic Strand

The President's Commission on the Status of Women.

Presidential candidate John F. Kennedy vowed, in 1960, that if elected he would establish a national commission to study the status of women in the United States. He won, and he did. The driving force behind both the promise and the commission was Esther Peterson, a long-time activist in the trade union movement, educational organizations, and the Democratic party. In 1961, Kennedy appointed Peterson to head the Woman's Bureau in the Department of Labor, a traditional source of political influence for women in the federal government. She was also named to the post of vice-chairman *(sic)* of the President's Commission on the Status of Women, with Eleanor Roosevelt as honorary chairman. From her previous experience in politics and trade unionism, Peterson was able to draw upon the pool of women described in chapter 1 as feminists in the "woodwork" of national politics—those who had singly and quietly risen to relatively high positions in the federal bureaucracy, political party hierarchies, and established women's organizations.

The composition of the commission was carefully drawn to represent a variety of interest groups and officials, including a large number of men. After almost two years of fact-finding, the commission's report—*American Women* (1963)—was presented to the president at a White House ceremony on 11 October 1963 (Eleanor Roosevelt's birthday). The report documented widespread discrimination against women, and made twenty-four specific recommendations for guaranteeing equal treatment, including requests for a Cabinet officer to follow up on the commission's recommendations, and for an executive order requiring equal opportunity for women in private firms that received federal funds. The remaining proposals leaned strongly on the existing legal system, urging women to use the courts to test their grievances.

Significantly, the commission did *not* endorse an Equal Rights Amendment, stating that equality was already embodied in the "equal protection" clause of the Fourteenth Amendment to the U.S. Constitution, and expressing the belief that legal challenges would soon lead the Supreme Court to affirm this interpretation. In sum, the commission's report presented a fairly optimistic view that once the facts were known, the established mechanisms of democratic government would remedy the situation.

Legislation: 1963–64. To a limited extent, this optimism was rewarded. A presidential order was signed, although no Cabinet-level official was appointed. The Equal Pay Act of 1963 embodied the principle of equal pay for men and women doing the same work but did not mandate equal access to jobs. In this respect, the legislation reflected union concern that employers not hire women at a lower rate of pay in order to replace men or to drive down male wages, though employers could still not hire women at all.

In 1964, the pending Civil Rights Act was broadened to include "sex" as well as race in the section (Title VII) concerning equal employment opportunity, largely through the efforts of Representative Martha Griffiths of Michigan, with the unwitting help of a very conservative Southern colleague (Howard Smith, D–Va.) who thought that including women in a Civil Rights Act would allow legislators to vote against it on grounds other than racism. The act, as amended, was finally passed in July 1964 and signed into law by Lyndon Johnson at a ceremony with no women present, and with no mention made of equal rights for women (Robinson 1979). The word "sex" would probably not have remained in the act had not a small group actively lobbied for it, including all but one of the few women in Congress (Freeman 1975; Robinson 1979). We must remember that this was before there was an organized woman's movement that could pressure legislators.

Favorable legislation is one thing; ensuring that it is enforced is quite another. The Civil Rights Act of 1964 provided for an Equal Employment Opportunity Commission (EEOC) to handle complaints brought under Title VII. From the beginning, a high proportion of the complaints pouring into EEOC offices were charges of sex discrimination. Yet, even the existence of an enforcement mechanism was no guarantee that women's rights would be taken seriously. It would take another decade to bring sex discrimination into the center of EEOC concern (Robinson 1979). Nonetheless, Congress had acted, and there was a potential federal presence for ensuring equal treatment in employment. It is doubtful that either would have occurred without the groundwork done by the president's commission and a growing network of feminist activists in government.

State commissions on the status of women. Perhaps the most important legacy of the Commission on the Status of Women was not in the area of legislation at all, but in the mandate to convene commissions on the status of women at the state level. Eventually, every state in the union would have such a body, although in some instances (e.g., New Hampshire) the governor would appoint active antifeminists. Most of the state commissions on the status of women were created at the urging of women already active in state politics, and in many cases this became a simple way for political leaders to pay off a debt to women who had worked in their campaigns (Freeman 1973). More importantly, the state commissions were almost entirely composed of women who had risen to the leadership of organizations representing various racial, religious, occupational, and ethnic constituencies.

The state commissions served a number of functions. Officially, they were charged with gathering data on the roles and resources of women and with documenting areas of discrimination in the laws and practices of the individual states. In doing so, many latent (unanticipated and unintended) consequences followed. First, the members of the commissions and their staffs (often also predominately female) came to know one another and to share a common concern with women in general. The data they gathered was often eye-opening, since many commission members had little awareness of the cumulative impact of discrimination on women. Additionally, in the process of data gathering, many other groups were drawn into the activities of the commissions, and began to identify their interests with those of other women. Publicity in the form of hearings, news releases, reports, and media interviews brought the work of the commissions to public attention.

As with the presidential commission, the emphasis was on legal remedies and legislative action, but the state units were likely to be—or become—more radical than the federal commission, pushing for state Equal Rights Amendments. The state commissions also created a "climate of expectations that something would be done" (Freeman 1973, 798). Moreover, the state commissions were linked through a Federal Interdepartmental Committee and a Citizens Advisory Council that became clearinghouses for information. In sum, a national network of activists was created—the commissioners,

their staffs, the groups that these individuals represented, other constituencies activated during investigations and hearings, and political and community
leaders.

The particular events that led to the formation of a social movement organization occurred in June 1966, when representatives of state commissions were meeting in Washington, D.C., for their third annual conference.
During the same month, Representative Griffiths charged that the EEOC
had failed to take its mandate seriously. EEOC's lack of interest in sex discrimination was well known; its commissioners made open jokes about the
topic; and in any event, EEOC had little enforcement power (Robinson
1979). When delegates to the conference of state commissions on the status
of women presented a resolution demanding that EEOC enforce the sex
clause of Title VII, conference officials refused to allow it to come to the floor
for a vote. Several angry women agreed that the time had come to organize
a group that could lobby for women in the same way that the National Association for the Advancement of Colored People (NAACP) worked on behalf
of blacks. Thus was the National Organization for Women (NOW) formed,
by two dozen delegates to the conference, and a woman who was gathering
material for her second book—Betty Friedan.

NOW and other bureaucratic organizations. As de-
scribed in chapter 2, Friedan's first book had brought feminist ideas into public discourse and given her personal visibility, access to the media, and
credibility with the public. She had been invited to the White House "when
token women were needed to give a Good Housekeeping seal of approval to
some new program" (Friedan 1976, 78). She was also connected to the nationwide network of persons linked to the state commissions. Moreover, the
events of the third annual conference convinced many network members
that they were not going to achieve their goals solely through established
government channels. Although EEOC was ultimately to become receptive
to feminist influence through guidelines issued in 1969, and again by legislation in 1972 that gave it enforcement powers, in 1966 a new organization
independent of government and political parties was needed to create pressure for that change in focus.

By the time of NOW's first organizing meeting in October 1966, the two
dozen founding members had grown to several hundred men and women.
The name—National Organization *for* Women—expressed a commitment to
recruit both men and women who shared a belief in women's equality. Members were primarily drawn from the ranks of the elite: articulate achievers
with little movement experience but good media presence and government

contacts, so that news of the movement traveled far in advance of NOW's ability to organize followers (Freeman 1973).

The new organization drew heavily on the resources of that elite: not only specialized skills but access to other organizations' budgets were essential qualities for leadership roles. Friedan (1976) recalls that a member of the United Auto Workers was NOW's first secretary-treasurer not only because of her commitment to the cause but also for her ability to use the UAW's facilities for printing, mailing, and maintaining membership lists. Other mailings went out from the offices of other board members in different parts of the country. Throughout this period, membership lists were kept secret to protect members from retaliation by employers.

NOW's first target was EEOC, in support of a sex discrimination suit brought by stewardesses against the airlines' policy of forcing them to retire at marriage or at age thirty or thirty-five. NOW also fought to reverse an EEOC decision that sex-segregated newspaper ads did not constitute discrimination. Television networks were invited to cover a few small demonstrations, embarrassing the commission into holding hearings on both issues. And in both cases, new rulings supported the NOW position. President Lyndon Johnson then issued an executive order barring discrimination by federal contractors.

When NOW sought membership in the Leadership Conference on Civil Rights, its application was refused on the grounds that women's needs were not a civil rights issue. Rather than one civil rights movement, there would henceforth be separate women's rights and black rights movements. Black women such as Pauli Murray and Aileen Hernandez, founding members of NOW, were placed in the awkward position of bridging the gap.

Almost as soon as NOW was created, it was torn by controversy: was its mission that of improving women's employment and education opportunities, or the broader and more controversial goal of confronting and eliminating sexism throughout society? This question of scope was raised by the issue of reproductive rights; namely, should NOW advocate repeal of then-current laws that made abortion illegal? When the 1967 NOW convention added repeal of antiabortion laws to its agenda, the women who sought to steer clear of such a divisive issue left NOW in 1968 to form the Women's Equity Action League (WEAL). WEAL is a national membership association devoted to lobbying for a range of feminist issues, especially matters of educational and economic equity, to monitoring the performance of state and federal legislators, and to supporting legal challenges to patterns of discrimination in universities, banks, and the media (Carden 1974).

Another early addition to the bureaucratic strand was the National Women's Political Caucus (NWPC), a bipartisan association of politically active women, who could place women's issues on the agenda of state and national political parties. NWPC also endorsed and supported particular candidates, a step that NOW in this period had refused to take. Leadership roles in NWPC are carefully divided between Republican and Democratic activists to ensure that support could be mobilized for feminist candidates regardless of party label. Since NOW's focus at that time was on lobbying elected officials, it seemed wisest to withhold organizational endorsements altogether.

All three organizations started as small groups of highly placed women and men coordinating their activities on a national level and only gradually expanding into membership organizations with local chapters that any interested person could join. At first, there was no effort to recruit members, but increasing media attention in 1970 brought out large numbers of women looking for something to join. In many cases the national organization could only reply, "Start a chapter yourselves." Even when a local unit was created, it was difficult for others to locate or find an appropriate way to participate (cf. Cassell 1976, 6). Jo Freeman's experience was typical of many women "looking for the movement": "I first read of the National Organization for Women—with feelings of delight and relief—early in 1967 in a newspaper interview. My letter to the interviewee was never answered. Nor were any of the other five letters I wrote during the next year to the other NOW addresses I read or heard about in varying places. Clearly, something was happening, but I couldn't find it" (1975, xi).

At this stage, the NOW leadership had not determined how to use the women flocking to join the movement, except as volunteers willing to devote their time to dealing with other new members. There was no real organizational role for a local member. Elites could lobby, and sympathizers could demonstrate, but what was an ordinary member to do? Yet increasing numbers of women wanted to join NOW to express their commitment to the feminist ideas circulating in the mass media, and for the instrumental, if vague, wish to somehow "help." Until a local chapter could find some effective way to deal with the influx of potential members, it could only rarely provide innovative ideas, leadership, or local organizational activity.

Once this first organizational hurdle was surmounted, and members could be effectively used in concrete projects, a second obstacle appeared: there was no real link between the national organization and its chapters. Communication was haphazard, duplication of effort commonplace, and controversy emerged over which unit, national or local, was responsible for the other. A compromise was finally reached that allowed substantial local autonomy, but at the cost of increased bureaucratization of the organization as a

whole. Rather than relying solely on national task forces, state-level committees were formed to coordinate local activities with national priorities, while
the national office (founded in 1969) prepared information packets that eliminated the necessity of each new local beginning from scratch. In this fashion,
NOW survived its first period of growth and became a national membership
organization with a democratic and largely decentralized power structure.

These early, tentative efforts to form a national movement proved more
successful than anyone had dared to believe. In the short period between
1968 and 1971, NOW, WEAL, and NWPC were joined by many other nationally organized groups representing specific constituencies and issues of
particular concern to members; for example, women in federal employment,
female athletes, older women, professional and other working women,
members of ethnic and racial minorities, and women in academic and intellectual fields. Groups sprang up faster than people could keep track. While
some came and went rather quickly, others survived to form the backbone
of the New Feminist Movement. As in the human backbone, the separate
elements remained discrete and flexible, and yet firmly linked to one another, lending to the whole a strength that could not be found in a single rigid
organization.

There is, however, a sense in which these bureaucratic organizations are
only the visible tip of the new feminism, surface manifestations of deeper
changes taking place within the society and in the consciousness of women
and men. To grasp fully the breadth and depth of the New Feminist Movement requires an examination of the strand described by Freeman (1973) as
the younger branch, by others as the women's liberation movement (Carden
1974; Cassell 1977), and by us as the collectivist strand.

The Collectivist Strand

The origins of the second strand of feminist activism lie not only in the
Southern civil rights movement of the late 1950s but also in the student-led
New Left movement of the 1960s in the North. In both causes, idealistic
young women were actively involved in creating change. Activist white
women rejected the privileges of class and race, and experienced the
strength of a small group engaged in community organizing. Especially in the
New Left, they also found themselves treated by their male counterparts
less as colleagues than as trophies. Male New Left "big shots" were expected to have a small horde of female hangers-on (Piercy 1970). Women's developing sense of independence, integrity, and power repeatedly conflicted

with their treatment as things, as prizes to be fought over by white and black men (Stember 1976).

Women in the civil rights movement.   As noted earlier, many black men had attitudes toward women very similar to those of white males. The aggressively sexist ("macho") style of the young black men who suddenly found themselves in positions of power in student-led organizations appalled their black female colleagues, who were the first to raise the issue of sexism in the student civil rights organizations. But it was more difficult for black women to break away from primary involvement in the civil rights movement than it was for their white sisters, not only because of their deep personal commitment but because of the hostility directed at them. Black feminists were called traitors to the greater cause of civil rights (Wallace 1982). Black women and white women often found a common cause in confronting the sexism of movement men, even though that sexism also drove a wedge between them.

One tense and crucial issue for the civil rights movement was that of interracial sexual relationships. Black men were accused of "talking black but sleeping white" (Stember 1976). White women would accept sexist behavior from black men that their black sisters would not tolerate. Black women, in turn, often resented the rivalry and the white women who "won" the sexual competition. Black men rationalized their dating of white women not on the grounds that race was irrelevant, but on the claim that since white women were the "possessions" of white men, interracial sex was a revolutionary act. Nonetheless, in the early days of the civil rights movement, both Zinn (1964) and Evans (1979) report several warm and loving relationships between black men and white women.

More often, however, the masculine ideology that sees women only as sexual objects was dominant. Grier and Cobbs argued, for example, that "the white woman represents the socially identified female ideal and thus an intensely exciting object for [black men's] possession" (1968, 91). When black women criticized their brothers' "coming down the streets with their African garb with a white woman on their arms," black males would reply that the relationship was not one of love but of possession, anger, and abiding hostility, with black male power depending on "conquest of the 'White Bitch'" (Brown 1968, quoted in Stember 1976, 111). Neither white women nor black women found their human identity affirmed in such an assertion. Such claims were most common among younger, radical black power groups, and did not represent the tone or feelings of leaders of the more established civil rights organizations such as the NAACP.

By the mid-1960s, white males also discovered that they were no longer welcome in the more radical black civil rights organizations. Most of the white former civil rights activists found new homes in the protest movements of the 1960s: free speech, student power, antiwar, and community organizing. As they joined the less structured world of the "youth movement," these women brought with them the legacy of their Southern experience: the dream of equality and the skills needed to fight for it. What they found were the same assumptions about women as the prizes and possessions of men that had poisoned their experience in the civil rights movement. Activist white women and some of their black "sisters" had been sufficiently radicalized to understand that if they were to pursue their vision of a moral community of equals, it would have to be with other women. Here, then, was a pool of women skilled in grass-roots organizing, who had learned how to build a movement from the ground up, and who were structurally available for co-optation to the ideas of feminism. The communications network established during these years would ultimately provide one national base of support for the New Feminist Movement.

Women in the New Left. The "New Left" is a term used to describe those loosely linked groups of predominately white college-age men and women engaged in challenging the basic institutions of American society in the 1960s. Among the many targets of the New Left were the universities, the military, racism, materialistic values, the political process, economic imperialism- -almost every aspect of the status quo except sexism. Their critique of existing institutions was "left wing" in the sense that the ideals of a restructured society were fundamentally anticapitalist, echoing many of the themes of the Old Left of the 1930s: brotherhood, equality, an end to exploitation, and a fairer distribution of societal resources. What was new was the emphasis on direct democracy. The Old Left had become authoritarian and inflexible, and so isolated as to be virtually invisible to the general public. The New Left followed no "party line" but instead consisted of political self-education and protest groups, and a variety of collectivist experiments, such as "free schools" and alternative newspapers. Nonviolent tactics were borrowed from the civil rights movement, although the New Left was ultimately to produce its own violent fringe.

New Left ideology viewed restrictions on sexuality as the reflection of a repressive society, seen as part of a broader complex embracing work discipline, deferred gratification, and political suppression of unpopular opinion—all of which combined to create "one-dimensional" obedient robots who had lost the capacity for questioning whether what they produced was worth their life's effort. "Question authority" was a key slogan of the New Left, and as authorities increasingly demanded the bodies of young people for the war in Vietnam, their legitimacy came under escalating attack from a student-age population that preferred to "make love not war." With the deepening involvement in Vietnam, the New Left found itself with a broad and growing constituency.

While there are important differences in structure and ideology between the Old and New Left, both attracted sizeable numbers of women activists, who became skilled organizers at lower levels of authority but who never held decision-making posts. According to Trimberger's (1979) analysis, the Old Left/Communist party provided an all-embracing community for its members. It created an important place for women, and supported those who were engaged in child care. The Old Left was also characterized by an ideological commitment to equality for women that was missing from the New Left, but Old Left women were expected to subordinate their personal needs to the broader movement.

The New Left, in contrast, did not subordinate the individual to the group; its structures were looser, the emphasis was on spontaneity and personal freedom; there was no ideological or organizational center and hence no source of discipline. Moreover, the range of human activities considered to be politically relevant was broader than the economic issues that composed Old Left agenda. In the 1960s, "free speech," nonconformist clothing, and unconventional sexuality were all defined as challenges to the political system. In this context, New Left women could be expected to be more self-aware than those of the Old Left for whom the political overwhelmed the personal (Trimberger 1979). To women in the New Left, the personal could become political, and they confronted growing male power in the movement, for "as the movement became more militant, many males found it an excellent arena for competitive displays of virility, toughness, and physical courage" (Flacks 1971, 118). These tendencies were reinforced when the focus of the New Left shifted from community organizing (in which the women excelled) to draft resistance (from which women were effectively excluded).

Having enlisted in the cause of personal freedom, women could not long overlook their lack of power within the New Left nor their treatment as mindless sex objects (Evans 1979; Freeman 1973). Movement demands for an end to sexual repression were not connected to a challenge of the double standard; liberation was defined as "free food, free chicks" (Piercy 1970). The "chicks" began to feel more abused than liberated. However, the New Left's linking of political and sexual repression provided a fruitful starting point for a feminist critique.

Here, then, was another group of women, knit into a national network of student activists, ripe for conversion to feminism. At first, groups of women met separately to discuss their grievances within the movement, and to compose resolutions demanding that movement men recognize how they were oppressing their female colleagues. Only later did these women extend their analysis and their demands from the New Left to the society as a whole.

The precipitating events for this shift in focus took place over several years in several different locations, but the pattern was constant: the women would arrive at meetings and conventions of New Left organizations seeking to place women's issues on the agenda only to be told that these were insignificant in comparison with matters of war and peace, race relations, draft resistance, or the cause of American Indians.

There was a limit to how much public ridicule New Left women of the 1960s would endure; they had already shed their "good girl" image to become "radicals"; and in city after city, individually or in caucuses, they decisively split with the New Left. Robin Morgan's "Goodbye to All That" (1970) and Marge Piercy's "Grand Coolie Damn" (1970) marked the end of a phase in which the collectivist strand of the new feminism had operated as the women's branch of the student left, and the beginning of an autonomous feminist movement at the "grassroots."

Their anger was liberating and invigorating. Out of the turmoil came insightful criticisms of the broader society. Summarizing the experiences of women in both the civil rights movement and the New Left, Wini Breines remarks:

In the midst of sexist movements, women were having experiences that transformed their consciousness and changed their lives. . . . [D]emocratic and egalitarian values inspired women and offered them an alternative vision of society. . . . When women acquired the experience and skills that enabled them to feel strong enough to move out on their own, it was with political ideas that they had inherited from the sixties. (1979, 504–5)

Unlike NOW, which was still an elite organization, the many, small, self-contained women's groups that now appeared throughout the nation were accessible to students and other women with New Left connections (particularly young housewives in university areas).

Also unlike NOW, small, autonomous "liberation" groups could experiment with such attention-getting devices ("zap actions") as picketing the Miss America Beauty Pageant in Atlantic City to protest the sexual objectification of women, or a sit-in at a male-only clam bar in Hoboken, New Jersey, or a "hairy-legs" demonstration in front of a San Francisco shop where an employee had been fired for not shaving her legs. It is difficult to imagine the women of the older branch engaging in street theater, holding "abortion raps" at a time when all abortions were illegal, or forming groups with such names as Redstockings, Bread and Roses, or W.I.T.C.H. (Women's International Terrorist Conspiracy from Hell). For several years, from 1968–1972, these groups and their actions added energy and zest as well as serious intellectual content to the emergent women's movement.

Yet by 1973, this phase of collectivist activity had run its course. The vital and influential liberation groups had either dissolved or lost focus, in what Cassell (1977) refers to as a "ripple effect"; that is, as their ideas began to spread, their original impact dissolved into ever-widening circles of feminist activity. Perhaps the event that symbolizes both the highpoint of collectivist influence and the absorption of its energies into a larger movement was the Women's Equality March in New York City in 1970, when tens of thousands of women and men, old and young, radical and reformist, joined in the first of many large-scale demonstrations of the strength of this new movement.

The structure and style of collectivist groups. As this brief history suggests, the women in feminist collectives differed in many respects from those who were the founders and the leaders of bureaucratic organizations. Most obviously, they were younger in age and came from the counterculture rather than from the establishment. Where the older women had mastered the techniques of bureaucratic organization, the younger ones were fiercely antielitist and antihierarchy. The older women had careers that gave them access to the system, but that also made them vulnerable to retaliation and fearful of "going too far." Students and young housewives in the younger branch enjoyed more flexible hours and fewer scheduled commitments, so that they could throw themselves into full-time "careers" in the women's movement. Their experience was most likely to have been in grass-roots organizing and staging provocative public demonstrations. Both strands were effective in using the media, but the events they placed before the cameras were very different.

This old/young distinction also reflects a difference in cohort membership. A cohort refers to a group of individuals who enter a given system at the same time and age together through a particular slice of history. The women who founded NOW and other bureaucratic strand organizations were members of the very small birth cohorts of the Great Depression, strongly influenced by the social activism of the New Deal, often daughters or granddaughters of feminists who took their own career commitment as self-evident. Because of the small number of college-educated women in their birth cohorts, they felt themselves to be part of an elite. They emphasized the autonomy and individuality of women, and were acutely aware of the nation's failure to realize the full promise of women's education and the suffrage. They had been personally successful and saw existing restraints as holdovers from a less enlightened era; thus, their faith in working through the system.

Collectivist strand women, in contrast, were the first of the "baby boom" cohorts to enter a greatly expanded educational system; they had grown up in the comfort of the relatively affluent 1950s; and were encouraged to achievement more as a matter of course than as a mark of distinction. Unlike the older women, they were reluctant to define achievement in purely material terms. The civil rights movement and the New Left provided a focus for their idealism, although neither movement fully recognized or used their talents. The New Left also offered an alternative education in critical social theory that gave many women basic insights into the dynamics of psychological and political oppression that they would later use to analyze their own situation.

In both movements, young white women found a personally important "community." Intense involvement in small group interaction among peers within the counterculture held enormous appeal, but it continued along patriarchal lines. Women, who were told that their role in the revolution was to make sandwiches for the "brothers" who were occupying the administration building, began to question the meaning of this revolution and of the "family" whose patterns it imitated. Ultimately, they insisted on the importance of traditional "female" values—interpersonal relationships, nonviolence, community service—for all people, not just women.

Activist women drifting out of the civil rights movement and the New Left did not give up their vision of a moral community, but they abandoned the possibility of finding it in existing movements. The impulse toward community, common to the New Left and the collectivist strand of early feminism, became embodied in the technique and structure of the consciousness-raising (CR) group and in the ideology of "sisterhood."

Consciousness-raising. The technique of CR was developed even before New Left women made the break into an autonomous women's movement. As simply "small groups" of women, they discussed the problems they were having with male dominance in movement activities, and sexual exploitation, and the fear that such problems were not really "serious enough" to deserve more attention than the "real revolution" of the New Left.

The CR process was essentially a four-step discussion. The first stage involves self-revelation, with each individual talking about herself and her feelings while other participants practice "active listening," or drawing her out and encouraging her. In the second stage, participants assemble experiences into a larger pattern. Third, these shared experiences are analyzed to find common causes in social arrangements. Finally, members reach the stage of abstraction where the group attempts to move to the level of social theory, linking their own analysis to other theories of oppression (Bunch-Weeks 1970, 190).

This process turned conventional New Left practice on its head; rather than starting with theory, as in Freudian or Marxist analysis, and then attempting to fit contemporary experience into the theoretical framework, New Left women started with their own experiences, developed theory from that, and ended up criticizing the "master." The response of New Left men was that the women were "navel-gazing" while the real revolution was going on without them (Fritz 1979).

The personal transformation of priorities produced by these discussions and the rapid word-of-mouth spread of information about consciousness-raising (greatly accelerated once the mass media picked it up), brought such a demand for CR groups that the resources of most women's groups were stretched thin. Membership in the feminist movement for collectivist women was largely defined as having participated in CR. Groups formed wherever young women came together. Participants discovered that women could be friends in more than a superficial way. The process of recognizing the oppression in their lives as part of a system-wide pattern rather than as an expression of their personal "failure" as women (or as revolutionaries) was also exhilarating, encouraging a high degree of commitment to the goals of the feminist movement—a conversion experience in an almost religious sense.

The process of self-discovery and the creation of new forms of community did not proceed without difficulty. Many groups failed because members could not control expressions of personal power or devise successful means of helping one another. Kramer (1970) presents a somewhat chilling account of consciousness-raising among a "founding cadre" of New York City feminists, as they pioneered an unfamiliar style of interaction while trying to set their own lives in order. Some women moved from group to group in an attempt to find a supportive network, and large numbers ultimately succeeded, but not without cost.

Sisterhood and power. The CR groups that formed the basic unit of the collectivist strand were deliberately nonhierarchical (without formal positions of power and subordination), a virtue established in the New Left. Collectivist feminists gave "hierarchy" the additional negative meaning of a basically male principle of organization in contrast to a female mode of equality, defined as "sisterhood," that is, a horizontal rather than vertical relationship. While rejection of any form of hierarchy and expertise could work for members of groups dedicated to exploring their own experience, problems arose when groups also attempted to engage in political action. There were no established mechanisms for the resolution of conflicts over goals and tactics. When informal leaders emerged to steer a group toward a decision, other members saw this as an illegitimate exercise of power.

Under these conditions, women who had special skills or abilities ran special risks. Although the group insisted that such women share their skills and dedicate their efforts to the cause, the radical vision of equality in these early years was directly opposed to the recognition of individual contributions, within the group as well as in public. Many women's articles were written anonymously or in the name of a collective, an ironic twist on the historical restraints that made it already true that "anonymous was a woman." Women who violated the unwritten rules of egalitarianism by appearing overly assertive or concerned with individual achievement could be subject to "trashing," a process Freeman describes as "a particularly vicious form of character assassination" (1976). Such women were accused of using the movement and other women's oppression for their own personal gain, and were either openly condemned or subtly excluded from group activities (for example, not being informed of the next meeting). If a group member achieved some degree of public recognition as a result of her feminist activities—that is, became a "media star"—she was especially vulnerable to trashing. The distrust of expertise blended into anti-intellectualism; "sisterhood" demanded that no woman rise above the mass in any way, making those with academic credentials automatically suspect. The trashing experience led many talented women to cut all ties with women's collectives, although not with the goals of the movement.

It is perhaps understandable that in the emotionally charged small group setting, women newly energized by personal awareness and revolutionary images should find themselves making the political personal; that is, reducing the big issues to personality problems (and, in the process, turning their own ideology upside down). Much the same pattern was evident among American socialists in the 1930s, and it takes place today within the New Right. Powerlessness makes it difficult to confront those who actually wield power,

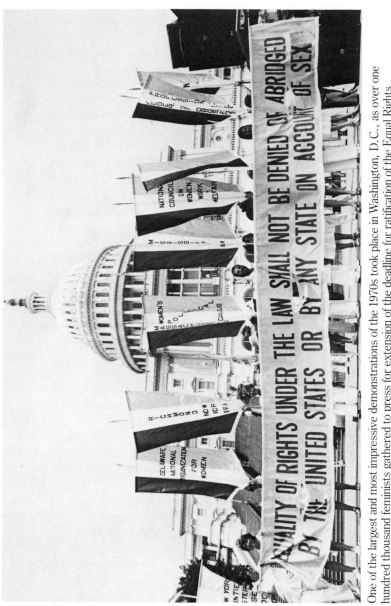

One of the largest and most impressive demonstrations of the 1970s took place in Washington, D.C., as over one hundred thousand feminists gathered to press for extension of the deadline for ratification of the Equal Rights Amendment. Marchers dressed in white and displayed the colors—purple, green, and gold—of the earlier movement for women's suffrage, linking past and present. *Photograph courtesy of Bettye Lane.*

and easier to displace anger horizontally. Existing on the radical fringe of social movements appears to produce a "siege mentality" that frequently leads to both personal and ideological attacks on comrades-in-arms. Although suspicions that getting ahead meant selling out were not always unfounded, holding women down to the lowest common level as a means of ensuring "equality" could in the long run only perpetuate powerlessness, breed resentment, and create divisions within the movement. In any event, personal trashing diminished as women became integrated into other social institutions, including a larger and more diverse feminist movement, and as local groups shifted from self-exploration to self-help and finally to providing community services (see Chapter 5).

Legacies of the Early Strands

Thus, by 1970, two very different age groups of women had produced two very different organizational modes based on divergent visions of appropriate goals and methods. Although it might seem that such a division would diffuse the energies and commitment of feminists, this structural diversity was a source of strength, allowing various women to find a place for themselves within the broader movement. Moreover, the two modes of activity provide a counterpoint, or "dialectic," in which each feeds and corrects the other. That is, the collectivist impulse ensures that humanistic concerns and nonhierarchical styles remain visible, not only as ultimate feminist goals but as a means of transformation now. However, collectivists have difficulty dealing with bureaucracies, and since most American institutions are bureaucratically structured, the possibilities for influencing these are limited. Bureaucratically structured organizations in the women's movement, conversely, can conduct the type of nationwide money-raising and lobbying activities that bring pressure to bear on other bureaucracies, including legislative and administrative bodies. Collectives are created in order to change institutional patterns directly, by providing alternative ways of meeting members' needs. Bureaucratic activists focus on indirect change, through lawsuits, political pressure, or "moral suasion" (mobilizing public opinion), and changing the ways existing bureaucracies function.

What we have been describing are "ideal types": polar opposites and pure examples. More often, the lines between the types blurred as groups originally based on collectivist principles were transformed into local units of a broad-based movement organization, or as local chapters of national organizations served the functions of a primary group. One such pattern can be found in the academic community, where women across a variety of departments first came together as an informal support network for one another, and to explore women's lives from a woman's perspective, before becoming part of a nationally organized "women's caucus" in their discipline, with the broader goal of encouraging a new perspective in their field of study. In this fashion many feminist organizations have been able to transcend conflicts between expressive and instrumental goals, successfully blending the personal and the political.

Still, the importance of collectivist groups in the New Feminist Movement declined in the early 1970s as all feminist organizations became increasingly goal-oriented, and the two strands grew closer together in both structure and style. One factor in this development was, quite simply, the time element involved in consensual decision making, often to the exclusion of accomplishing concrete tasks. Another factor was the immediate need for women to organize effectively around certain real and symbolic political goals: the Equal Rights Amendment and the protection of reproductive rights. The tendency toward bureaucratic domination, however, is far from total. The movement then and now embraces a spectrum of organizational modes, with the national mass-membership organization (often asking only for money in their direct mailings) at one pole, and community-based women's centers, health or music collectives at the other. In between, one can find thousands of separate groups of women engaged in the work of the movement, in one form or another, for any or all of the stated goals of contemporary feminism. This diversity and creativity gave the emergent movement a strength and resilience that attracted an outpouring of support in the early 1970s. The feminist boast that "we are everywhere" could no longer be taken lightly.

The number and diversity of feminist publications, as illustrated in this collage, are unequaled by any other contemporary social movement. The New Feminist Movement has attempted to address both the range of women's experiences and their common interests.

CHAPTER FOUR

Dilemmas of Growth:
The Promise of Diversity

Social movements typically originate in the activities of a small nucleus of people who share similar backgrounds and experience. To become an effective agent of change, the movement must expand this base, adapting its ideology and structures to take into account the experience of others. As the movement reaches out to others, its own publications and the mass media are needed to spread the word beyond the range of interpersonal contacts. This task demands new resources and new structures.

The first major challenge to any social movement is surviving this transition from a small core of activists to a complex and varied set of organizations, representing a diverse and widespread constituency. The second major challenge is to reflect this diversity in the formulation of goals and priorities for the movement as a whole.

As described in the previous chapter, the New Feminist Movement developed from two very different groups of activists, leading to the creation of two organizational strands: the bureaucratic and the collectivist. From the beginning, both types of organizations attempted to reach a broader audience, in order to influence public opinion and attract new members. In this chapter, we examine these outreach efforts, their successes, and the dilemmas that these successes posed for the movement. Our first focus is on how word of the movement spread from the initial networks of interpersonal influence to the public at large, and, second, on public response in the form of changing opinions on women and the feminist movement. As rising proportions of the public supported change in women's status, a constituency was created that could be mobilized for more specific demands.

But even in the increasingly favorable climate of opinion, not all sympathizers are equally willing or able to become activists. In the second half of this chapter, we look at the processes of mobilization that lead people to become personally involved in movement activities, whether for a single demonstration or in an ongoing group context. In the New Feminist Movement, as in all social organizations and movements, these processes of mobilization are biased in certain predictable ways. Some people stand a much greater chance than others of being mobilized, and in the last section of this chapter we examine these biases and their meaning for contemporary feminism.

Publicizing the Movement

Feminist publications.   It used to be said, before the day of the photocopier, that the most important piece of equipment for any social movement was a mimeograph machine. Most movements for change, precisely because they are outside the established networks of influence and communication, must find an inexpensive but effective way of reaching and maintaining contact among widely separated individuals and groups. In common with members of the other social movements of the 1960s, feminists first kept in touch through flyers announcing important events, mimeographed newsletters, and photocopied manuscripts.

By the late 1960s, several radical feminist groups were publishing newspapers and magazines. The first of these was a six-page mimeographed newsletter, *Voice of the Women's Liberation Movement,* published by Chicago feminists in early 1968 and distributed across the country. Although *Voice* soon faded away, it was quickly succeeded by many others. By 1971, over 100 women's liberation journals and newspapers were in circulation (Hole and Levine 1971), only some of which have survived to the present, among them: *Women: A Journal of Liberation* (1969); *off our backs* (1970); *Second Wave* (1971); and *Southern Feminists* (1970). These periodicals today have circulation rates ranging from 20,000 for *Women: A Journal of Liberation,* to 350 for *Feminary,* the new name for *Southern Feminists.* [Information in this section not otherwise attributed comes from the 1982 edition of *Ulrich's International Periodical Directory.*]

Also, in the late 1960s and early 1970s, in addition to National NOW's organizational newsletter, *Do It NOW* (1968), a number of local NOW chapters published newsletters and newspapers that circulated among chapters and to the general public. Feminist newspapers were established in Milwaukee, Wisconsin (*Amazon,* 1972), Westchester, New York (*Westchester Woman,* 1972), and Cleveland, Ohio (*What She Wants,* 1973).

These early efforts were quickly augmented by a veritable explosion of feminist publishing between 1972 and 1978. Each special interest group established its journal or monthly report: women in the arts, in literature, and the media; Jewish women, black women, older women; women in various academic disciplines and professions; working women and neighborhood women. But there was as yet no general-interest publication that could link already committed feminists across their special concerns or reach out to a potentially sympathetic public. This gap was filled with the introduction of *Ms.: a Magazine for Women* in 1972. As the most successful mass-circulation feminist publication, *Ms.* today has a press run of 400,000, and a readership of over a half-million, since many copies are shared or in libraries (although some public schools have been under local pressure to cancel subscriptions). To place this figure in context, *Cosmopolitan* magazine has a circulation of 2,250,000, and *McCall's,* 6,500,000. At the other end of the ideological spectrum, the major women-published antifeminist newsletter, the *Phyllis Schlafly Report* (1967), has a current circulation of 30,000.

The second most widely circulated feminist publication is a tabloid-format newspaper called *New Directions for Women,* with a national circulation of 55,000. *New Directions* began in 1972 as a fourteen-page mimeographed newsletter for feminists in New Jersey, with a press run of 2,000 copies, most of which were hand delivered to libraries and other public places (one of the authors was present at the first editorial meeting; it took place in a neighbor's kitchen). The growth of *New Directions* exemplifies the gradual but persistent spread of a feminist media presence, from local to national, from narrow concerns to an ever-widening range of topics, from limited appeal to a broad readership, and from outside to almost inside the mainstream—*New Directions,* for example, has received a grant from the Ford Foundation to expand its readership base.

The mid-1970s also saw the publication of several periodicals of high intellectual quality, most notably, *Feminist Studies* in 1972, *Quest* in 1974, and *Signs* in 1975. Contents range from original poetry to analyses of literature to academic research reports. These journals provide a publication opportunity often denied to articles on women's issues in other professional publications, and they have become lively forums of feminist debate. Because they cover the entire range of women's concerns, these journals allow readers from one field of interest to follow developments in other areas.

The emergence of a national audience for feminist writing and information encouraged the creation of women-owned and operated publishing houses and collectives. Among the earliest of these was KNOW, Inc., founded in the fall of 1969, and soon followed by the Feminist Press. KNOW's early list contained a large number of reprints of articles that had already appeared in the academic and alternative press, and that could now reach a wider audience. KNOW also served as first publisher for a number of feminist essays that had previously circulated only in mimeograph. Soon, feminist publishers were putting together anthologies and soliciting new manuscripts, so that today there are a half dozen publishing houses operated for and by women.

Finding an outlet for these publications was another difficult hurdle, as most chain bookstores reserve their shelves for mass-appeal books. One response was to establish women's bookstores. These bookstores, similar to those of the Old Left in the 1930s, serve as general meeting places and rallying grounds for community feminists. A list compiled in 1980 includes over seventy women's bookstores in thirty states, primarily in college towns or large cities (*Women's Action Almanac* 1980).

However, as feminism itself moved into the mainstream of American culture, established publishing houses became interested in tapping this new market. The success of Friedan's *Feminine Mystique,* Millett's *Sexual Politics,* and Germaine Greer's *The Female Eunuch* (1970) encouraged major publishing houses to create or expand their "women's issue list." A number of anthologies appeared that brought articles from the alternative press into mass-market availability. *Sisterhood is Powerful* (Morgan 1970), *From Feminism to Liberation* (Altbach 1971), and *Women in Sexist Society* (Gornick and Moran 1971) were three early collections that combined underground "classics" with new pieces, and made them accessible to a mass audience. With the expansion of women's studies programs and courses in higher education, every important academic publisher has attempted to reach this market with at least one book on "sex roles." In sum, what had been esoteric knowledge in 1969 was broadly available in 1972 and commonly recognized by 1974.

While books, magazines, and newsletters were important elements in spreading the word, they tended to reach primarily those already active in the movement. Coverage by the mass media was even more crucial in reaching a wider audience.

Mass media coverage of the movement. As attention shifted from the civil rights movement to the ghetto riots of the late 1960s, and as the student movement and New Left dissolved under the guns of the National Guard and in factionalism over "revolutionary violence," the media discovered the New Feminist Movement. In large part, this was intentional. Women in the bureaucratic strand were both media-wise and media-conscious; some were from the communications industries, others had extensive contacts in publishing and news services. The younger women, despite an antimedia ideology, had also learned how to catch public interest for New Left activities through media events such as protest marches, mass demonstrations, and "street theater" episodes.

Between the carefully prepared conference papers and press handouts of the older women and the "zap" actions of the collectivists, the media had much to report in the late 1960s and early 1970s. Rather than having gradually increased their coverage of the movement through its years of growth, the media treated the New Feminist Movement as a sudden discovery. Mentions of the women's movement in the national press increased tenfold between May 1969 and March 1970 (Morris 1973). Media interest picked up sharply in mid-1969; NOW's executive director reported that her office "went crazy" trying to answer media inquiries that August (Carden 1974, 32) and in the "grand press blitz" of early 1970 the stories began to appear (Freeman 1975). Features about women and the feminist movement on television newscasts almost tripled (from 18 to 53) between 1969 and 1970 (Cancian and Ross 1981). Not only did the number of stories increase, but there was a distinct change of content and tone. Coverage of women by the *New York Times* shows an increase from 168 stories in 1966, to 603 in 1970, and 1814 in 1974, with a general shift of focus to feminist concerns. Items on the legal and political aspects of women's rights and on nontraditional roles jumped from 27 percent of all coverage of women in 1966 to 46 percent in 1970 and 56 percent in 1974 (Cancian and Ross 1981, 23). Most of these articles, however, are still found on the *Times*'s "Style" page, otherwise devoted to fashion and news of high society.

As the New Feminist Movement attracted the mainstream press, an important strategic decision was made by collectivist leaders, already angered over the ridicule of feminist goals by New Left men. Women activists refused to speak to male reporters, forcing the press to send female reporters to cover demonstrations and news conferences. While this might appear to be a logical editorial decision, the American press was slow to see the connection between feminist analysis and its own news-gathering practices. Some newspapers even claimed they had no women reporters or that they were all busy covering weddings or testing recipes. The press modified these habits only under pressure. As VanGelder observed:

The parallel between women and blacks in journalism is worth noting. Until the mid-Sixties, news of the black community was virtually ignored by the press, and black reporters numbered a handful . . . [but] as the value of black news accelerated, people like SNCC and the Panthers did a wicked thing. They started banning honkies from their press conferences. Tsk, tsk, said all the editors as they madly hired up every black journalist they could find. . . . Come the women's revolution, an awful lot of talented women are going to be hauled away from their steno pads, research jobs, and fashion columns—to explain it in print. (1970, 85)

Although some of the newly authorized women reporters may have been selected in hopes that they, too, would trivialize the movement (the *New York Times* assigned the wife of a senior editor), many newswomen found themselves personally affected and transformed by their contact with feminists and feminism. Not only did they file sympathetic reports, but they began to organize for changes in their own workplaces—more women in responsible positions, greater control over editorial content, and increased attention to topics of feminist concern (in the news sections as well as the social or "women's" pages [Tuchman 1978]).

Staff writers on traditional women's magazines also struggled to raise the awareness level of publishers and the public. They demonstrated and lobbied for articles on working women, the New Feminist Movement, nonsexist child rearing, violence against women, the women's health movement, and the Equal Rights Amendment. Feminist-inspired social science research began to be reported in their articles and editorials. In this fashion, 1969–70 marked a turning point not only in quantity but quality of media coverage. Ideas that had previously circulated only by word-of-mouth or among the small number of subscribers to "alternative" publications, now appeared in mass circulation newspapers and magazines, reaching millions of women without personal links to the tiny feminist groups that existed in major cities.

This media coverage was essential to the success of the new feminism. For any social movement to expand its base and to develop latent support from the public at large, the initial network of activists must be able to communicate to a potentially sympathetic public. The movement ideology must be widely broadcast, so that individuals throughout the society can see that what they thought were personal problems are not at all unique. These effects are reflected in actual patterns of recruitment. One study of movement members found that all who joined before 1969 had heard about the movement from personal contacts, while among joiners in or after 1969, about one in four had been activated soley on the basis of media reports (Carden 1974).

In addition, as more books are published and reviewed, as more magazine articles appear, as more mention is made on radio and television, as newspaper coverage expands, the movement itself becomes "institutionalized"; that is, it becomes a "normal" part of the social landscape. In this way, media attention creates reality, validating the existence of whatever it covers. Even though it had been a growing force for several years, the New Feminist Movement became "real" as soon as the reporters and cameras focused on it (just as, a decade later, the movement lost much of its "thereness" when the cameras and reporters turned away).

The reality created by the media was, in many ways, a different one from that experienced by members. Indeed, the most memorable media image was of an event that never actually occurred: the "bra burning" during a protest against the Miss America contest in Atlantic City in 1968. And what an image! Here is the distillation of resentment over the status of women as sex objects, over the need to contort one's natural shape to fit a culturally defined ideal; and, yet, how easily ridiculed and trivialized the movement can be made to appear through such images. The glare of publicity exaggerates both the strengths and weaknesses of a social movement and its membership. In these early years of the new feminism, media attention undoubtedly served to spread the word and activate constituencies, making the movement appear more powerful than the actual numbers of committed feminists would suggest, an impression that probably accounted for many early legislative gains, but that also awakened countermovement forces.

Demonstrations and the media. Media attention can spread the message, letting potential recruits know they are not alone, but there must be something to join—a local organization or CR group—before the feeling of solidarity can be translated into active support. Here is where local groups or chapters of national organizations assume critical importance. They are rallying places of activated commitments and visible symbols of a movement's vitality. Demonstrations also serve this function, while at the same time contributing to the "newsworthy" quality of the movement, attracting even more media attention.

A demonstration operates at several levels. In addition to the obvious appeal to those who watch on television or read about the event in magazines and newspapers, there is also the effect on participants. Marching together creates a sense of solidarity, deepening one's commitment to the movement; if the situation has an element of danger, there is the additional exhilaration of risk-taking on behalf of the cause. Just being with others who feel as you do helps to legitimize your feelings; the shared ideals can become an important part of your identity. If as a demonstrator one is heckled or attacked, awareness of the opposition is heightened, an experience "worth perhaps a hundred CR sessions" (Fritz 1979) in creating insight into the conflict and stimulating loyalty to the cause.

The New Feminist Movement has orchestrated a number of demonstrations that have served the dual functions of broadcasting a message and reinforcing the allegiance of participants. The 1970 New York City march for equality, for example, exceeded the expectations of its organizers when 20,000 took over Fifth Avenue in the first show of feminist strength, to the general amazement of onlookers and the police. For participants, the experience of finding so many others willing to give visible support to the movement reinforced a feminist identity. The demonstration, then, is a mobilization tactic, providing an occasion for the periodic reactivation of commitment.

Not all sympathizers become personally involved. The vast majority of Americans who think of themselves as feminists have probably never attended a meeting or taken part in a demonstration. Their commitment is largely expressed in their voting behavior and their willingness to provide financial support to specific movement causes. These men and women constitute a latent force that can be mobilized periodically on behalf of a particular candidate or piece of legislation. This constituency is kept abreast of the movement primarily through the media. therefore, keeping the movement in the news is an essential element in retaining this base of support, provided, of course, that the news being reported does not ridicule or trivialize.

In other words, the audience for many media events may not be the announced targets as much as bystander populations outside the arena of action, such as politicians, employers, "closet feminists," potential sympathizers, and media executives who need to be convinced that the movement is still alive and well and living in towns and cities across the nation.

Sympathizers and Activists: Problems of Mobilization

Public attitudes toward women and women's issues. By the early 1970s, through their own publications and the attention of the mass media, "women's liberation" had become a household word. While some of this attention was negative if not outrightly hostile, as in the use of such terms as "women's lib" and "libbers," much of the response to the New Feminist Movement was astonishingly positive. No one was more surprised than the feminist organizers and activists themselves when hundreds showed up at events where only a few dozen had been expected, and thousands appeared where hundreds had been anticipated. Public lectures, women's studies courses, and CR groups were all overflowing. Even so, those who came out were but a small fraction of the movement's potential constituency: the 51 percent of all Americans who are female, plus a sizeable proportion of male sympathizers. The general population was certainly aware of feminism after the media explosion of 1969–70; how did they respond to this information?

Public opinion data available from this period indicate a basically favorable response. It is difficult to tell how much these attitudes differed from those held before 1970, since questions on feminist issues were not asked in the 1950s or 1960s. As feminist activities and media interest mushroomed, so too did the monitoring of attitudes by national opinion polling organizations. Most comparisons of opinion change therefore cover only the period between 1970 and the present.

There are, however, a few studies that include data from the 1960s. Mason, Czajka, and Arber (1976) were able to assemble a set of questions about women's roles in the labor force and the family that had been asked of women in special surveys in 1964, 1970, and 1973–74. While none of the surveys reached a representative sample of respondents, the researchers were able to piece together evidence of significant attitude change in virtually every subpopulation of women questioned. For example, disagreement with the statement "a man can make long range plans for his life, but a woman has to take things as they come," increased by over 30 percentage points among college-educated women between 1964 and 1970. The attitudes of non-college-educated women changed little between 1964 and 1970, but in subsequent years kept pace with changes among college-educated women. At all periods, respondents were less aware of problems in women's role as primary caretaker of the family than they were of inequalities in the workplace, but over time both attitudes became substantially more feminist, and the two "sets" of attitudes became more closely linked. In other words, the message that women's roles in the family and in the labor force are manifestations of the same structure of inequality was apparently being received.

Another extended time series of opinion data comes from Detroit women, initially interviewed in 1962 and contacted again in 1977 (Thornton and Freedman 1979). Four questions were asked: about male authority in the family, men doing housework, women's activities outside the home, and sex-segregated roles in general. In 1962, the proportions giving "nontraditional" responses to these questions ranged from 32 percent to 56 percent. By 1977, no item received less than 60 percent egalitarian response. Attitude change was most marked among younger and better-educated respondents, and least among fundamentalist Protestants, but all subgroups showed increased support of feminist goals. Those women who had returned to school or entered the labor force in the period between the two surveys became even more feminist than comparable women without such experiences.

These same women were reinterviewed in 1980 along with the children born to them in 1962, who were, therefore, eighteen years old (Thornton et al. 1983). The researchers found no signs of backlash: changes in mothers' attitudes between 1977 and 1980 continued at the same rate as between 1962 and 1977. In addition, egalitarian mothers tended to have egalitarian children. Sons were more traditional than daughters, but both were less traditional than their mothers had been in 1962. Differences between the generations were small, and children were not always more egalitarian than their mothers. For example, mothers were more likely than their children to say that family decisions should be shared. Thus, although the conceptions of appropriate and desirable sex-role behavior held by young people in 1980 differed greatly from those held by their mothers in 1962, there is less disagreement now between mothers and children than commonly assumed.

One frequently used index of support for equal rights is a willingness to vote for a female candidate for president of the United States (or at least a reluctance to tell an interviewer that you would not). Up to 1969, only 55 percent of the American public indicated a willingness to vote for a "qualified" female nominee, a percentage that had remained virtually unchanged since 1958 (Ferree 1974). In 1972, a full 70 percent of both male and female respondents answered affirmatively. Prior to 1972, acceptance of a female candidate was not related to age or education, even though younger and better educated persons are typically more "tolerant" on a wider range of issues. From 1972 on, these expected patterns appear. By 1972, also, acceptance of a woman candidate was strongly related to willingness to support a black nominee, suggesting that the minority group analogy had influenced public attitudes. Support for a woman candidate continued to increase until 1975, when it leveled off at 78 percent (Schrieber 1978; Davis and Taylor 1977), and rose again between 1978 and 1982, reaching 82 percent, with no difference between female and male respondents (Cherlin 1982). Such equal unwillingness to express prejudice in an abstract question may not translate into equal support for real candidates. While Geraldine Ferraro was being considered for the 1984 Democratic vice-presidential nomination, hypothetical runoff questions showed her to attract about five percentage points more support to the Democratic ticket among women, but to lose an approximately equal amount from men (Clymer, 1984).

Not only has there been a rise in favorable opinions toward feminist issues, but respondents are increasingly linking their attitudes one to another, and connecting these to their own experience. Feminist positions became not only more widely accepted but also more internally coherent, making it easier for individuals to "choose sides" by adopting a consistent feminist or antifeminist stance (Thornton et al. 1983). The general direction of change, however, was clearly toward the feminist position, while evidence of increasing linkage among attitudes strongly indicates that the status of women had become an important public issue.

As attitudes became more structured, differences among subgroups emerged more clearly. Variations by education, age, and social class are particularly pronounced today in contrast to the period before 1970 (Thornton et al. 1983). In part, this may reflect differences in the perceived consequences of change for one's own life (Spitze and Huber 1982; Ferree 1980, 1983b). For example, Spitze and Huber found that women who believe that the Equal Rights Amendment will make it easier for men to evade the responsibility of supporting their families, and who are themselves dependent upon male support, are especially likely to oppose the ERA.

Group differences in support of feminist issues may also be related to exposure to different social networks, information, and social pressures. Thus, employed women embedded in friendship networks at their place of work are more feminist on average than are other employed women, while housewives embedded in home-based friendships are less feminist than other housewives (Ferree 1980). Contrary to the assumption that feminist awareness would stem from higher levels of dissatisfaction, working-class housewives were more dissatisfied but less feminist than their employed counterparts. These findings suggest that employment exposes women to ideas favorable to feminism, and provides a context in which discontent can be attributed to political rather than personal causes.

Indeed, one of the strongest and most consistent predictors of nontraditional attitudes is women's own labor-force participation. Women who are employed—regardless of occupational status, income level, or being in a traditional or nontraditional job—are more likely than nonemployed women to favor further sex-role equality (Mason et al. 1976; Cherlin and Walters 1981; Thornton et al. 1983). Returning to the labor force, for whatever reason, predicts an increase in feminism (Thornton et al. 1983). Paid work and feminist attitudes then reinforce each other (Molm, 1978; Ferree 1981; Macke 1982).

Attitudes toward the New Feminist Movement itself also changed over the decade. In answer to a question about "most of the efforts to strengthen and change women's status in society," 40 percent of the general population replied favorably in 1970, compared to 57 percent in 1974 and 64 percent in

1980 (Roper 1980). This question did not use the terms "feminist" or "women's liberation," either of which might have increased the proportion of negative responses. However, in a series of surveys done for the American Council on Life Insurance concerning attitudes toward seven social movements, including "women's liberation," respondents "completely for" the New Feminist Movement increased from 17 to 25 percent, those "more for than against" remained essentially stable (32 to 35 percent), and those mostly or fully opposed dropped from 41 to 32 percent between 1972 and 1978.

Contrary to the stereotyped view that feminism appeals only to white middle-class women, black women are more likely than white women to have favorable attitudes toward the movement: 60 versus 37 percent in 1970, and 77 versus 65 percent in 1980 (Roper 1980). Moreover, women's attitudes toward feminism or sex roles are not influenced by their husband's income or occupational status as a blue- or white-collar worker (Mason and Bumpass 1975; Welch 1975; Scheppele 1977; Spitze and Huber 1982; Burris, 1983), or the status of their own jobs (Thornton et al. 1983). The effect of education, however, has become more pronounced over time; in 1970, 44 percent of college graduate women and 36 percent of women who had not graduated high school favored efforts to change women's status; by 1980, these proportions were 73 and 54 percent, respectively. Notice that in 1980 the level of support for feminist goals by the less educated women was higher than support by college graduates had been in 1970, but that over the decade the difference between the two groups had widened from eight to nineteen percentage points.

Although attitudes on employment and feminism became more closely linked through the 1970s, attitudes toward reproductive rights remained largely separate. A feminist analysis of abortion based on the principle of a woman's right to control her own body emerged during the abortion reform debates of the late 1960s (see Chapter 6), but public attitudes were more influenced by perceptions of abortion as a health and family planning issue.

Public opinion polls show a dramatic increase in support of a woman's right to a safe and legal abortion, even before the 1973 Supreme Court decision in *Wade* v. *Roe*. For example, in 1965, 71 percent of the population approved of legalizing abortion when a woman's health was seriously endangered by pregnancy, a percentage that rose to 80 percent by 1972 (before *Wade*) and to 88 percent by 1980. Approval of abortion in less extreme circumstances increased more in the period before 1972 than afterward—in the case of an unmarried women from 18 percent in 1965 to 41 percent in 1972 and 48 percent in 1980; and in the least-favored circumstance—no more children desired—from 16 percent approval in 1965 to 40 percent in 1972 and 47 percent by 1980 (Deitch 1982; Jaffe et al. 1981). Deitch also notes that respondents' attitude toward legal abortion is associated with attitudes on other feminist issues, but the relationship is not strong, nor did it increase in the period 1972–80.

Other research, reported by Mueller (1983), also indicates that abortion remained something of a "single issue" throughout the 1970s. In general, attitudes on abortion showed the same trend toward increasing internal consistency that we have noted in attitudes on female role issues (e.g., voting for a woman for president, opinions on women's employment, and so forth), and both sets of beliefs have consistently moved in a feminist direction, but have not become more closely linked. Black women, who are more supportive of women's rights in general but less supportive of abortion rights, typify those for whom the two issues remain separate (Combs and Welch 1982).

Mueller further notes that while very religiously involved respondents are less likely to take a consistently feminist position on either set of opinions, they did not become more antifeminist over the decade. In other words, the New Right and other backlash forces have had less impact on public opinion than commonly believed, and far less influence on attitudes than the New Feminist Movement displayed at the beginning of the 1970s. Despite increasingly organized opposition from the Catholic church hierarchy, support for abortion rights among Catholics has actually increased between 1975 and 1983, from 67 percent to 79 percent who believed abortion should be legal under at least some circumstances, according to Gallup poll figures (Jaffe et al. 1981, 105; *Conscience* 1983, 13).

By 1980, the *New York Times*—in its "Home" and "Style" sections, of course—was reporting recent survey results as heralding "major shifts in attitudes of women" (13 March 1981, C1), and announcing "a new view of women" (6 January 1981, C11). For the first time, a majority (52 percent) of respondents said that their ideal way of life would be a marriage in which both breadwinning and housekeeping/child-care responsibilities were shared. Between 80 and 95 percent would ask both male and female children to perform previously sex-linked tasks, and large majorities endorsed sharing responsibility for even the most traditional tasks such as mowing the lawn and mending clothes (Roper 1981).

In summary, the decade of the 1970s was a period of striking change in the public perception of women, of the feminist movement, and of its specific goals. Most of the change in attitudes was recorded at the beginning of the decade, undoubtedly as a direct result of feminist activism—the books and pamphlets, meetings and demonstrations, and media coverage described earlier in this chapter. Moreover, these gains in public acceptance have either remained stable or showed small consistent increases over the rest of the decade and into the 1980s, despite an antifeminist counterattack and an indifferent federal administration. Finally, feminist attitudes have become anchored in demographic realities: age and education now predict feminist support as they did not two decades ago.

As women's levels of educational attainment and labor force participation continue to rise, and as younger cohorts of women are heard from, we can expect further steady, if slow, increases in nontraditional attitudes. It seems safe to conclude that feminist ideas have spread well beyond the ranks of movement members and become part of the taken-for-granted world of most Americans. This is a remarkable achievement in itself, and it provides the backdrop against which both strands of the organized movement reach out to new constituencies and handle the inevitable internal stresses of growth.

Biases in mobilization. Members of the two original strands were recruited through existing social networks; that is, by word of mouth among women already organized for other purposes. These existing cooptable networks were essential to the early growth and survival of the movement, but they were also narrow bases of recruitment. In the early years, many women were "left out" of the movement because they were not linked to either the bureaucratic organizations or the collectivist groups of the 1960s. As a result, recruits for both strands were disproportionately drawn from the ranks of urban, educated women, with older ones located in the bureaucratic-legal structures that gave birth to NOW and similar organizations, and younger ones in the student/intellectual milieu of radical politics. In either case, few working-class women—old or young, black or white— were available for mobilization via these interpersonal influences.

Although the movement is often described as being "white and middle class," nonwhite women have always been represented among its leadership; most notably, Pauli Murray, a black writer, attorney, and ordained Episcopal priest; Aileen Hernandez, an attorney and past president of NOW; and Florynce Kennedy, also an attorney, whose outspoken views and flamboyant personality have attracted much media attention. These women, and other black and Hispanic professionals, were already integrated into the network of bureaucratic activists. It is, however, accurate to note that virtually all of the leading figures of the New Feminist Movement, black and white alike, were college-educated. Such women are likely to be found in the vanguard of change for the same reasons that most social movements have depended on a middle-class educated elite to provide organizing skills and to publicize the cause. People involved in a struggle for daily existence can only rarely afford the time and energy required for movement organizing; they are also more vulnerable to the risks that movement activity entails.

Not only do middle-class women have these resources, but they are encouraged to have high aspirations. It is very difficult, over the long run, to educate people for positions and responsibilities that they are not permitted to assume without generating grievances that feed into a social movement. In turn, the movement rewards organizational skills and the ability to articulate movement goals. Middle-class women have developed these abilities, even in sex-stereotyped jobs and volunteer activities. Working-class women may have such skills, but they are rarely recognized and encouraged.

All social and political organizations therefore find it easiest to mobilize their middle-class sympathizers (Verba and Nie 1972). Critics of the New Feminist Movement invariably refer to this recruitment bias in order to discredit the entire movement, claiming that it cannot speak for all women, and most especially for the doubly oppressed: women of color and of the working class. Curiously, although this charge is most often leveled against the bureaucratic feminist organizations, it was the collectivist groups that displayed greater homogeneity in membership. This is so, according to Rothschild-Whitt (1979), because value agreement and normative consensus are essential to the success of collectives, while in hierarchal organization, order can be imposed from above by impersonal rules despite individual differences. One can be more confident that others share one's values when they are similar in social background characteristics. In addition, friendship networks rather than organizational memberships were the primary recruitment channels for the collectivist strand.

It would be a mistake, however, to continue to perceive feminism in the United States today as a middle-class phenomenon. The 1970s were a period in which many other constituencies saw themselves as beneficiaries of movement goals: women of color (black, Native American, and Asian), Hispanic women, and most working-class women. From their earlier position of outright hostility, many labor unions have turned to open endorsement of feminist goals, while working-class women have moved from a position of distanced neutrality into organizing on their own behalf. As a result, the racial and class composition of activist feminists has changed greatly, making the New Feminist Movement one of the most broad-based and diverse movements in American history.

Recruiting black and ethnic women. For black and Hispanic women, feminist participation is rendered more difficult because of a primary identification with others of the same racial or ethnic group, and because of the often unconscious racism of some white feminists. Nonetheless, black women have long been aware of gender inequality, and on most issues hold more feminist positions than those of white women. Black women, however, also place high priority on ending racism. Not only does this mean that they may, at any given time, prefer to work on problems of race rather than those of gender, but also that they will generally prefer to work with those who share an awareness of racism that many white feminists lack.

Awareness of oppression, from whatever source, also does not automatically confer the ability to do something about it. Movement activity takes time that might otherwise be devoted to survival: earning money and/or child rearing. One must also be in a position to be recruited, that is, in contact with others able and willing to join a movement. For these reasons, it is typically the more affluent and socially integrated who join movement organizations, while the most burdened and deprived do not or cannot. In addition, since most social contacts remain within racial bounds in a segregated society, white feminists have not always recognized the type of effort required to involve more than a token number of minority women. This is one reason why separate black and Latina feminist groups are so important to the integration of the movement as a whole.

Despite the many barriers to mobilization, black and Hispanic women have been attracted to the New Feminist Movement. As early as 1971, Chicana feminists in California opened a center for working women. The National Conference of Puerto Rican Women was founded in 1972, and the Mexican American Women's Association in 1974. The first American Indian Women's Conference was held in New York City in 1975, providing an organizational base for the American Indian/Alaskan Native Caucus that emerged at the National Women's Conference in Houston, Texas, in 1977.

Among black women, the National Council of Negro Women, a long-established leadership group, was an early endorser of the Equal Rights Amendment and other mainstream feminist goals. More explicitly feminist organizations appeared in the mid-1970s: San Francisco's Black Women United for Action and the National Black Feminist Organization, both in 1973; and, in 1977, the National Alliance of Black Feminists and the National Association of Black Professional Women. Until this point, activist black women had worked in organizations devoted to the advancement of their race in general, or in the women's movement, or in both, separately. Diana Lewis (1977) suggests that middle-class black women, in particular, may have been responding to the realization that the gains of the civil rights movement were being realized primarily by black males. Through their involvement in black feminist organizations these women could now combat both racism and sexism with others who shared their priorities.

Within the movement, problems persist. Women of color remain "invisible" despite their presence; that is, there is a tendency for whites to speak as if all the women are white, and all the blacks are men, leaving the black woman without an identity of her own (Hull, Scott, and Smith 1982). White feminists must also confront evidence of unconscious racism, so deeply embedded in the national psyche and its institutions that one is hardly aware of it. As Simons (1979) illustrates, the classic writings of contemporary feminism, while making much of the analogy between racism and sexism, fail to deal specifically with the condition of black women. Rather than turning away from the New Feminist Movement, however, a number of black and other minority feminists are attempting to bridge the two movements by their very presence; indeed, a recent collection of writings by minority women is titled *This Bridge Called My Back* (Auzaldua and Moraga 1981).

For Hispanic women, a somewhat different set of problems limits their involvement in the movement. They face greater cultural and structural barriers to independence than is the case for black women, more used to fending for themselves and their children. The power of the Catholic church and traditional patriarchal values is particularly strong. But perhaps the major impediments are structural: the extremely low level of educational attainment among Hispanic women, and the fact that the types of jobs that do not require skilled training (domestic service, farm labor, textile production, and garment sewing) are declining sectors of employment, leaving women struggling just to survive. Nonetheless, especially where Hispanic women have become involved in civil rights activism, they, too have been drawn to feminism.

Recruiting poor and working-class women. For many poor women, regardless of color, some stated goals of the movement appear narrow and class-bound—legal abortion, equal pay, professional concerns, and an emphasis on individual achievement. Although, on a statistical basis, the "body issues"—rape, abortion, and domestic violence—affect minority and working-class women even more than their middle-class white counterparts, these concerns are perceived as basically elitist in comparison to matters of race and class inequality that affect both men and women. For many poor women, caring for the children they do have is the crucial family issue, and efforts at family planning have been interpreted, with good cause, as attempts to control fertility among the "lower classes." Moreover, when middle-class feminists call for enhanced work and educational opportunities they are not typically thinking of the kind of schooling and jobs available to minority women (Gittell and Naples 1982). There are, of course, some exceptions, as described in Mary Walshok's (1981) study of women in nontraditional blue-collar jobs.

Social class differences in focus are nicely illustrated in the contrast between two feminist organizations devoted to reproductive rights: the Committee for Abortion Rights and Against Sterilization Abuse (CARASA) and the National Abortion Rights Action League (NARAL). CARASA's definition of "reproductive rights" includes the right to *have* children, to be protected against involuntary sterilization (not an uncommon fate for poor black women in the South, even today), and to *resist* the pressure on unmarried women to have abortions. In contrast, NARAL, an organization heavily supported by middle-class feminists, is devoted to the single issue of legal abortion, even to the point of mentioning the "social costs of uncontrolled childbearing" among the poor in some of its literature.

With respect to working-class women, there is the pervasive belief that the organized feminist movement has overlooked their interests in favor of individualistic and personalized achievement goals for more advantaged women (Sidel 1978; Luttrell 1984). Nonetheless, there was sufficient concern and energy among some working-class women to form a National Congress of Neighborhood Women in 1974, now offering college degree courses, a job development program, and various other services from its Washington D.C., office.

A recent study by Gittell and Naples (1982) of 110 activists in either women-oriented bureaucratic organizations or in grass-roots organizing in low-income and minority communities, found little contact between the two groups. That is, the community activists felt alienated from the broader movement, while feminist activists had failed to identify with the kinds of problems around which neighborhood women organize: housing, public schools, unemployment, and crime. Both groups of activists have much to gain from bridging the gap that currently separates them: feminists have technical skills and networks of influence unavailable to community women, and the latter have established bases of support lacking to most feminist organizations. By pooling these different sets of resources, and forming coalitions around common goals, women's political power could be greatly enhanced (see also Haywoode 1977). Indeed, there is already one powerful issue around which all women can unite: the increasing "feminization of poverty" (Pearce 1981; Hess 1983).

Organizing working-class working women has not been an easy task. Most are concentrated in "pink collar" service jobs (as workers in restaurants and bars, in beauty shops, health-care facilities, stores, shops, and offices) or in low-skill factory employment, and until quite recently, there was very little support among the major unions for organizing in these sectors. Since the 1920s, the Women's Bureau of the Department of Labor had been the only organization serving as watchdog and voice for unorganized female workers, but the Bureau's commitment rises and falls with each new federal administration. For example, the Bureau celebrated its fiftieth anniversary in 1970 with an endorsement of the Equal Rights Amendment, but during the Reagan years has withdrawn from any profeminist commitments, or, indeed, any visible effort on behalf of working women. Today, however, there are a few small nonprofit organizations, such as the National Commission on Working Women, devoted to the needs of women in the pink- and blue-collar work ghettos. For those in unionized workplaces, the Coalition of Labor Union Women (CLUW) was formed in 1974, with three thousand delegates from fifty-eight unions attending. Also in 1974, women in various cities formed associations of office workers: Women Employed (Chicago), Women Office Workers (New York), and 9 to 5 (Boston). By 1979, many of these groups joined in creating Working Women: A National Association of Office Workers. Their organizing activities were greatly helped by the popularity of the movie *9 to 5*.

The success of "reaching out" efforts by feminist organizations in the mid-1970s was forcefully demonstrated in the composition of delegates to the National Women's Conference in Houston, Texas, in 1977. White middle-class women were actually underrepresented among elected delegates. In fact, white at-large members had to be added to several state delegations in order to meet the racial balance requirement of the legislation creating the conference (Van Gelder 1978). The emotional highpoint of the meeting was the presentation of a minority women's resolution by one representative each from the black, Native American, Hispanic, and Asian-American caucuses, symbolizing their shared commitment to the new feminism, and evoking sustained applause from thousands of participants, including even members of the antifeminist delegations from Utah and Mississippi (Van Gelder 1978; Rossi 1982).

Realizing the Promise of Diversity

Despite many barriers to the participation of minority and working-class women, the New Feminist Movement today embraces over two dozen organizations devoted to their concerns (*Women's Action Almanac* 1980). Minority and working-class women are active in all facets of the movement, but only recently has an effort been made to integrate their needs and concerns into the movement's overall goals and strategies. Constructive criticism of the middle-class assumptions underlying certain feminist demands has already led several organizations to reformulate their goals—for example, to include sterilization abuse with barriers to abortion as a denial of reproductive rights, or to call for women's entry into apprenticeship programs along with an end to quotas in professional schools. But the issues of greatest importance to black, Hispanic, and white working-class women have yet to be fully understood or accepted throughout the movement, in part because the voices of these women are only now being heard.

Incorporating such different perspectives will eventually broaden the vision of the New Feminist Movement as well as expand its base, but diversity also brings conflict, pain, and anger. The phenomenal growth of feminism in the past two decades has been accompanied by considerable organizational stress and strain. As women joined the movement, they brought with them their own deepest needs and dreams, as well as experiences that challenged existing assumptions about what was true for all women. New issues sometimes spawned new organizations, and at other times led to changes in existing groups, and sometimes did both. It is to these problems of organizational change, conflict, and growth that we turn in the next chapter.

A "Take Back the Night" march in Washington, D.C., one of many around the country through which feminists have drawn attention to commonplace violence against women, an issue that crosses lines of race, class, and ethnicity. *Photograph courtesy of Joan E. Biren.*

CHAPTER FIVE

Feminist Organizations in Transition

As word of the movement spread and its ideas exploded into public consciousness, its organizational life in all its variety mushroomed. By 1973, the *New Women's Survival Catalogue* listed hundreds of groups in dozens of different areas. The next edition, in 1975, called itself a "sourcebook" rather than catalog since it was no longer possible to list all the rape crisis centers, health clinics, art galleries, credit unions, child-care facilities, research libraries, bookstores, restaurants, self-defense studios, lobbying organizations, schools, task forces, retreat houses, divorce clinics, film cooperatives, theater groups, therapy collectives, career counseling enterprises, women's studies programs, record companies, and other businesses and services through which the movement established a local and national presence. The sourcebook editors referred to this proliferation of feminist groups as "militant pluralism," that is, a positive affirmation of the variety of life-styles and interests of women. In the first half of this chapter, we will look at the varied organizations created by feminists to express their values and to realize their goals.

Rather than insisting on any one correct strategy or ideological position, the New Feminist Movement encourages any and all efforts by women to take control of the institutions that affect their lives. Since there is no institution in our society free of the effects of male dominance, feminist groups will be as diverse as the society itself. Such diversity inevitably breeds conflict. In the second part of this chapter we examine some of these conflicts and their implications for the future of the movement.

Proliferation and Consolidation

While the abundance and variety of feminist groups continues to defy efforts at cataloging, it is possible to identify several general strategies for challenging male dominance. In this section we will examine three basic forms developed in the 1970s: self-help groups, educational/political organizations, and cultural/entrepreneurial establishments, each of which has made a distinct and important contribution to the growth of the New Feminist Movement.

Direct action/self-help.   Direct action groups represent a strategy of collective organization and self-help. Their message is that sisterhood is already powerful: that women can act together and create immediate change in their lives. Self-help is a way for people who have defined themselves as powerless and oppressed to realize that they do have options and the ability to change things. Direct action groups are an appealing strategy for both radical and socialist feminists because such groups offer a partial realization of the ideal of the new feminist community. The ideal community of socialist feminists includes new relationships of equality between women and men, whereas radical feminists are primarily concerned with relationships among women, and their ideal community is often separatist.

Direct action groups have been most effective in the areas of law and medicine, precisely where male domination of the system has generated widespread and recognized problems for women. Most begin with self-help and expand to other collective strategies.

Law.   The deficiencies of our law-enforcement system were first recognized in cases of rape and sexual assault, where the prevailing tendency to blame the victim forced a woman to endure a second ordeal in which police, lawyers, and judges discredited her testimony on the basis of past sexual activity (real or implied) and her "failure" to defend herself successfully. As many feminist analysts have pointed out, a woman's right to safety on the streets or in her own home has never been taken seriously, although the criminal justice system vigorously pursues this right on behalf of men (Brownmiller 1975; Griffin 1971; Russell 1975). Rape is treated as a joke, a sexual turn-on, and even as a sign of male accomplishment, but rarely as a physical assault, psychological trauma, or major crime.

Two early forms of antirape action were hot-lines, offering immediate support and advice to assault victims, and self-defense training, especially karate. Self-defense training allows a woman to protect herself instead of depending upon a male "protector" (who may himself become an attacker).

Because self-defense techniques compensate for differences in size and strength, women develop the ability to walk without fear, and to feel self-confident in a way that should spill over into other areas of life.

In addition, women who had previously been victims of sexual assault began to speak out about their trauma. They refused to be made to feel "dirty" and guilty about their experience, and offered their advice and support to current victims via hot-lines and rape crisis centers, even accompanying victims to hospital emergency rooms. The use of former victims was gradually supplanted by trained feminist counselor/advocates. In many cities and towns, such a person has been added to the staff of hospitals and police departments. In its third phase, antirape organizing focused on institutional changes that would make rape cases easier to prosecute. Many states have changed their laws to eliminate the need for witnesses or evidence of a struggle, and the use of information on the victim's previous sexual history. Some states have even removed the rule that exempts husbands from prosecution for sexual assault on their wives. Other local efforts have attacked the cultural supports for violence against women, such as media depictions of rape as sexually gratifying. Across the country, "Take Back the Night" demonstrations have focused public attention on the inability of women to enjoy the same freedom of movement that men take for granted.

Self-help groups have also been organized for victims of violence within the family. These efforts also began with hot-lines and crisis centers, such as Casa de las Madres in San Francisco or Transition House in Cambridge, Massachusetts, where the provision of immediate shelter was combined with consciousness-raising on the roots of male violence, and where victims helped staff the shelters. The publication of feminist analyses, particularly Martin's *Battered Wives* (1977), brought the problem to widespread public attention, so that shelters and services for battered women multiplied far beyond those that could be provided by movement members. By 1978, the U.S. Commission on Civil Rights listed over 300 shelters, hot-lines, and groups acting as advocates for victims of family violence (Tierney 1982). Although fewer than half of such shelters were explicitly feminist in orientation, the presence of a feminist group in the community was one of the strongest predictors of the existence of a program for battered women (Johnson 1981; Tierney 1982).

Another legal area in which direct action through self-help has proliferated is that of family law in general. Collectives have been formed to help women negotiate the legal system with or without a lawyer, as, for example, in filing a *pro se* divorce petition, thus avoiding legal fees. Other groups provide information and emotional support to those involved in custody disputes (especially lesbian mothers) and to women in prison. In some states, feminists have sought the decriminalization of prostitution, often defined as a crime that only women can commit, and where enforcement has exclusively focused on the provider rather than the purchaser of sexual services.

In all these ways, women have become more skilled in dealing with the system, created new ways of meeting needs outside the system, and provoked changes in the law and its enforcement. These activities have been experiences of empowerment for participants, bringing benefits to many other women who may never recognize their debt to the feminist movement.

Health.   The second major area in which self-help has been an essential component of feminist strategy is that of physical and mental health. A number of important studies in the early 1970s (Broverman et al. 1970; Bart 1972; Chesler 1972) strongly suggested that mental health professionals perceived a "normal" woman as characterized by dependence, low self-esteem, anxiety, and insecurity. Women without these traits were subjected to "cures" for their "masculine protest" and inability to "adjust" to their natural roles. Feminist therapy clinics refused to accept this definition of mental health for women; they began with the assumption that the same qualities of assurance, independence, and self-esteem that were "mentally healthy" for men applied to all human beings. Therapy collectives helped women to direct their own lives and to make their own choices. The expertise of mental health professionals was challenged by nonprofessional "facilitators" who taught women to stop blaming themselves for being unhappy or deviant.

In the field of physical health, resistance to male professional judgments was carried out on a range of issues, most of which were related to sexuality and reproduction. For example, the process of childbirth had come to be defined by the obstetrical establishment as an illness to be managed by drugging, restraint, isolation, and surgery. It was the doctor, typically male, who then "delivered" the baby to a grateful mother. The medicalization of childbirth had replaced the natural process of labor with the support and assistance of other women (Arms 1975; Rich 1976; Rothman 1982). Self-help groups promoted the advantages of home births, lay midwives, and breast feeding and found allies among existing mainstream advocates of natural childbirth such as Lamaze and La Leche League. Unlike their allies, feminists also note that this emphasis on breast feeding and natural childbirth can produce new standards of "true femininity" to which women can be pressured to conform. In an era of declining overall fertility, many hospitals and physicians have become so concerned about the competition from home-births and midwives that they have made limited concessions in the form of hospital "birthing rooms," natural childbirth clinics, and nurse-midwives as labor attendants.

Self-help also meant self-examination. So mystified and medicalized had women's sexual organs become, that few had ever seen them for themselves, or even wished to. It was a daring act, therefore, for one NOW member, at a 1971 meeting, to take a plastic speculum, insert it in her vagina, and invite her friends to take a look. The idea rapidly spread. Women who had been socialized to think of their bodies as unclean and to be ignorant of the most elementary physical facts, found self-examination an exhilarating experience. This hands-on relationship to health, begun collectively and continued individually, soon included menstrual extraction, tracking ovulation by measuring vaginal temperature and secretions, and breast self-examination. For example, use of the diaphragm, the female contraceptive with the fewest serious side effects, increased substantially as women felt more comfortable handling their own bodies. Women's health centers also fostered consciousness raising through self-knowledge. All of these activities presented a direct challenge to the medical monopoly of health care: why go to a physician for something one can do for oneself, quickly, painlessly, and inexpensively?

Actual health-care services provided by direct action groups began in the period before 1973 with the need to provide medically safe abortions to women who could not afford to go abroad, or who might otherwise die or be mutilated by self-induced procedures or the work of illegal abortionists (Fruchter et al. 1977). In addition to providing an essential service, members of the collective gained a sense of personal competence and demystified medical skills for themselves and others (Schlesinger and Bart 1981). Even after the Supreme Court decision that legalized most abortions, many self-help clinics and women's health centers have continued to provide abortion services because local hospitals and physicians refuse to do so.

A number of feminist health clinics provide primary care for a range of common problems, as well as preventive care, health education, and information sharing. Information flows both ways, with "providers" eager to learn from "clients" about side effects and the overall success of various treatment modes (Fruchter et al. 1977).

The transformation of many women from passive patient to assertive consumer created a need for accurate, easily understood information on women's bodies and on existing medical procedures. This gap was partially filled by the publication in 1976 of *Our Bodies, Ourselves* by the Boston Women's Health Book Collective, which has invested profits from its book in a clearinghouse for women's health information. Other collectives operate national coordinating systems for research and lobbying (e.g., Healthright, and the Women's Health Network).

In general, the growth of legal and medical self-help groups gave women a sense of personal mastery and collective power by dealing directly with a problem rather than seeking help from establishment organizations. In the process, existing institutions were forced to respond more appropriately to women's needs. Thus, although institutional change was not the original goal of direct action groups, they helped bring about major reforms in both the criminal justice and health-care systems, although ultimate control remained in the hands of the "experts." From their involvement in self-help, some women went on to acquire professional training; how much of their feminist orientation will survive this training remains to be seen, especially as the line between being a professional nurse or lawyer and being a movement activist increasingly blurs. The express goal of creating cooperative, nonhierarchical, women-controlled alternative settings for providing services was only partially realized, but even partial realization would have seemed utopian in 1969.

Educational/political groups. Educational and political groups are the organizational expression of a strategy for change that emphasizes pressures on existing social organizations, from the federal government to a local employer. As such, they are particularly attractive to liberal and socialist feminists. Part of this strategy is to educate decision makers and the general public about the current system's effects on women, thus generating a desire for change. Another, equally critical, part of the strategy is to organize people who want change and so become a political and economic force. A reliance on joint rather than individual action is the key. The most prominent organization of this type is NOW, with its special interest task forces. We will discuss NOW and similar groups composing the women's policy network at the national level in the next chapter.

But the New Feminist Movement has also spurred the creation of numerous special-purpose and single-interest groups with educational and political goals. Among the earliest were Federally Employed Women, formed in 1969 to improve the position of women in the civil service system, and the National Coalition of American Nuns, also founded in 1969 to speak out on civil rights, urge the ordination of women, and "protest any domination . . . by priests, no matter what their hierarchal status." In addition, organizations formed at the turn of the century in response to the earlier feminist movement, such as the National Federation of Business and Professional Women's Clubs, emerged from hibernation to become active on issues of women's rights.

Many of these organizations were formed to push for changes in particular occupations and by specific employers. Clerical workers in Boston, for example, began to organize on a city-wide basis for maternity benefits and regulation of temporary employment agencies. Women Employed, in Chicago, began with a survey of working conditions, and went on to file sex-discrimination suits against such major employers as Kraft Foods. Other occupational and professional caucuses were quick to respond to the feminist message, with the Federation of Organizations of Professional Women serving as an umbrella unit able to coordinate the efforts of many of these groups on issues of common concern.

Academic women also organized. Indeed, the spread of feminism through American colleges and universities illustrates the process of proliferation, followed by consolidation and institutionalization. The "take off point" was in 1970–71 when the rate of formation of feminist groups accelerated dramatically across the country, off campus and on. This organizational explosion both fed and reflected the burst of media coverage described in the last chapter. Between 1968 and 1971, academic women had formed at least fifty organizations to deal with the status of women within particular disciplines, and to bring a feminist perspective to their field of study (Klotzberger 1973). In 1970, also, the American Association of University Professors, the leading professional organization of faculty members, reactivated its Committee on the Status of Women (Committee W) that had been "excused from further service" in 1928. Committee W immediately embarked on investigations of grievances relating to sex bias in hiring and promotion policies at a number of universities, as it had done five decades earlier.

At a number of colleges and universities, pressure from female faculty led to the formation of committees on the status of women that subsequently documented inequities, demanded reforms, and precipitated change. In many universities, new coalitions of women crossed traditional boundaries between faculty, students, and staff, as well as departmental divisions, to demand day-care facilities, gynecological services, improved campus security, and scholarships and fringe benefits for part-time workers and students, the great majority of whom are women. On some campuses, women's centers were established to house and coordinate the dozens of services and activities that sprang up almost overnight. Most centers were collectively organized and oriented to self-help projects, and some offered noncredit courses in car repair, carpentry, and other nontraditional skills.

At the same time, women's studies as an intellectual specialty was being transformed from a set of collectively run noncredit courses on the fringes of academe into fully institutionalized programs, with departmental status at some universities. The first accredited course in women's studies, "Evolution of Female Personality," was offered at Cornell University in 1969. By December of the following year, there were at least 110 women's studies courses in the catalogs of American colleges and universities, and by the end of 1971, more than 600 such courses at almost 200 institutions of higher education (Howe and Ahlum 1973). In 1982 there were innumerable courses and over 300 degree-granting programs in women's studies on American campuses.

Increasingly, the directors of these programs found themselves playing university politics: lobbying for resources, for curricular reform, and for research funding and facilities; organizing conferences; and managing institutes and journals. Partially to keep track of these diverse organizations and programs, the National Women's Studies Association was founded in 1978. In addition, the National Council for Research on Women is a consortium that coordinates the work of institutes involved in feminist research and policy analysis. The most recent focus of women's studies organizations is "mainstreaming," that is, the incorporation of new research and perspectives on women into the rest of the curriculum rather than being confined to "women's courses." This, too, requires skill at lobbying and organizing women to act collectively.

The experience of women on college campuses is an example of the processes taking place in a variety of settings, as the movement's ideas spread through the society. The explosive growth of women's groups in 1970–71, the discovery of their common concerns, alliances with others of varied backgrounds, the rejuvenation of organizations from the earlier wave of feminism, the gradual growth of coordinating organizations, and the achievement of semi-institutionalization are all typical of the history of feminist political/educational organizations.

The academic example also illustrates the blurring of distinctions between self-help collectives and the bureaucratically organized lobbying organizations, the original two strands of the New Feminist Movement. In recent years, mutual respect has grown as differences in style between the strands have diminished and as both types of groups increasingly combine organizing for institutional change with providing women-run alternatives. The new organizational style could be described as a flattened hierarchy, with elected leaders, and even paid staff, but in which making decisions and setting priorities are democratically decentralized to a far greater extent than is found in traditional academic departments, labor unions, or political interest associations.

The existence of thousands of local and special interest groups across the country gives the movement a diversity of focus and organizational flexibility that makes it unusually open to grass-roots input. By the same token, problems of coordination are magnified; resources are increasingly diverted to maintenance activities such as sharing information among groups. This extensive network ensures the presence of the New Feminist Movement in every area of society, but does not guarantee group effectiveness. Obstacles to success include competition between groups, co-optation by established institutions, and goal displacement, that is, a shift in goals from accomplishing concrete changes to maintaining the organization and enjoying the company of other members. Nonetheless, the existence of a feminist organizational structure capable of applying significant pressure for social and political change is an enormous and meaningful accomplishment.

Cultural/entrepreneurial groups. From its beginning, the New Feminist Movement has given birth to a wide variety of cultural and entrepreneurial groups more concerned with self-maintenance and sociability than with exerting pressure on existing institutions. Founders of these groups interpret their very existence as a key aspect of social change, as "alternative institutions" whereby women can provide service to other women. Rather than developing women's individual resources through collective action, as self-help groups do, these enterprises focus on developing the community through women's individual contributions. The basic argument is that as long as women patronize male-run banks, restaurants, or gas stations, the money does not recirculate among women, nor is it likely ultimately to be donated to feminist causes. In the same way as black or ethnic businesses serve local needs, prosper individually, and contribute to the financial stability and growth of the community as a whole, women-owned businesses are targeted to a particular clientele: the "feminist community." Because they provide an outlet for individuals to act on their commitment, they appeal particularly to career and radical feminists.

Among the first such specialized feminist businesses were bookstores that carried feminist material not available in mainstream shops, and also provided a meeting place for poetry readings, rap sessions, and casual encounters. Other feminists opened restaurants and coffee houses where women could go alone without fear of harassment. The goal of one such restaurant, Full Cycle, in Minneapolis, was to "recycle feminist energy by serving nutritious food, providing women with employment and skills and returning any profits into other feminist projects." (Grimstad and Rennie 1975). Some restaurants are run as collectives, others are profit making, but all combine vegetarian food, feminist politics, and community service, while struggling with defining the conditions under which men would be welcome as guests.

Later, feminists began to offer not only a place to eat, but a place to stay, such as the Retreat for Women in rural Connecticut. Short-term feminist gatherings—music festivals, worship services—were organized, some of which evolved into full-time institutions such as Olivia Records, a women-managed music distributing company, or the Mother Thunder Mission, a feminist church in New York City. Theater groups, film collectives, and feminist art galleries can be found throughout the country. In Los Angeles, a number of activities can be found under one roof in the Women's Building.

Individual feminists have offered their services to the community, as tax consultants, car mechanics, therapists, midwives, and physicians. A recent issue of *Sojourner*, a Boston-based feminist newspaper, carried dozens of advertisements for women health-care professionals, a women's gymnasium, a feminist law firm, a typesetter, a clothes designer, a "performance space" for music, three restaurants, several auto repair shops, and four inns/retreat houses. Nationally recognized musicians such as Holly Near and Sweet Honey in the Rock combine feminist themes and other political songs in concerts that bring feminists together and raise funds for national and local feminist causes.

Cultural activities also include organizations centered upon women's spirituality. Some of these may be found within traditional religious denominations, while others attempt to discover and define a new spiritual direction for women, as in the revival of "pagan" rituals expressing closeness to and dependence upon nature. The emergence of explicitly feminist covens of witches reflects a desire to affirm women's history as healers and rebels, and to reclaim the old religion of "wicce," or witchcraft, persecuted and displaced by Christianity many centuries ago. While their reconstruction of history is not entirely accurate, the idea of creating rituals and structures that affirm women's bodily and spiritual needs and strengths is important (Adler 1979; Ruether 1983). Producing nonsexist liturgies and supporting individual women in the ministry are ways in which feminists have sought to realize these goals within traditional religious structures.

These various cultural and entrepreneurial activities not only serve the feminist community but create it. By bringing women together to enjoy each other's company, and by providing services and support for one another, cultural/entrepreneurial feminists re-create a base of interaction and interdependence that had almost disappeared when women were confined in isolated nuclear households. These ties create bonds of experience and mutual reliance that could support direct action but are more commonly used to build a distinctive "feminist community" that in the long run could become cut-off from the world of other women. At the same time, such supportive communities focus members' energies on feminist issues and help to prevent burn-out among activists.

Conclusions. In sum, the proliferation of feminist groups in the early 1970s afforded expanded opportunities for mobilizing women. Feminists with broad concerns could be active in dozens of narrow-focus groups, creating dilemmas of priority and allocation of energy. By the end of the decade, a web of national, state, and local women's organizations was able to provide the coordination necessary for broad-based coalitions around single issues.

Carden (1981) notes that the proliferation of differentiated groups encourages a flexibility in ideas, activities, and organizational forms that reflects the movement's dual emphasis on autonomy *and* sisterhood, on cooperation *and* achievement. The range of such groups is impressive and most have achieved at least some of their primary goals. Activists also realize "secondary gains" in enhanced feelings of competence, the development of skills, and the sheer pleasure of being with like-minded individuals and "fighting the good fight." Both the primary and secondary gains of movement involvement continue to attract a broad spectrum of support, mobilizing women of all ages and social backgrounds.

The problems associated with proliferation, however, are not minor. Although loosely linked under the banner of women's rights, these groups and organizations do represent divergent ideologies and constituencies. Energies may be deflected from the larger struggle, and some members may become personally estranged, by dissent from within, by compromises made in the name of coalition, or by failure to agree on priorities. As Carden (1981) also concludes: the diversity, creativity, and enthusiasm associated with proliferation are crucial assets, but a great deal of energy can be siphoned off in trying to accomplish too many goals with too few resources. Proceeding in many directions at once, as the New Feminist Movement has attempted to do, helps bring the movement into contact with virtually every aspect of women's lives, but by the same token makes it difficult to point to any single accomplishment as the movement's primary achievement.

While the decade of the 1970s was a period in which the movement's base was broadened and its diverse goals and strategies defended in the name of "militant pluralism," internal dissent has periodically threatened its fragile unity. In the next section we examine some of these conflicts and their implications for the continued growth of the New Feminist Movement.

Internal Conflict in the Women's Movement

At various times in its brief history, the New Feminist Movement has been torn by internal disputes. Many early conflicts were related to structural factors, as in trashing described in chapter 3. Other conflicts reflect disagreement over priorities. We have selected a number of these—lesbianism as a feminist issue, pornography, the centrality of abortion rights, political endorsements, and the interplay of racism and anti-Semitism—as illustrative of the dynamics of conflict within the movement. Inevitably, in a movement as open and media-oriented as this one, each dispute has been aired in public. The ways in which conflict has been resolved have not always been ideal, yet in each case potentially destructive issues have been successfully managed. This is not to say that strains do not continue, but only that their negative impact has thus far been limited, and that the process of self-examination engendered by divisive issues has often strengthened the movement.

Lesbianism.   One of the earliest internal debates centered on the issue of lesbianism: namely, what degree of recognition was to be given to the double oppression of homosexual women? The locus of this debate was NOW as the most visible and broad-based feminist organization (even though, at that time, it had only a few thousand dues-paying members). The question was raised at NOW's 1971 national conference over the strong objections of representatives from the South and Midwest, and of Betty Friedan, a NOW founder and past president. Their argument against recognizing lesbian interests as a feminist issue was based on the fear of losing whatever legitimacy the fledgling organization had worked so hard to obtain. The "lavender menace," according to Friedan, threatened NOW's public image by evoking the great American fear of homosexuality. The argument *for* raising the issue was precisely that the fear of homosexuality (homophobia) and the hatred directed toward homosexuals has been used throughout our history to enforce conformity to "proper" feminine or masculine behavior. For example, parents continue to discourage boys playing with dolls and girls with trucks for fear that such atypical behavior will lead to homosexuality, even though family roles, job interests, and choice of sexual partner are actually quite separate preferences.

"Compulsory heterosexuality," or the belief that homosexuality is so abnormal as to be almost unthinkable, has particularly negative consequences for women. It means not only punishment for sex-inappropriate behavior but also reinforces the assumption that a woman without a man is necessarily incomplete, immature, sexually frustrated, and "fair game" for male attacks (Rich 1980). The male response to feminism, typified in statements such as "all she needs is a good fuck," increased many women's awareness that their claim to independence was already being interpreted in sexual terms. Feminists were thus placed in the position of either having continually to deny that they were lesbian (regardless of their actual sexual orientation), which could only affirm and perpetuate the idea that every woman needed a man, or having to attack head-on the definition of lesbianism as bad or sick.

Faced with these alternatives, a majority of delegates to NOW's 1971 convention passed resolutions approving "a woman's right to define and express her own sexuality and to choose her own life-style," recognizing "the oppression of lesbians as a legitimate concern of feminism," and supporting the child custody rights of lesbian mothers (Carden 1974, 113). The endorsement of these resolutions by NOW's national board was not followed by a wave of resignations, nor was the public response unexpectedly harsh. As Carden (1974) points out, the issue has already been resolved in local NOW chapters where gay and straight women engaged in dialogue and mutual exchange. Debate and discussion continue over questions raised by lesbian feminists: the value of separatism, the costs and benefits of loving women, the privileges heterosexual women take for granted.

Although there are undoubtedly many women in the movement for whom the issue remains personally distasteful, most objections are based on the political consequences of linking feminism and lesbianism; for example, one feminist speaker at the 1977 Houston conference referred to lesbian civil liberties problems as an "albatross around the neck of the movement" (Van Gelder 1978). In Rossi's study of delegates to the Houston conference, 73 percent agreed that one can be a feminist without working for lesbian rights, but only 39 percent said that the lesbian issue has done more harm than good to the movement (1982, 93). Clearly, the issue of homosexual rights remains a powerful weapon of the antifeminist backlash, but equally firmly, lesbian oppression has become one legitimate concern of the New Feminist Movement.

Pornography.   As one of the least debatable goals of contemporary feminism is an end to violence against women, and as there is increasing evidence linking pornography to such violence (e.g., Donnerstein 1980), it may seem strange that pornography has become a point of conflict among activist women. For some feminists the key issue shaping their attitude is the sexual content; for others, it is the antifemale violence found in most pornography. The former are reluctant to condemn pornography; the latter have no hesitation in doing so.

The law reflects the sexual view; pornography is legally defined in terms of explicit sexuality offensive to community standards. As sexual taboos have weakened, "normal" nonviolent sexuality has become progressively less offensive, so that what receives the label pornographic today is increasingly violent and women-hating. Yet, outside feminist circles, objections to pornography still largely focus on its explicit sexuality. Feminists who share this focus are likely to see pornography as a positive force in liberating women's repressed sexuality.

Movement women who wish to protest the dehumanization and violence against women in contemporary pornography often hesitate to make common cause with antisexuality campaigners who have in the past used antipornography statutes to suppress birth control information and otherwise to keep women ignorant of their bodies (Diamond 1982; Bessmer 1982). Nonetheless, radical feminists and right-wing moralists find themselves on the same side of the pornography issue, although their reasons differ: traditionalists are worried about pornography's threat to the sexual control and moral purity of the male consumer, while feminists fear that this material legitimates and encourages violence against women in general. Yet feminist resistance to pornography could provide a way to mobilize those whose oppositions to dehumanization and the degradation of women is based on moral and religious grounds, as has recently occurred in local antipornography campaigns in Minneapolis and Indianapolis (Shipp 1984).

The pornography debate within feminism has also taken on another, more troubling dimension as feminists on all sides of the issue have accused the others of betraying the movement by adopting the sexual ethics of patriarchy. This debate reflects a basic tension within contemporary feminism between its moral reform and liberal traditions. Moral reformers affirm a personal, caring, nonexploitive vision of sexuality, and therefore campaign against dehumanizing pornography, while also emphasizing the value of sexuality to the development of the whole person. Sexual liberationists reflect a hands-off stance, bolstered by the liberal ideology of individual choice and appeals to freedom of expression.

At this moment, there is no single "feminist" position on what to do about pornography, other than to deplore the sexual exploitation of women. In the 115 recommendations of the National Commission on the Observance of International Women's Year, presented to President Ford in 1976, there was no mention of either pornography or violence against women except in the case of rape. At the National Women's Conference in Houston in 1977, resolutions were offered on rape, battered women, and violence against women in the media, but no statement on pornography. It has been left to women's groups in various cities to raise consciousness on the links between pornography and rape, and to organize their own campaigns against pornography and antiwoman violence, with assistance from several national clearinghouses that provide newsletters, slide shows, and speakers.

Reproductive rights. One of the fundamental goals of the New Feminist Movement is to ensure women's control over their own bodies. The Supreme Court decision in *Wade* v. *Roe* (1973) appeared to provide constitutional protection to the privacy of reproductive decisions, but a powerful backlash by Catholic and fundamentalist Protestant clergy, and by conservative legislators at the local, state, and federal levels, with committed grass-roots support, have gradually whittled away at these guarantees—for poor women, minors, and those seeking abortions after the first trimester (twelve weeks). Feminists who had wanted NOW and other organizations to avoid the issue of abortion law repeal in the 1960s—before the *Wade* decision—are now fully determined to ensure that reproductive freedom is not erased by acts of Congress or constitutional amendments declaring the personhood of fertilized ova.

The ferocity of the opposition to abortion rights has served to solidify commitment to reproductive freedom within the New Feminist Movement, as exemplified in the 1981 legislative agenda of WEAL—an organization founded by women who had broken away from NOW over the abortion issue in the mid-1960s—that contains a strong statement of support for government funding of contraceptive research and family-planning programs, vowing to fight all attempts to restrict reproductive rights. But this agreement on the principle of a legal "right to choose" should not be interpreted as signifying a shared position on abortion. A wide spectrum of feminists—from women on the Catholic Left to Marxist feminists—have strong personal and political objections to the way in which the abortion issue has been presented.

Rosalind Petchesky (1980), for example, points out that the "right to choose" is meaningless when women are powerless to change the context in which their choices are made; poor women in the United States operate under very different conditions of choice than do the nonpoor. Analyzing what she calls the liberal feminist and Marxist views on reproductive freedom, Petchesky finds that each is incomplete as a basis for feminist theory and action. The classic liberal position—control over one's body as an extension of the right to privacy and personal integrity—ignores the social relationships of reproduction, atomizes the individual, and fails to provide moral guidance for one's decisions. In the Marxist view—recognizing the importance of the sexual division of labor in society—the right to choose is not an absolute but an historical necessity that could change when women are no longer charged with the sole responsibility for child care. This means that, once political leaders declare that the socialist revolution has succeeded, as in several Eastern European countries today, they then make rules governing reproductive choice in the name of the community as a whole. An authentic feminist politics of reproduction must attempt to reconcile the rights of the individual with the good of the community, so that even when the responsibilities of child care are shared with men or the group as a whole, the needs of individual women are respected.

Despite the failure to develop fully such a theory of reproductive freedom, and despite the personal misgivings of individual feminists over the subject of abortion, there is no controversy today within the movement over the necessity of maintaining and expanding existing legal guarantees of control over one's own body, whether this involves the right to refuse sterilization or to terminate an unwanted pregnancy. Even within the American Catholic community, where the church hierarchy has taken an uncompromising position against abortion, reproductive rights have been supported by the National Coalition of American Nuns and through an organization called Catholics for Free Choice. There is also scattered evidence that Catholic and non-Catholic women are similar in behavior as well as belief; the proportion of Catholic women obtaining abortions in many states is no less than the proportion of Catholics in the local population (Jaffe et al. 1981).

Political endorsements. To the extent that the New Feminist Movement seeks to be a truly national movement, and to the degree that most feminist goals must be accomplished through legislation, it would be advantageous to have allies in both major political parties and to avoid making enemies among sitting legislators. Whether or not to endorse specific candidates thus becomes a strategy issue.

This was the major policy dispute between NOW and the National Women's Political Caucus in the early 1970s. For many years, the NOW leadership successfully fought off efforts to endorse specific candidates, while NWPC not only endorsed but contributed talent and funding to selected recipients. This led to conflicts within NWPC over which candidates deserved a share of these very scarce resources (women's campaigns being typically underfunded), and to charges and countercharges of "careerism," that is, of using the movement for personal advancement (the same type of dispute that characterized collectivist organizations). Other divisions centered on the differences in priorities among three subgroups: those who wanted more women in politics regardless of their positions on the issues; those who would support pro-women candidates regardless of their sex; and those who were willing to support any generally progressive political stand or candidate. The outcome in many instances was simple indecision.

By the mid-1970s, however, NOW reversed its policy as the organization became increasingly active in mainstream politics. The results have been mixed. In the 1980 national elections, for example, NOW was left without anyone to endorse, having declared in the primary election period that they would not support Jimmy Carter, who ultimately became the Democratic candidate. The Republican choice, Ronald Reagan, not only repudiated all feminist support but took the Republican party with him, when, for the first time in decades, the Republican platform did not contain a plank supporting the Equal Rights Amendment.

The endorsement issue still presents problems to feminist organizations, particularly when state and national units disagree, as happened in the 1982 senatorial election in Connecticut, where national NOW supported one candidate (Lowell Weicker, a strong ally in protecting abortion rights), while Connecticut NOW endorsed his opponent (Toby Moffett, who was more progressive on a range of issues). In general, national organizations cannot and do not wish to impose their will on local units—agreeing to disagree, as it were. These differences in priorities produce more ineffectiveness than anger among feminist organizations, even when different candidates are endorsed in the same election. Such was the case in the New Jersey senatorial election in 1982 when NWPC endorsed the Republican Millicent Fenwick, while New Jersey NOW supported her Democratic opponent, Frank Lautenberg. The candidates held similar strongly feminist positions on most issues, but Fenwick, even though a female role model of national reputation, would have voted to organize the Senate on Republican lines, thus placing powerful antifeminists in the chairs of committees dealing with women's issues. Obviously, the choices that feminist organizations are called upon to make in giving or withholding endorsements are difficult, but the feminist movement may be unique in its ability to tolerate this level of diversity within and among its component parts.

Anti-Semitism and racism.   The most recent, and perhaps most divisive issue in contemporary feminism is that of anti-Semitism. Fear and hatred of Jews is, of course, not new in the world. What makes anti-Semitism so dangerous for the New Feminist Movement is that it threatens the

fragile links between white and minority women. Far beyond their proportion in the general population, Jewish women have been prominent in the
movement as well as in the New Left and the civil rights movement. For
many, their Judaism and feminism are of a piece with their commitment to
civil rights for blacks and to movements of national liberation in the Third
World.

Although the Third World issues have been manipulated by some governments into an extension of the Arab-Israeli conflict, in which blacks tend to
identify with less-developed Arab countries, the basic tension between black
and Jewish women in the United States is rooted in their actual status as
members of a "minority group." Both black and Jewish women are well
aware of the effects of discrimination and marginality, but Jewish women
have attained a level of economic security and educational privilege from
which black women remain excluded. For Jewish women, being a "minority"
is defined in terms of their psychological status as "outsiders" in a Gentile
culture; for black women, minority status refers to legal and social disabilities, to poverty and oppression. Black women often fear that affirmative action and other too-little, too-late programs targeted to "minorities" will be
co-opted to the further advantage of Jewish women.

In addition, much vocal opposition to affirmative action today comes from
Jewish men, lending support to black fears that the Jewish community's concern for civil rights extends only to the limit of self-interest, and that black
entry into the professions will be resisted and resented. In essence, black
and Jewish fears are based on historical experience, resulting in expressions
of black anti-Semitism and Jewish racism that have strained the relationship
between black and Jewish feminists.

Additional attacks on Jewish women have come from the extreme left
wing of the feminist movement, whose members identify with the Palestin-
ian cause against Israel. At the 1975 United Nations Women's Conference in
Mexico City, for example, a resolution equating Zionism (the desire of many
Jews to have a homeland in Israel) with racism was passed overwhelmingly.
Again, in a follow-up conference in Copenhagen in 1980, a Program of Action
calling for the elimination of Israel was passed by a vote of 94 to 4. Non-
Israeli Jewish women were repeatedly subjected to openly anti-Semitic at-
tacks from delegates from every part of the world, including some from the
United States (Pogrebin 1982).

While this type of behavior may be expected on the international scene—
it happens at the United Nations every day—similar feelings have been expressed within the New Feminist Movement, and not only from the far left,
typically in terms of charges that Jews dominate the movement and thus

reduce its chances of success (a charge also leveled against lesbians). This is a potentially destructive situation for the New Feminist Movement, if the price for maintaining minority group and radical representation is the exclusion of Jewish or lesbian or any other group of women. A feminist movement without the likes of Bella Abzug is as unimaginable as one without women of color or a Marxist presence. A diverse feminist movement must not only welcome women of various backgrounds and perspectives, but also encourage every woman to contribute all she can and to listen sensitively to the concerns of others. This is why racism, agism, homophobia, discrimination against the physically handicapped, and, most recently, anti-Semitism, have been seen as fundamentally incompatible with a feminist commitment to respect for all women.

Summary and conclusions. The spread of feminist ideas and groups in the early 1970s allowed the movement to reach heretofore untapped constituencies. Organizations that had lain dormant since the suffrage struggle were reactivated on behalf of women's rights. What had been the preserve of educated, urban women became a movement by and for women of many different backgrounds and perspectives. With such a diversity of participants, it was inevitable that internal dissent would emerge. Such conflicts have forced movement activists to clarify and consolidate their positions.

So far, the movement has proved remarkably resilient to internal dissent. Conflicts have spawned new groups and new efforts at consciousness-raising. The feminist agenda has grown and diversified to the point where no one person could work effectively on all its issues. This diversity has allowed each feminist to decide where she wishes to put her energy, and to trust that her personal priorities will be integrated into a feminist whole. To an increasing degree, this task of integration has been assumed by NOW, as the largest mass-based national organization. If feminists spend more time arguing about the correct course of action than in acting as they believe best, then the movement's diversity—its source of strength heretofore—becomes a threat, and flexibility could degenerate into factionalism.

In the course of these conflicts, mainstream organizations such as the Young Women's Christian Association and the Business and Professional Women's Foundation, church-related groups such as United Methodist Women and the National Council of Jewish Women, and even the Girl Scouts of America, all became increasingly radicalized in their positions on women's issues. Conversely, many feminist organizations on the radical fringe became somewhat more conservative in their image and actions.

In ideology, then, there has been a "coming together" around certain shared goals—equal opportunity, equal pay, reproductive rights, and the Equal Rights Amendment—but organizationally there has been an extraordinary growth of diverse associations and activities. The paradoxical situation of a social movement both coming together and growing apart has thus far been a positive feature of the new feminism, although strains persist. We look at this transformation more closely in the next chapter.

Although it is commonly assumed that feminism is a young women's issue, this delegate to the International Women's Year conference in Houston illustrates the universality of concern for equality. *Photograph courtesy of Bettye Lane.*

CHAPTER SIX

Interest-Group Politics: Triumphs and Tensions, 1973–83

Despite the conflicts of the past decade, a broad consensus on priorities and goals has been forged. From this base, remarkable in its breadth and depth, the New Feminist Movement continues to press for change. In doing so, many of its educational and political groups have coalesced into an interest group of national scope. Working within the system, however, presents problems of co-optation and goal displacement at all levels, from the international to the local. Yet, remaining outside mainstream politics could lead to impotence and public indifference.

In this chapter we trace the transformation of the educational and political organizations of the movement from their origins as small, radical groups to their current presence as an increasingly powerful political force or "interest group" (Costain 1981), focused on the crusade for an Equal Rights Amendment and the struggle to preserve reproductive rights.

Just as these issues became rallying points for feminists, they also served to awaken and unite a backlash movement. Organized antifeminism has become closely identified with the far right of the American political spectrum and with extremely traditional religious denominations. The struggle between the two has increasingly been fought on conventional political terms. New problems of coordination and co-optation emerge from this focus on interest-group politics, while the old issues of recruitment and structure fade. But as the movement confronts its opposition politically, it also faces the problem of defining its own goals. This has led to considerable debate within the movement regarding the nature of feminism and femininity. Thus,

115

the New Feminist Movement enters its third decade organizationally stronger than ever before, but faced with new challenges in plotting the course of further action.

Entering the Political Arena

Transforming the movement. In a democratic society, the ultimate success of a social movement depends upon the ability of its organizations to use and manipulate the political system. Otherwise, members continue to be outsiders without a voice in policy-making, and movement issues are perceived as irrelevant or illegitimate. To the extent it succeeds, however, a movement is transformed into an "interest group" participating in the regular political process.

There were many reasons for believing that the New Feminist Movement could never become incorporated into mainstream politics. Generating a sense of solidarity and shared fate among American women has been a long and slow process. Most women, even today, do not perceive themselves as having common interests as women that transcend other roles (Gurin 1982). There was also early resistance to lobbying on the grounds that this would only fragment rather than unify an already diverse movement. Then, too, interest group politics requires a more bureaucratic organizational model than many feminists were willing to accept.

Another source of resistance to conventional politics lies in the nature of the movement itself. If movement goals could have been achieved through normal channels, there would have been no need to organize outside these channels in the first place. Thus, social movements must pioneer nonconventional means of expression: both a politics of disorder—such as media events and demonstrations—and the formation of alternative social institutions, and also attract members who are willing and able to participate in such nonconventional politics. Conventional political tactics such as lobbying (direct persuasion of legislators), then, seem to negate the uniqueness of the movement, turning it into a feminist equivalent of the American Medical Association. Under these circumstances, the transition from social movement to interest group is not simple. Some feminists view the transition as essential, while others consider it "selling out."

Changing circumstances, however, made the transition to interest group politics increasingly likely. Costain (1981) lists three conditions under which a movement is likely to gain effective access to legislators: (1) a major change in the external environment that diminishes resistance to lobbying; (2) the assistance of other groups; and (3) supportive members of Congress.

The changes in the external environment were those recorded by public opinion polls discussed earlier. Further, with only a low-level lobbying effort by NOW, WEAL, and NWPC, Congress had already passed legislation designed to improve the status of women. The Equal Rights Amendment was approved by a vote of 354 to 23 in the House of Representatives in October 1971, and by 84 to 8 in the Senate in March 1972. Indeed, the ERA was viewed as so noncontroversial at that time that no polls were done; the earliest public opinion poll on the ERA was done in 1974. Skeptics in the movement saw that lobbying could pay off and that a majority of Americans would support feminist goals when traditional tactics were used.

By 1973, NOW, WEAL, and NWPC had all established Washington offices in order to be closer to the action. From this beginning, a "women's lobby" quickly developed (Costain 1981), as they were joined by other national women's voluntary associations in attempts to build grass-roots support for certain issues and to influence legislators. Most notable among these established allies were the National Federation of Business and Professional Women's Clubs, the League of Women Voters, the American Association of University Women, the National Council of Jewish Women, and United Methodist Women. Since each of these organizations had originally developed out of a concern for women's needs and problems, the emergence of organized feminism reactivated a commitment that had become muted over the years. The similarity in social background characteristics among both feminist and traditional organization members made possible a shared realm of discourse (Costain 1981). There was also a co-optable network of friendships and common organizational memberships between women in the established and the new women's groups (Gelb and Palley 1982; Rossi 1982).

The established women's organizations had mastered the art of lobbying. They put their knowledge and expertise, and the political legitimacy of their large memberships, to the service of feminist goals. They also provided a large pool of community activists, women well versed in local politics and organizing. This coalition achieved a number of significant victories in the mid-1970s: minimum wage for domestic workers, educational equity, access to credit, admission to military academies, job protection for pregnant workers, and funds for the observance of International Women's Year. Major defeats included failure to override President Nixon's veto of comprehensive child-care legislation or to preserve federal funding for abortions for poor women. The importance of the coalition between feminist groups and traditional women's organizations is underscored by the fact that at this time the movement received little support from such powerful sectors as the business community, unions, or the national administration.

Table 6.1.
Growth of NOW: 1972–82

	1972	1977	1982
NOW Membership	15,000	40,000	220,000
Annual Budget	$160,000	$500,000	$13,000,000
Political Action Committees (PACs)	0	0	81 in 40 states
Public Support for ERA	(not available)	56%	63%

Source: National NOW Times *October 1982; Carden 1974, 196.*

The third condition for lobbying success, supportive members of Congress, was also available in the mid-1970s: a dozen activist congresswomen and several male allies, who introduced and guided bills through the complex legislative processes. At the same time, groups such as the Center for Women's Policy Studies were established to undertake policy research for congressional allies, and to monitor enforcement of laws already passed (Gelb and Palley 1982).

These successes in lobbying and coalition building coupled with the loss of momentum in the drive to ratify the Equal Rights Amendment, spurred some Washington-based feminist organizations to expand their membership, funding, and staff. This marked a major shift for NOW. Just as the mainstream women's organizations moved to more activist positions, NOW came in from the fringe. Despite fears that many members would leave the organization, the long-range outcome for NOW has been positive in terms of organizational growth, as seen in Table 6.1:

Clearly, NOW has not only grown, but has become a basically political organization. It appeals for funds through its PACs and distributes these to feminist candidates throughout the nation. Not all members are pleased with NOW's increasing emphasis on electoral politics, however, and their discontent was evident at NOW's 1982 national convention, where a new president was to be elected. The women who sought a return to more radical positions and unconventional tactics rallied behind the candidacy of Sonia Johnson, a former Mormon who was excommunicated for defying her church's opposition to the Equal Rights Amendment. Johnson was narrowly defeated by Judy Goldsmith, the candidate of NOW members committed to pursuing a pragmatic electoral strategy.

Other hints of disunity surfaced during floor debates and informal caucuses, especially on lesbian rights and minority women's issues. In part, the tensions reflect NOW's strategy of incorporating principles of participatory democracy and egalitarian sisterhood in a structure that is basically bureau-cratic. The organization itself considers persistent conflict as a healthy sign that grass-roots sentiments are not being stifled and that the membership as a whole can still set goals and strategies despite NOW's hierarchical struc-ture (Carden 1978; Gelb and Palley 1982).

Playing party politics. NWPC, NOW, and abortion rights orga-nizations have also been active at the level of national party politics. Follow-ing changes in Democratic party rules governing national conventions, minority and female representation was much greater than in the past. The burning issue for women at the 1976 Democratic convention was whether future party conventions would have *equal* numbers of female and male del-egates from each state. A compromise on this and other topics of concern to women was worked out with nominee Jimmy Carter, and hailed as a victory for politically organized feminism (Freeman 1976).

By 1980, however, Jimmy Carter had lost the support of NOW and many other feminist organizations. At the same time, his relatively impressive re-cord in appointing highly qualified women to cabinet posts, the federal judici-ary, and administrative departments meant that there were a number of pro-Carter feminists at the 1980 Democratic convention, the first in American history at which the number of women delegates equaled that of men. Al-though Democratic party leaders are now in the process of undoing these rule changes, feminists cannot make credible threats to withdraw their sup-port as long as the Republican party is even less sympathetic to feminist goals.

At the Republican party convention of 1976, NWPC and its allies, includ-ing Betty Ford, wife of the presidential nominee, pressured delegates into endorsing the Equal Rights Amendment, but were greatly outvoted on other topics of concern to women. Unlike the situation at Democratic nominating conventions, there was no sustained floor debate on feminist issues. By 1980, the political climate within the Republican party had grown increasingly chilly for reproductive rights and affirmative action. The convention that nominated Ronald Reagan not only refused to endorse the Equal Rights Amendment, but called for a constitutional amendment banning all abortions, and favored the suggestion that federal judgeships be given only to persons who opposed reproductive rights, causing some Republican feminists to leave the party.

In the presidential election of 1980, there was for the first time a signifi-cant gender difference in voting preferences, with women more likely than men to favor the Democratic candidate. This "gender gap" showed up even more strongly in the Congressional elections of 1982, and continues to appear across a range of issues in public opinion polls (Thom 1984). These findings provide the first solid clue to a "women's vote" based on economic self-interest as well as traditional women's concerns—for example, care of the elderly, education, and peace (Erie, Rein, and Wiget, 1983). We cannot know the degree to which feminist political organizations and public relations contributed to the gender gap, but there can be no doubt that the opportunity exists today, as never before in American history, for the creation of a voting bloc of immense power.

Struggling for influence. As the movement groups entered the political arena, they encountered both support and hostility not only from political party organizations but from other groups representing both established interests and new contenders for power. In one recent study, when compared to members of other elites (party, labor, farm, business, media, and minority group leaders) heads of feminist organizations held comparatively radical views of equality, tended to explain poverty in terms of social structural conditions, supported affirmative action for both women and minority group members, and favored greater wage equality for all workers (Verba, Orren, and Ferree 1985). While most of these goals are held in common with blacks and organized labor, neither the black nor labor leaders saw feminists as particularly helpful allies in their political struggles. Conversely, leaders of feminist organizations saw labor unions and black organizations as potential allies, supported their goals, and felt that these groups should have more political power. But the black and labor leaders did not believe that feminists really shared their goals, that the New Feminist Movement represented all women, that existing feminist organizations had much political influence or deserved more. Members of conservative elites (business and farm leaders, Republican party officials), not surprisingly, were strongly antifeminist in their views of equality and willingness to support or seek the support of feminist organizations, but the reluctance of liberal groups to join forces with women's organizations requires explanation.

One reason why black and union leaders failed to recognize the potential value of feminist allies in the mid-1970s is that feminist groups had been hesitant to use their influence on issues not having a direct impact on women. In addition, women's organizations were, and are, relatively weak, so that feminists gain more from alliances with more established organizations than the reverse. As "the new kids on the block," feminists had to show that they could muster enough support—in letter-writing, fund-raising, and votes—to be taken seriously. Not only did feminist organizations need to establish credibility in their own right, but it was also necessary to build working relationships with other groups whose goals they could support.

Feminist ties to black civil rights groups, to organized labor, and to the Democratic party have strengthened over the past few years but remain somewhat fragile. In part, this weakness reflects differences among feminists. Rossi (1982) identifies a subgroup of feminist with strong economic and social welfare priorities but weak ties to other parts of the movement. Conversely, the subgroup of feminists most involved in issues of sexuality and violence have few links to groups working on matters of economic welfare. These differences reflect the various routes by which women came into the movement, and led to diverse alliances. Feminists with experience in the civil rights movement, unions, or the New Left tend to be sympathetic to a socialist analysis in which class and race are important variables. As they themselves are more likely than other feminists to be minority or working-class women, they value links to organized labor and black groups for their own sake as well as for their potential contribution to feminist goals.

Radical feminists, particularly those from the moral reform tradition, are most deeply concerned with women's special qualities and experiences, particularly those of exploitation and violence. Many are also members of world peace and disarmament groups, and active in the ecology and antinuclear movements. It is in these directions that they then look for allies; in turn, long established women's peace groups (e.g., Women Strike for Peace) have drawn new support from the revitalization of feminism.

Liberal feminists are most likely to favor alliances with established civil rights organizations, particularly the American Civil Liberties Union (which has funded a women's rights project), and with the family planning movement, as exemplified by Planned Parenthood. On other issues, liberals have made joint cause with minority lobbies—blacks, the aged, the handicapped, and children's rights advocates.

As a consequence of all these different interests among feminists, the New Feminist Movement has established a broad range of links to other political interest groups, but these alliances typically do not encompass the entire movement. While there is a vulnerability to such "weak ties," there are also strengths (Granovetter 1973): greater flexibility for broad-based feminist organizations such as NOW to maneuver among potential allies and to balance goals and priorities of the many constituencies within the movement. An important aspect of NOW's activities in recent years has been to educate its own members to expand their vision to encompass a variety of feminist perspectives, and to support one another.

Co-opting the Movement

Playing politics increases the possibility of "co-optation," that is, being absorbed into the policy-making structures that one has been fighting against. When the feminist movement receives official sanction, or when its leaders are used to promote the goals of other groups and political leaders rather than those of women, co-optation has taken place. This may happen at a number of levels.

At the international level. The two United Nations Women's Conferences illustrate one way in which co-optation can endanger both national feminist movements and efforts to create an international women's alliance. In both Mexico City and Copenhagen, official delegates selected by their governments rarely criticized their own nations, and women's issues often took second place to such international concerns as racism in South Africa, colonialism, disarmament, the Arab-Israeli conflict, and the world economic system.

In Mexico City, in 1975, 2,000 delegates from 150 nations sat through two weeks of speeches not very different from those presented at any United Nations meeting. Delegates praised their own country's efforts to assist women, and then tackled whatever issue their government wanted to bring to public attention. Although male delegates were outnumbered six to one, the men had great influence on working committees and in preparing the conference agenda. Ultimately, a ten-year World Plan of Action for International Women's Year was hammered out, but apparently no one expects the member nations or the United Nations itself to do much in the way of implementation (Reid 1975).

A second conference to assess progress on the World Plan was held in Copenhagen, Denmark, in 1980, and again became a forum for the airing of international disputes that, although they do affect women, are not inherently feminist. As Bunch (1980, 83) put it: "Copenhagen is a government conference about women—not a women's conference." But if the conferences were not exactly conducted by, for, or about women, they did encourage a shared consciousness and placed national governments on record as planning to improve the position of their female citizens.

Neither conference was entirely devoid of feminist content, although this did not appear in the official sessions. In both cities, an alternative meeting was staged by nongovernmental organizations (NGOs) such as the Young Women's Christian Association, International Planned Parenthood, and the like. In Mexico City it was called the Tribune, involving several thousand interested individuals and representatives of the NGOs. The Tribune attempted, in a way that the official conference did not, to encourage a genuine dialogue among women from nations at very different stages of economic development. The barriers to an international women's movement are not only political but economic; there is a vast gulf in needs and problems between women from the industrialized West and those from less developed countries. International women's conferences—formal and informal—at least provide an opportunity to recognize these differences in perspective, and, for some, to realize that their cause is being co-opted by nonfeminist national leaders.

In Copenhagen, the unofficial conference was the Forum, also sponsored by NGOs, and open to anyone who could afford the trip. The alternative sessions were critical of the World Plan and the lack of implementation, and, as was the case in Mexico City, the unofficial meetings also became occasions for the expression of violent anti-Semitism, to the great discomfort of American Jewish feminists (Pogrebin 1982).

Speaking of both Mexico City and Copenhagen, Tinker (1981) concludes that since neither the male establishment nor the international media take women seriously, the impact of such conferences has been more negative than positive. Both the politicization of the official meetings, and the confusion of the alternative sessions, serve only to trivialize women's concerns. Possible responses include participation only in international meetings on specific issues, or continuing to exploit any opportunity to build bridges among women, or refusing to take part in co-optable events (McIntosh et al. 1981). Since another International Women's Conference is scheduled for Nairobi, Kenya, in 1985, there is not much time left for feminist leaders to decide

At the national level. Among the few clearly positive outcomes of the United Nation's Decade of the Woman and the observance of an International Women's Year in 1975, was the requirement that national governments fund research, publications, and meetings in preparation for Mexico City and Copenhagen. An executive order from President Ford established a national commission, under the leadership of Jill Ruckelshaus, perhaps the most openly feminist of Republican women, to study and report on the status of women. From its research, public hearings, and miniconferences, the commission produced its report, "To Form a More Perfect Union . . . Justice for American Women" (1976), amply documenting the continuing barriers to equal opportunity for American women.

All this information provided the background for the culminating event: a

National Women's Conference in Houston, Texas, in 1977. Although most of the delegates were feminists, organized antifeminists dominated a few state delegations. In addition, women of ethnic and racial minorities were represented in greater measure than their proportions of the general population, making diversity both in attitudes and social background the hallmark of the conference (Rossi 1982). There was also an alternative conference, sponsored by antifeminists under the leadership of extremely conservative religious, patriotic, and political groups. Although the counterconference was unofficial and much smaller than the official one, it received equal attention from the media, in the name of the "fairness doctrine."

The formal, as well as informal, structure of the Houston conference was similar to that of a political party convention, with most participants organized into state delegations, and much of the action on the floor orchestrated by "backstage" influentials. Consequently, some delegates (20 percent in Rossi's survey) felt that resolutions composing the Plan of Action were "railroaded through" in an undemocratic manner. Nonetheless, a majority of delegates rated themselves as "very satisfied" when they left Houston, expressing a firm resolve to work for the implementation of resolutions when they returned home. On the national level, this commitment has led to the formation of a continuing committee that launched a five-year program of action to be capped by a second conference in 1985 (Rossi 1982).

It is still a matter of debate whether the Houston conference should be seen as co-opting feminists to other national political agendas or as having placed feminist issues on these agendas. Both Republican (Ford) and Democratic (Carter) administrations had attempted to control the mood and direction of the conference by their selection of commissioners and at-large delegates, and state-level politics undoubtedly influenced the makeup of state delegations. Yet the overall plan was clearly an expression of feminist goals, with both mainstream political activists and members of feminist organizations collaborating to achieve its ratification. As Rossi notes, there were some instances in which personal reservations were set aside and controversial points endorsed (particularly on the sexual preference and reproductive freedom sections) in order to present a broad and unified feminist front.

Since it was the more radical rather than the more conservative positions that were endorsed, there is little evidence that feminists were co-opted into the nonfeminist political mainstream. It appears that conferees obtained endorsement of positions they were willing to fight for and simply refrained from actively opposing those on which they were ambivalent. Interestingly, programs to aid female victims of violence received more promises of future support from women already concerned with economic issues than the reverse, suggesting the gradual entry of specific issues into the national feminist agenda (Rossi 1982, 314).

Not only are all attempts at co-optation not successful, some may backfire. The National Advisory Committee on Women, established by President Carter in 1978, with Bella Abzug and Carmen Delgado Votow as co-chairs, undertook a detailed and highly critical analysis of the impact on women of Carter's budget proposals for 1980. As a consequence, the president fired Abzug, and most feminists on the advisory committee resigned. When the Carter White House downgraded the role of Midge Costanza, its resident expert on women and minority issues, NOW declared that it could not support his candidacy for a second term.

Clearly, the Carter White House resented women's attempts to influence administration priorities, and believed that there were more votes to be gained from increasing defense outlays than from maintaining, much less expanding, social welfare programs (of which women and their children are the major beneficiaries). This was, of course, the same conclusion reached by the Reagan administration in 1980–84, under which the projected military budget rose to 600 billion dollars while programs assisting women were slashed. In other words, as long as a "women's vote" is not taken seriously, administrations at best make gestures of support for feminist goals, but do very little to change policies.

At the state and local level. Among the earliest mainstream feminist organizations were the state commissions on the status of women, but they were also most vulnerable to outside political pressures, as their members were political appointees, serving at the pleasure of the governor. In some states, commissioners were vigorous advocates of feminist concerns; in others, they were less active; and in a few instances governors replaced activist commissions with antifeminist ones. When the ex-commissioners reconstituted themselves as commissions-in-exile, they found that their unofficial status now allowed them to be more openly critical of state policy. The official commissions were sometimes rendered ineffective by the appointment of a few antifeminists who tied up meetings in endless debates (Lindsey 1980; Rossi 1982).

Independent feminist organizations have typically been structured into national, regional, and even local components before developing at the state level. This was clearly a major handicap in the Equal Rights Amendment ratification drive. Recently, however, there has been a rapid growth in state level coalitions of feminists and traditional women's organizations (Boles

1980). In nonratified states, these coalitions focused narrowly on the Equal Rights Amendment, while in other states they found common ground in supporting legislation in areas of concern to women in general—day care, marital rape, and pension equity. Co-optation remains a risk for these relatively new and still weak state-level organizations.

At the local level, feminist groups have tended to focus on matters relating to sexuality, including sexual violence, rather than the political and economic concerns of state and national units. Local feminist groups are more likely to engage in direct action than in lobbying. Yet, direct action groups, including rape hot-lines, shelters for battered women, and health-care clinics, share problems and needs that render them vulnerable to co-optation and distortion of priorities ("goal displacement").

One factor is the sheer cost of direct action. Whether resources are given as in-kind services (volunteer labor, rent-free space) or in cash (from foundations or government agencies), group members must direct their energies to keeping these resources flowing. The time spent on fund-raising and public relations comes at the expense of the group's original goals.

Often, the problem is more subtle, involving the crucial distinction between self-help and community services (Withorn 1980). Feminist principles of community organizing emphasized the need to develop structures in which women could help themselves resist their subordination. Hot lines, shelters, and clinics relied on the voluntary labor of women rather than on the services of certified "experts." In addition, programs were to be run collectively by staff and clients alike. Volunteers were to engage in consciousness-raising, helping victims to place their personal experience in a larger political context, and encouraging them to build self-esteem through helping themselves and others.

These egalitarian self-help principles were rarely shared by the funding sources to which the feminist groups appealed. Foundations, charitable organizations, and government agencies demanded clear lines of accountability, evidence of expertise (degrees, diplomas, certificates), and rigorous bookkeeping, all of which gradually introduced bureaucratic norms into a collectivist structure. Moreover, the longer feminists worked in these settings, the more they came to distinguish service providers from clients, and to approve increases in staff power. Once such compromises are made, few obstacles remain to the transformation of the original radical organization into a conventional community service, complete with an executive director, a board of trustees, and a fund-raising/public relations specialist. Such changes often provoked angry confrontations among staff members, some of whom would move on to other, purer feminist community projects (Ahrens 1980).

Foundation funding poses another set of problems. As a rule, foundations prefer to grant "seed money" to experimental projects rather than to support established and successful programs. As a consequence, many feminist community organizations lost their funding when they were no longer new; unable to replace these funds, the services were discontinued. Other organizations struggled to find new projects to interest foundation sponsors, or tailored their programs to the current fad among funders; either way, priorities were distorted. Very few local action groups have been able to survive and maintain their original goals for as long as five years, but new groups continue to form around a growing range of issues.

These examples suggest the dangers involved in trying to work within the system at any level: co-optation, trivialization, banishment, and goal displacement. Yet, remaining on the outside also has its hazards: ridicule, indifference, and impotence. The leaders of organized feminism have moved in the direction of creating a political constituency out of the diverse elements of contemporary feminism. Yet as feminist mobilization brings women's issues into mainstream politics, a countermobilization by groups opposed to these goals is activated (Mueller and Dimieri 1982). Such polarization may work to the disadvantage of feminists, whose goals may now appear more controversial and less consensual than originally perceived (Boles 1979; Gelb and Palley 1982). The controversies over an Equal Rights Amendment and abortion rights illustrate these dynamics.

The Battle for the Equal Rights Amendment

The emergence of an effective women's lobby has been overshadowed by the defeat of its central symbol: an Equal Rights Amendment (ERA) to the U.S. Constitution. First introduced in Congress in 1923, the ERA was the brainchild of Alice Paul, an important figure in the suffrage movement and founder of the National Woman's Party. For almost five decades, the amendment was buried in the Judiciary Committee files. Then, in 1970, Congresswoman Martha Griffiths called it out of the committee onto the House floor, where it was overwhelmingly approved after an hour's debate.

The Equal Rights Amendment

Sec. 1. Equality of rights under the law shall not be denied or abridged by the United States or by any State on account of sex.

Sec. 2. The Congress shall have power to enforce by appropriate legislation the provisions of this article.

Sec. 3. This Amendment shall take effect two years after the date of ratification.

Senate approval in 1972 was followed by its relatively speedy endorsement in thirty-four of the thirty-eight states required for final passage. The amendment then became stalled in fourteen, mostly Southern, state legislatures. The emergence of serious opposition to what had appeared to be smooth sailing for the amendment marked an important turning point for the New Feminist Movement (Boles 1979). The unexpected strength of resistance to the ERA established the movement and its opposition as serious political forces, and led to a reappraisal of priorities among feminist groups. In the summer of 1973, a coalition of thirty organizations including the League of Women Voters, the American Civil Liberties Union, the United Auto Workers, and the American Association of University Women was formed to press for ratification. With limited funds, this ERA Ratification Council began a fund-raising campaign and a low-level research and lobbying operation.

Over the course of the decade, these efforts expanded and accelerated, so that by 1980 the list of major American organizations supporting ratification was impressive in its range: unions, working-women's federations, professional caucuses, women's clubs, most mainstream Protestant and Jewish organizations, and racial and ethnic associations. From the Amalgamated Clothing Workers of America to Zonta International, from flight attendants to coalitions of Catholic nuns, the list includes over 100 organizations with national membership (Boles 1979).

Despite such widespread support, it became clear by 1978 that the original seven-year period for ratification would expire without the needed approval. After intense lobbying from the pro-ERA coalition, as well as the first massive demonstration in years—over 100,000 ERA supporters marching on the Capitol in Washington—Congress extended the deadline for three more years. But by 30 June 1982 the amendment still lacked the necessary state ratifications, having been narrowly defeated in Florida and Illinois. That evening, "Over the Rainbow" parties were held by those who had worked long and diligently—and successfully—for its defeat.

Curiously, it was not the original opponents of the ERA who were celebrating. In the late 1960s and early 1970s, opposition came from unions and the political left, who feared that women workers would lose workplace protections, but this resistance ebbed as the "protections" were shown to deprive women of high-paying jobs. By the mid-1970s, however, the apparent strength of feminist organizations had awakened the fears of many who held deeply conservative views about the appropriate roles of women and men. The Supreme Court's 1973 ruling on abortion activated additional resistance from church authorities and laypersons who felt that the ERA, by reaffirming women's rights, would remove entirely existing controls over women's reproductive choices.

In one state legislature after another, religious and political conservatives reminded their colleagues that "you can't fool mother nature," and warned that if the amendment was passed, men could no longer control their daughters or wives. Opposition to the ERA was mobilized around issues such as single-sex toilets, women in combat, homosexual marriages, and men supporting their families, issues that tapped a well of anxiety about sexuality in our culture, and fed fears regarding the changing division of labor between men and women. Although each of these charges could be accurately refuted, advocates for the ERA were at a disadvantage, as it is typically more difficult to demonstrate the advantages of change than to awaken anxiety over loss of the familiar (Conover and Gray 1983).

Not only did the remaining state legislatures fail to ratify the amendment, but several passed resolutions rescinding their earlier approval (the legality of which remains untested). Furthermore, in 1975, state-level ERAs were rejected by the voters of New Jersey and New York, two relatively "liberal" states, where feminists underestimated the skills and passion of their opponents. The message was clear: the ERA was in trouble, both from the strength of antifeminist forces and from the inability of supporters to mobilize effectively. It was only in 1979 that supporters of the amendment moved into high gear: forming coalitions, appealing successfully for funds, and preparing a public relations campaign. Ratification became NOW's priority goal, a cause and a consequence of its transformation into an interest group. Ironically, the losing struggle for the amendment marked the high point of feminist organizing. Membership gains and financial support reached new peaks; cooperation among women's groups was stronger than ever; and public opinion polls recorded high levels of support for ERA.

Why, then, was failure possible? Just as feminists made the ERA a central symbol of their crusade for equality, so did the forces of antifeminism give great symbolic value to its defeat. Public policy analysts suggest that such highly polarized symbolic issues are rarely won by those favoring change, even when their opponents are a small minority (Coleman 1957; O'Brien 1975; Conover and Gray 1983). If ratification is ultimately achieved, it will be as the outcome of a long hard struggle to re-create a national consensus. The passage of the Women's Suffrage Amendment, for example, took over thirty years of concentrated, organized effort. Efforts to obtain passage of the ERA continue today. On 3 January 1983, the first order of business of the House of Representatives was to reintroduce the Equal Rights Amendment, with 230 co-sponsors, but the bill has thus far failed to win congressional approval as antifeminists seek to add clauses prohibiting women in combat, upholding single-sex schools, and otherwise limiting the guarantee of equal rights in the original text.

The Politics of Abortion

The other major focus of resistance to feminism emerged after the 1973 Supreme Court decision in *Wade* v. *Roe* and *Doe* v. *Bolton* that declared existing abortion laws in Texas and Georgia to be unconstitutional. These and similar state statutes had denied abortions under *all* conditions, leaving both the pregnant woman and her physician open to criminal prosecution. At the time of the Court's decision, the movement to reform state abortion laws had made slow but steady progress; by 1970, one third of the states had adopted statutes that were less restrictive than in the past, but these were based on medical considerations and not upon women's rights.

By the early 1970s, several major feminist groups had made abortion law repeal a central feature of their program, and a dramatic change in public opinion had been registered, from overwhelming opposition to changing the laws in 1965 (85 percent) to a slim plurality in favor of leaving the choice to a woman and her doctor. This opinion shift followed widespread publicity about the effects of illegal abortions and the plight of women bearing deformed fetuses due to the use of the drug Thalidomide and to an epidemic of German measles in the 1960s.

On 22 January, by a 7 to 2 vote, the Supreme Court declared that expectant mothers enjoyed a "right to privacy" under the Fourteenth Amendment—but only up to a point. The point was after the first three months of pregnancy, when the state had an interest in protecting maternal health and could enact regulations only for that purpose. The Court acknowledged the state's right to protect a potential human life by forbidding an abortion during the final twelve weeks of pregnancy except to preserve the health or life of the mother. In this way, the Court sought to reconcile the rights of women, the public's interest in adequate standards of medical care, and the state's concern for the protection of a viable fetus. The decision had the immediate effect of striking down the most repressive state statutes, but it fell short of a full guarantee of the right to control one's own body.

Another immediate effect was to activate an organized opposition. Under the leadership of the Catholic church's hierarchy, the newly prominent Protestant fundamentalist preachers of the "electronic ministry," and the founders of an ultraconservative New Right movement, antiabortionists united in a National Right to Life Committee (Jaffee et al. 1981). Their symbol of a red rose, stitched on a lapel or ceremoniously presented to legislators every 22 January, has become as familiar an image as the feminists' coat hanger representing the dangers of illegal abortions. By appropriating the labels of "pro family" and "pro life," the opponents of feminism seized the initiative from the New Feminist Movement, forcing feminists to spend a great deal of time denying that they are antilife or antifamily, and trying to establish themselves as "pro choice" rather than pro-abortion.

The antichoice faction has been remarkably successful in influencing federal, state, and local legislators to enact laws and administrative guidelines that increasingly erode the guarantees of *Wade* v. *Roe*. At the national level, Congress has denied Medicaid funds (for the health care of the poor) for abortions, and has attempted similar restrictions on military and federal employee health insurance coverage. State and local authorities have passed equally restrictive Medicaid regulations, and many hospitals have refused to have the procedure performed in their facility. Moreover, the Supreme Court has upheld these regulations, effectively denying to poor women a right that the Court once extended to all.

In addition, antiabortion forces have attempted to impose restrictions on the availability of abortions even in the first trimester. But in 1983, the Supreme Court reaffirmed its support of a woman's right to privacy by finding most of these restraints to be unconstitutional. In many ways, the Court extended the guarantees of the *Wade* decision, but only for those women not dependent upon Medicaid.

This latest setback has led abortion opponents to renew their efforts for a constitutional amendment forbidding all abortions, thus placing the issue beyond the reach of the courts. Other antiabortion activists have resorted to the "politics of disorder": family planning clinics have been fire-bombed and otherwise damaged; a clinic director and his wife were kidnapped; clients have been harassed by picket lines as they enter the facilities, and by subsequent phone calls in which they have been called "murderers." In many sections of the country, therefore, legal abortions are simply not available. However, in contrast to the ERA battle, the status quo favors the prochoice, feminist position. Organized attempts to change the status quo (e.g., pro-ERA, antiabortion) operate at a disadvantage since their cause is usually perceived as less urgent, more risky, and less important than the defense of existing rights (Conover and Gray 1983).

Although the antiabortion movement is dominated by right-wing political organizations, some opposition has also emerged from the political left, based on ideals of pacifism and nonviolence, and of concern for the poor and handicapped (Lowell 1980). More typically, left-wing groups and individuals

accept the necessity for legal abortion while deploring the economic and social injustices that make it the only alternative for some women. Both the
socialist and moral reform traditions in feminism also encourage a distinction
between the legal right to a safe abortion and the desirability of abortion per
se (Petchesky 1980). The need for abortion, they point out, is socially determined by poverty, by the stigma attached to unmarried motherhood, by the
anonymity of current adoption practices, and by repressive sexual attitudes
that limit the use of reliable contraception. For feminists in the socialist and
moral reform traditions, the way to reduce the incidence of abortion is not
through restrictions that drive needy women to risky alternatives, but
through change in the social/economic factors that have produced the need
for an abortion in the first place.

The success of STOP-ERA and Right-to-Life however, direct our attention to the extent of the antifeminist backlash and the deeper currents of
feeling it represents.

The Backlash Movement

Social movements invariably produce countermovements based on resistance to change. Countermovements share many of the characteristics of
primary movements (Mottl 1978), but are often reactive or defensive both
in structure and ideology, focusing on narrow goals rather than a broad plan
of transformation (Mueller and Dimieri 1982; Conover and Gray 1983; Ferree and Miller 1984). If the countermovement is successful, the status quo
is restored; if not, resistance may continue at the local level. The antifeminist
backlash, however, is not simply a movement opposed to the ERA and legal
abortion, but, rather, part of a larger countermovement with a broader set
of goals—the New Right.

Organized antifeminism. The New Right, as defined by one of
its leading figures, Richard Viguerie (1980), consists of all those opposed to
high taxes, government regulation, sex in the media, abortion, and weakness in foreign policy. The New Right espouses traditional conceptions of
masculinity including displays of strength, control over others, willingness to
use violence, and competitive success—all of which are rejected by the new
feminism. The New Right program calls for a return to an idealized past
when government was small, our military the envy of the world, when children obeyed their parents and wives depended on their husbands for financial support, and when Protestant prayers were in the schools and sex

education was out. In essence, they seek a massive repeal of real and imagined social trends of the past four decades.

Many of their fears are shared by Americans dismayed over what they perceive to be a breakdown of all social institutions, but most particularly the family. In the face of what is seen as a collapse of traditional authority, even some social scientists blame feminist critics for undermining the power of men as husbands and fathers (e.g., Lasch 1977). There has also been a flood of articles and books on the "new" science of sociobiology, the most recent attempt to root human behavior in biological forces such as genes and hormones, thus limiting the kinds of changes that can be imposed at the cultural level, particularly in the area of gender roles (cf. Breines et al. 1978). Popular magazines have given these "findings" extensive and uncritical coverage (Beckwith 1984).

The sociobiological position can be carried one step further to suggest that feminist goals are not only unrealistic but positively destructive. George Gilder (1973), one of the New Right's favorite philosophers, speaks of "sexual suicide" if women forsake their essential tasks of keeping men under emotional control, fed and clothed, and anchored to the home. In a later book, Gilder (1982) argues that a wife and children in the home are the bedrock of the free enterprise system, the only motivation for men to work hard and to accumulate profit.

Other analysts of the American scene point to our current low birth rates as contributing to the coming crisis in the Social Security system, to a lowering of consumer demand, and to a potential shortage of military conscripts. The common message is that many current economic problems could be solved if only American women would return to the kitchen and bedroom, and produce record numbers of infants—for their own good as well as that of the nation, and even Western civilization. "Sociobiological" arguments are now, as in the past, more often grounded in contemporary economic considerations than in biological data (Sayers 1982; Gordon 1977).

Opposition to feminism also arises from a romanticization of the family. When the family is perceived as the only legitimate source of sexual and emotional fulfillment, anything that threatens its stability is a personal loss and a public danger. Since women are charged with the maintenance of family life, it is they who bear responsibility for its apparent breakdown. Blame is then placed on the promises of feminism: that women can have an identity apart from family roles, that they can find fulfillment in the world of work, that marriages should be egalitarian rather than patriarchal, that relationships with other women could be as satisfying as those with men, and that one's body need not be placed at the service of God or country. These promises are seen as tempting but ultimately dangerous. No wonder, then, that the New Feminist Movement has aroused such a passionate backlash!

Opposition to the ERA began with the John Birch Society, an ultraright-wing organization devoted to saving America from communism. Since the John Birch Society has limited influence even within the New Right, the anti-ERA cause needed a more mainstream image and charismatic leadership, both of which were provided by Phyllis Schlafly, an energetic and articulate Republican party activist from Illinois. When her efforts to influence defense spending, foreign policy, and other "men's" issues were rebuffed by Republican party leaders in the early 1970s, she picked up the Birch Society suggestion that women themselves could provide the troops needed to defeat ERA. Schlafly formed an organization called the Eagle Forum, with branches across the country, and assumed a leadership role in the STOP-ERA coalition. At the Washington, D.C., "Over the Rainbow" celebration, Schlafly was the undisputed star of the evening.

How did she do it? Her resources included legions of women organized at the grass roots; money from various New Right funding sources (including the owners of Amway Enterprises and Coors Beer, and members of the National Chamber of Commerce); assistance from Birch Society branches and organizations such as the Knights of Columbus, the American Legion, and Daughters of the American Revolution; and the support of fundamentalist Protestant ministers, leaders of Orthodox Jewry, and large segments of the Catholic hierarchy. It was a formidable alliance. In addition, some feminist analysts (e.g., Langer 1976; Conover and Gray 1983) believe that the driving force behind the defeat of ERA was business interests, particularly insurance companies, whose profits would be reduced by equal pay or equal benefit provisions. Yet no amount of business support could have defeated so popular a proposal without the help of deeply committed, locally organized women who appeared at every public meeting, pressed candidates for answers, handed out literature, wrote letters to the newspapers, and showed up at the voting booth on election day.

Who are these women who actively oppose feminism? Several studies of active antifeminists agree in describing them as disproportionately likely to be married, to be involved in church activities, and to be conservative in both religious ideas and politics in general (Mueller and Dimieri 1982; Brown 1984). The consistency with which they support the fundamentalist view of biblical truth, for example, is greater than the consistency of their opinions on women's issues, some being willing to support equal pay or antirape programs while being firmly opposed to reproductive rights or equality in hiring

(Rossi 1982; Mueller and Dimieri 1982). In studies of public opinion, strongly antifeminist attitudes are related not only to religion and marital status, but also to more general beliefs, such as denying the social causes of poverty, and opposing black civil rights (Smith and Kluegel 1984), and anxiety over trends that legitimate open expressions of sexuality (Ferree 1983a). Some fear that advances for women will come at the cost of men's status (Spitze and Huber 1982), while others are afraid that feminism will result in women being exposed to the same exploitation as men on the job or in the armed forces. Indeed, the "women in combat" issue has been a powerful organizing weapon for antifeminists (Stiehm 1982). In general, those who have actually mobilized to act on these beliefs are, like active feminists, a selective sub-sample—in this instance, drawn from the co-optable social networks of fundamentalist Protestant and conservative Catholic churches, and from the extreme right of the political spectrum (Mueller and Dimieri 1982).

To a surprising extent, antifeminists recognize many problems that feminists also address, but frame their proposed solutions quite differently. The antifeminist view of men, for example, is in many ways more mistrustful than that held by feminists. For example, popular self-help books such as Marabel Morgan's *The Total Woman* (1973) play on women's fears that husbands cannot be trusted to remain in a marriage, but women are then advised to hold on to their husbands through total obedience, including a willingness to play out the latters' sexual fantasies. STOP-ERA leader Phyllis Schlafly plays eloquently upon women's economic dependence and consequent fear of divorce by demanding a return to punitive alimony for "guilty husbands" and urging women to be "better," that is, more submissive, wives, while feminists see economic independence and marriage based on affection rather than fear of punishment as the solution for the same insecurities.

Phyllis Schlafly's genius was to recognize the political implications of the traditional homemaker's question: how can I keep my husband from involvement with younger, sexier women? Rather than simply urging individual women to feel better by striving for perfect femininity—including spotless glassware, an ageless, odorless body, and cheerful, conforming children—Schlafly mobilized these anxieties in defense of traditional conservative economic, political, and sexual arrangements. Women who fear the consequences of their inevitable failure to attain perfect femininity feel perpetually vulnerable and can be activated to oppose changes that bring males and females into close contact and potential economic or sexual competition.

STOP-ERA also benefited from the opportunity to enlist the support of other constituencies already alarmed about nonfamily issues. There was no shortage of New Right groups devoted to particular causes: against gun control, communists, unions, and busing for racial balance; and for school prayer, tax credits for private education, and a strengthened military. Of course, not everyone involved in these causes is a member of the New Right, any more than those in organizations opposing these positions are all left-wing radicals. Yet the single-interest groups associated with extremely conservative positions provided crucial recruits, money, and moral support to STOP-ERA and Right-to-Life (O'Reilly 1982). Indeed, so strong and obvious is the link between antifeminism and right-wing politics, that several feminists analysts have suggested something more than a pragmatic decision by the New Right to enlist the support of fearful women.

The most systematic of these analyses is that of Petchesky (1981), who claims that the New Right seeks to destroy liberal democracy as it has developed since the 1930s, and is using women's issues as a lever for the return of patriarchy and militarism. That is, by reducing rather than expanding options for women, by denying access to family planning services, and by eliminating public support for social welfare programs, women will once more be totally dependent upon men, and men will not need to fear competition from women.

In this view, the antifeminist backlash is more than a reaction to the idea of female equality. It is a powerful last-ditch effort to preserve a system of domination that extends far beyond the family. Similar to other "nativistic revivals" that occur when a traditional way of life is disintegrating (e.g., the Native American Ghost Dance of the 1880s), a powerful yearning for the "good old days" leads to celebrations of traditional ways and fierce resistance to change. History is distorted and romanticized and the real problems of the past are forgotten. The New Right, for example, deplores female-headed families, while overlooking the fact that not so long ago mothers left alone were forced to place their children in orphanages or watch the entire family starve (Vandepol 1982). Government assistance today actually keeps the family (mothers and children) together.

The strength of the New Right's response is evidence of the importance of the issues raised by feminism: not simply jobs, or pay, or child care, but an authentic liberation of women from dependence upon men, from involuntary childbearing, and from confinement to the home. The New Right recognizes that, when carried to its logical conclusion, the feminist agenda is challenging every established male-dominated authority structure: religious hierarchies, governing bodies, corporations, financial institutions, and school systems. It should be no wonder, then, that the backlash has been so intense and relatively successful in delaying the full implementation of laws already enacted and in inhibiting further changes, despite overwhelming public support for most feminist goals.

Nonorganized antifeminism. While public opinion polls record majority support for such specific feminist goals as equal pay and economic opportunity, reproductive rights (under most conditions), willingness to vote for women candidates, and greater participation of fathers in child rearing, only a minority of respondents actually identify themselves as "feminists." This discrepancy characterizes even women in public office (Mueller 1980). In one study of 219 officers of women's organizations in Chicago (e.g., PTAs, church guilds, charitable groups) over 70 percent said they were not feminists, although 57 percent were "sympathetic" to movement goals, and higher percentages took profeminist positions on specific issues (Bers and Mezey 1981). The researchers conclude that there are allies in the community, but on specific issues only.

Why are so many women reluctant to be identified with the movement? One factor is fear of male disapproval or retaliation. Another is lack of *group consciousness,* defined by Gurin (1982) as (1) awareness of similarity and a feeling of belonging to a certain group; (2) becoming discontented with that group's power; (3) feeling that this lack of power is unfair; and (4) approval of collective action to improve the status of that group. While identification with the group "women" has doubled in less than a decade (from 34 percent in 1972 to 67 percent in 1979), discontent with the power of women as a group is "peculiarly lacking" (Gurin 1982, 4). However, there has been a substantial rise in the proportions of women who blame discrimination rather than themselves for differences in job status and pay scales (from 33 percent in 1972 to 55 percent in 1979). Still, on the question of organizing to bring about change, only 15 percent of women in 1972 and 1979 endorsed collective over individual effort. Gurin notes that many women find gratification in their traditional roles, and that they typically do not live in close association with one another—both conditions tht inhibit the development of shared consciousness (Hacker 1951).

The relatively low level of collective consciousness among women is reflected in the absence of significant sex differences in most profeminist attitudes, from support for the ERA to approval of women in politics (Smith and Kluegel 1984; Spitze and Huber 1982; Cherlin and Walter 1981). But while the absence of a distinctive consciousness among women, as women, is clearly a handicap for the movement, similarity in levels of support for feminist goals from women and men may be taken as a hopeful sign. Married men, who increasingly rely on women's wages to maintain the family standard of living, for example, should be particularly aware of the problems faced by employed wives, and therefore more supportive of change than are nonmarried men (Smith and Kluegel 1984). A question repeatedly raised within the movement is whether changes that empower women must necessarily come at the expense of men, or if both men and women can benefit from changing structures and attitudes. Men and women in the general public, who support the movement in roughly equal numbers, appear to have agreed that, at least for now, changing roles and responsibilities will also bring benefits to men.

For whatever reason, the New Feminist Movement has found a generally sympathetic audience but has failed to engage the strong commitment of a majority of women, causing considerable soul-searching among feminist leaders. In her most recent book, *The Second Stage,* Betty Friedan (1981) argues that the movement should reclaim the family as central to its vision of a new social order, and accomplish its revolution by replacing masculine ("alpha") modes of interaction with a feminine ("beta") style based on intuition, caring, and a "contextual" frame of reference. While also criticizing the movement's failure to appreciate family values, Elshtain (1981) rejects Friedan's views as too supportive of an oppressive political and industrial system. Rather, Elshtain (1982) claims that the movement must recapture a "women's world of concern and care," challenge a society that denies female values, and use family strengths to save communities from destruction by nonaccountable business and political forces. Other feminists find both these prescriptions dangerously supportive of the "two worlds" doctrine that has been used to limit women's sphere of action and, by reromanticizing the family, deny its oppressive aspects (Stacey 1983).

These and other discussions of the current state of the New Feminist Movement have been framed by the phrase "femininity v. feminism" (Costain 1982) in which the new emphasis on women's distinct characteristics— their special needs as bearers of the young, and their capacities for intimacy and empathy—could provide more ammunition for the backlash movement, encouraging women to leave the labor force and return to the nursery and kitchen. Or, conversely, the current debate could energize the movement not only to a final assault on all bariers to full participation, but also to a transformation of social structures more generally.

Within the movement, debate centers on the role of women entering the "man's world" of politics. How critical can women be of the rules of the game while they are playing it to win? Does women's exclusion make it easier for them to take moral postures condemning war, cut-throat competition, and sexual dehumanization? If so, should women seek to change the system from the outside or try to get in? Although the dangers of co-optation are real, so are the possibilities of influence and change. In the next chapter, we turn to a consideration of the accomplishments of the movement and some of the further questions facing feminists today.

Geraldine Ferraro, shown here addressing a NOW convention, broke new ground for women both politically and professionally when she was nominated as the vice-presidential candidate of the Democratic party in 1984. As women work together to accomplish their common goals, increasing recognition of their collective political strength has affected both major parties. *Photograph © Taylor/Sygma.*

CHAPTER SEVEN

Aims, Accomplishments, and Emergent Issues

In previous chapters we have described the origins and development of the New Feminist Movement over the past twenty years. But the picture is still incomplete. If the movement were as dead as the media have often proclaimed, then it might be time for an autopsy. Despite media "obituaries" (in 1982 *Ms.* published a collection going back to 1971), organized feminism is very much alive and developing in directions that may or may not prove fruitful in coming decades. While it is far too early to draw up a balance sheet of successes and failures, by looking at the progress that has been made and the struggles currently going on, we may at least have a better sense of the energy and diversity of the movement.

Diversity is really the key, since feminists differ over both goals and methods of change. Career and radical feminists see the means of change in women realizing their own power and potential; socialist and liberal feminists stress transforming social institutions, such as the law, the economy, and the schools, in ways that would liberate women. Disagreement about goals appears as career and liberal feminists urge eliminating restrictions on individuals, so that women can participate in society in the same way as men, but radical and socialist feminists seek a fundamental restructuring of society itself to create new forms of community.

These differences are echoed in the diversity of feminist organizations. Gerlach and Hine (1970) have argued that such diversity and decentralization is advantageous for social movements in that a variety of strategies can be pursued simultaneously, and if one strategy reaches a dead end, others may

Table 7.1.

Women Employed in Selected Occupations, 1970 and 1981
(Numbers in Thousands)

Occupation	Number 1970	Number 1981	Women as Percent of All Workers in Occupation 1970	Women as Percent of All Workers in Occupation 1981
Professional-technical	4,576	7,173	40.0	44.7
Accountants	180	422	25.3	38.5
Computer specialists	52	170	19.6	27.1
Engineers	20	65	1.6	4.3
Lawyers-judges	13	80	4.7	14.0
Physicians-osteopaths	25	60	8.9	13.8
Registered nurses	814	1,271	97.4	96.8
Teachers, except college and university	1,937	2,219	70.4	70.6
Teachers, college and university	139	202	28.3	35.3
Managerial-administrative, except farm	1,061	3,098	16.6	27.4
Bank officials-financial managers	55	254	17.6	37.4
Buyers-purchasing agents	75	164	20.8	35.0
Food service workers	109	286	33.7	40.5
Sales managers-department heads; retail trade	51	136	24.1	40.4
Sales workers	2,143	2,856	39.4	45.4
Sales clerks, retail	1,465	1,696	64.8	71.3
Clerical	10,150	14,645	73.6	80.5
Bank tellers	216	523	86.1	93.7
Bookkeepers	1,274	1,752	82.1	91.2
Cashiers	692	1,400	84.0	86.4
Office machine operators	414	696	73.5	73.7

continue to be successful. A review of the aims and accomplishments in each of the four basic directions taken by the New Feminist Movement provides a sense of the diversity of the feminist program for change and of the broad scope of concerns being actively pursued today.

Career Feminism: Desegregating the Labor Force

As the name implies, career feminists attach highest priority to achieving equality in the labor force. While this may seem a simple goal, the realities of

Table 7.1.

(continued)

Occupation	Number		Women as Percent of All Workers in Occupation	
	1970	*1981*	*1970*	*1981*
Secretaries-typists	3,686	4,788	96.6	98.6
Shipping-receiving clerks	59	116	14.3	22.5
Craft	518	786	4.9	6.3
Carpenters	11	20	1.3	1.9
Mechanics, including automotive	49	62	2.0	1.9
Printing	58	99	14.8	25.0
Operatives, except transport	4,036	4,101	38.4	39.8
Assemblers	459	599	48.7	52.3
Laundry and dry cleaning operatives	105	125	62.9	66.1
Sewers and stitchers	816	749	93.8	96.0
Transport equipment operatives	134	304	4.5	8.0
Bus drivers	68	168	28.5	47.3
Truck drivers	22	51	1.5	2.7
Service workers	5,944	8,184	60.5	62.2
Private household	1,132	988	96.9	96.5
Food service	1,913	3,044	68.8	66.5
Cooks	546	723	62.5	51.9
Health service	1,047	1,752	88.0	89.3
Personal service	778	1,314	66.5	76.1
Protective service	59	145	6.2	10.1

Source: U.S. Department of Labor 1982.

job segregation and discrimination are actually quite complex, and solutions more difficult than implied in the slogan "equal pay for equal work." In the first place, women are already segregated in a relatively small number of poorly paid jobs. The "big ten" are familiar: nurse, elementary school teacher, secretary, bookkeeper, typist, sales clerk, waitress, cashier, sewer/stitcher, and domestic worker. Over 40 percent of all working women are concentrated in these ten jobs alone (U.S. Department of Labor 1982). Second, women are typically found in the lowest-paying jobs within any given occupational category, even those that are female sex-typed. Thus, waiters predominate in elegant restaurants and male hairdressers in the swanky shops, while waitresses staff the corner diner and female hairdressers work in less pretentious establishments.

The female job ghetto. In the past decade, some headway has been made in opening up traditionally male occupations, but women in these fields remain only a small fraction of all women workers. Table 7.1 shows that there has been a dramatic increase in the number of women working in the financial sector and in certain professions. Moreover, the numbers of women enrolled in law, medical, and business schools suggest that these proportions will continue to increase for some time to come. In the decade between 1970 and 1980, women went from 4 to 25 percent of business students, from 9 to 23 percent of medical students, and from 7 to 31 percent of law students (WEAL 1983). In addition, when schools are willing to admit more women, more women apply, thus increasing the proportion admitted, enrolled, and graduating, which reinforces the school's willingness to admit women (Haignere 1981). As proportions of women medical school students increased, however, the percentage of women on the faculty declined from 15 percent in 1965 to 10 percent in 1979 (Association of American Colleges 1982).

There have also been notable increases in the numbers and proportions of women in traditionally male skilled-craft jobs, but as the numbers were very small to start with, even large percentage increases do not mean very large numbers. The number of women in all skilled-craft jobs doubled from 1972 to 1980, an increase of 365,000 in just eight years, but the percentage of craftworkers (e.g., carpenters, millwrights) who are female is still only 6 percent (up from 3.6 percent in 1972). These gains are not as secure as those made by women in the professions, due to "last hired, first fired" seniority rules recently affirmed by the Supreme Court. Women and minority men who have recently entered occupations that were previously closed to them are the most vulnerable to being laid off or fired in times of recession. For example, all the gains made by women in the steel industry in the late 1970s were wiped out in the layoffs of the early 1980s (Deaux and Ullman 1983). Women entering apprenticeship programs in declining occupations (such as machinists and printers) face especially difficult prospects. But women who have entered nontraditional blue-collar jobs report great satisfaction with the pay, the challenge, and the variety of the work (Walshok 1981; Deaux and Ullman 1983).

Despite clear gains in women's share of certain better-paying jobs, why is it that the average earnings of full-time year-round women workers remain lower than 60 percent of men's? One major reason is that the vast majority of women entering the labor force continue to be channeled into the traditional sex-typed jobs. Thus, while the absolute number of women lawyers rose from 13,000 to 80,000 between 1970 and 1981, the absolute number of women secretaries and typists increased by over one million in the same period (U.S. Department of Labor 1982; Leon 1982). The prospects for increasing wage equity for women depend both on raising wages for "pink-collar jobs" and on increasing the numbers of routes by which women can move into better-paying employment (Rytina 1981).

Unions and women. Until recently, many of the jobs in which women are concentrated have been ignored by male dominated labor unions. Today, women workers increasingly look to unions as a way to press their demands for increased pay and respect, and unions have discovered women as a new source of members in a period of reduced blue-collar employment. Although unions today represent a declining proportion of all workers, nurses, teachers, secretaries and retail clerks have all become *more* unionized in the past decade (LeGrande 1978; Moore and Raisian 1982). Some women's professional associations, such as the American Nursing Association, have taken on collective bargaining as part of their responsibility, negotiating over issues such as the respect and authority accorded nurses in patient care as well as better pay. Women office workers are affiliating with unions as a way to accomplish their goals (Koziara and Insley 1982; Goldberg 1983), and the Coalition of Labor Union Women (CLUW) continues to make male union leaders more aware and responsive to women's needs in both traditionally female and nontraditional jobs. Nonetheless, only 15 percent of women clerical workers were unionized in 1980, and only 19 percent of all women workers, compared to 31 percent of men (U.S. Department of Labor 1980). One barrier is the continuing male leadership and male-defined priorities in even those unions with a majority of women members.

Networking and mentoring. Women often do different types of work than men do even in the same fields, and they also find fewer opportunities for advancement. One recent study suggests that women's low wages partly reflect their lesser likelihood of getting on-the-job training or of being in positions to exercise authority over the hiring and pay of others (Corcoran and Duncan 1983). Despite the American belief in merit as the deciding factor in getting ahead, most employees also realize that "who you know" is often more important than "what you know," suggesting the importance of making contacts with other women to share advice, information, job offers, or additional contacts. By building networks of connections across jobs, firms, and levels, women can more effectively pool resources and so help themselves and others up and out of dead-end jobs. One problem with this strategy is that there are relatively few positions at the top. Another problem is that more highly placed women have more to offer others in the network than do women in lower-level jobs, creating a differential incentive to participate.

Most of the women at the top who help other women advance do so as *mentors* rather than in networks of mutual assistance. A mentor is a person, male or female, who helps and encourages younger or newer workers to learn the important informal rules of a job. Compared to men, women may have fewer mentors and less effective mentoring, because top-ranked men do not yet see women as their colleagues or successors. Women are therefore encouraged to mentor other women, but as long as men control the high-level jobs in our society, most women will still have to rely on male mentors, especially in nontraditional fields.

Famous firsts.   One very visible aspect of career feminism is the increase in the number of "first women" to hold a particular job, whether as Supreme Court justice, astronaut, coal miner, or sportswriter. In most of these cases, the sheer weight of tradition and prejudice held women from these positions. While the New Feminist Movement created the pressure to dislodge this weight, it is obvious that the abilities and efforts of the "first woman" are also crucial. Women in such positions soon realize that their success or failure will be taken as an indication of the capacities and accomplishments of all women. Kanter (1977) points out that the high visibility and the representative function of "first women" are also experienced by any woman who is greatly outnumbered in the workplace, whether first or fourteenth. Such women, whom Kanter calls "tokens," therefore face far greater stereotyping (either as "just like a woman" or as "unfeminine") and more intense performance pressures than do men, or women who are not so outnumbered. Women, like other minorities on a job, need a critical mass before their work conditions become normal. However, token women may be more aware today than in the past of the impossibility of conforming to conflicting stereotypes (e.g., to be aggressive yet ladylike), less anxious about the negative social consequences of their career success (cf. Horner 1968; Caballero, Giles, and Shaver 1975), and more willing to help other women follow in their footsteps (Laws 1975).

Sexual harassment.   Despite the common belief that women encourage and enjoy the sexual advances of coworkers, the evidence suggests instead that some men consider themselves entitled to "make passes," regardless of what the women do to discourage them (Schneider 1982; Jensen and Gutek 1982). Sexual advances are typically directed at lower-status women workers, because higher-status women have the power to retaliate against lower-status harassers (Tangri, Burt, and Johnson 1982). When women are subordinated to men (student to teacher, employee to employer, worker to supervisor), it is risky and difficult for women to resist such harassment, so that changing jobs may be the most common escape route (Jensen and Gutek 1982).

Sexual harassment is not a rare event. A survey of government employees done for a congressional committee found that 42 percent of the women reported experiencing sexual harassment on the job (U.S. Merit Systems Protection Board 1981). Other research suggests that women who are trying to advance within their firms are more likely to encounter sexual harassment than are women without such ambitions (Collins and Blodgett 1981). Sexual harassment may also be more common in nontraditional jobs. In one study, 31 percent of women in male-dominated jobs, but "only" 18 percent of those in traditionally female jobs, reported sexual touching at work; 11 percent compared to 6 percent reported that dating or having sex was demanded; and twice as many (21 versus 9 percent) quit jobs on account of sexual harassment (Gutek and Morash 1982). Women in male-dominated jobs also face nonsexual harassment. O'Farrell and Harlan (1982) note, however, that while male coworker hostility was a significant cost, experienced by nearly a third of the women in their study who were in nontraditional work, its frequency was actually less than women expected, and was outweighed for them by the other advantages of nontraditional work.

Once the federal courts ruled that sexual harassment was a form of sex discrimination (1976), women could protect themselves and their jobs through the courts, a difficult and costly route. Only a few employers have internal grievance procedures with sanctions to punish sexual harassers (Livingston 1982). However, women are finding that even informal resistance can be effective (U.S. Merit Systems Protection Board 1981). Such confrontation requires a change in consciousness, so that a woman no longer blames herself for men's behavior (Jensen and Gutek 1982; Benson and Thomson 1982). As women assert their right to a safe working and learning environment, they can "take back the day" as well as the night.

Assimilation or transformation? Many of the new books and magazines aimed at career feminists assume that their goal is to be accepted on the job with a minimum of disturbance to the status quo. Thus, women are advised to "dress for success" by creating a slightly feminized version of standard male business suits. Women are also expected to carry the burden of any conflict between business norms and their own needs and interests, by "coping with stress" and "balancing your time budget." Career feminism may encourage this superwoman syndrome, but it is not the only goal. Many career feminists believe that women can and will challenge and change the occupations they enter, as illustrated in two of the male sex-typed occupations that women have entered in recent years—the police and the ministry.

Women have held restricted positions in police forces. Fewer than 2 percent of all officers in 1970 were women and they were typically segregated in a separate women's division (Martin 1980). Since 1972, when Title VII of the Civil Rights Act was amended to cover public employees, it has been illegal to deny women equal opportunity in a law enforcement career, but women have found it difficult to realize this opportunity as departments argued that women were not large enough or strong enough to perform regular duties. Women candidates sued, claiming that the testing criteria that excluded them actually had no bearing on their ability to do the work. The courts, starting in 1975, upheld the women and struck down certain height and weight rules (Martin 1980). Finding that there had been past discrimination, the courts then ordered police departments to make special efforts to hire and train women for all their positions.

Women officers still face difficulties in conveying authority to suit the conventional "macho" image of the tough cop (Martin 1980). But this image neglects such important, nontraditional elements of good policing as skills in conflict resolution and empathy in dealing with victims. One study of male and female trainees suggests that women are actually superior in certain key abilities, including marksmanship and high-speed driving, while men are stronger and run faster (O'Connell 1980). Fair evaluation demands that all these skills be taken into consideration because they all relate to effective and safe police work.

Women's entry into the ordained ministry has also been accompanied by questions about traditional roles and beliefs. While religious traditionalists may not literally believe that God is male, they continue to assert that men are more like God in important ways—as authority figures and spiritual beings not "corrupted" by the physical processes of menstruation or pregnancy (Hewitt and Hiatt 1973; Ruether 1983). Feminists challenged the way biblical texts were being used to support these ideas, with some success (Ochs 1977). The first women rabbi in the Jewish reform tradition was ordained in 1972; the first women Episcopal priests were ordained in 1974; and increasing numbers of women entered the Protestant ministry in many denominations. Although only 4 percent of the clergy in 1982, women are now one-fourth to one-half the students in master of divinity programs in mainline Protestant seminaries (Carroll et al. 1983). Hymnals and prayerbooks have been revised to eliminate sexist language, and feminists in the churches have begun to challenge some underlying traditionalist ideas. For example, Ruether (1983) notes that the belief that authority in this world reflects divine authority is not true to the Bible, in which God rebukes rulers on behalf of the poor and oppressed. Many women preparing for the ministry today not only want to be accepted into existing church hierarchies, but to create more egalitarian religious institutions, dedicated to serving the poor and willing to confront injustice (Maitland 1982).

As these two examples illustrate, career feminists themselves have somewhat divergent goals. On the other hand, they would like to enter the same professions and occupations men do, with the same opportunities to be successful. On the other hand, they also see the need to move away from sex-typed and inappropriate job definitions and toward recognition of the full range of skills they possess. Female sex-typed jobs, such as nursing, lack the respect and pay they merit; male sex-typed jobs are defined in overly authoritarian or competitive ways. Career feminists often need to make hard choices as individuals between conforming to the existing structure of the job, or attempting to transform it. Advancing feminist goals within an organization, whether by simply encouraging one's company to provide day care or by trying to change its broader priorities, may not be compatible with "getting ahead" individually, but could be essential for other individual women to break through. While the push for assimilation and the desire for transformation are both important elements in the career feminist agenda, how well either will be accomplished remains for the next generation to determine.

Liberal Feminism: Equal Rights Under Law

Many of the advances women have made in the last fifteen years have been in the area of legal rights, and yet major differences in the status of men and women persist. Can equal treatment under the law bring authentic equality? With reference to both women and blacks, conservatives have argued that "stateways cannot change folkways," that is, that customs are stronger than laws, and so effective legislation can only follow changes in custom or sentiment. Liberals, including liberal feminists, argue that "stateways," or laws, can actually change behavior and, ultimately, attitudes. When equality is a principle of law, "folkways" begin to change, because the law alters the system of rewards and costs that influence people's choices.

Liberal feminists believe that only when men and women are treated equally can they realize their individual potential.

Defining discrimination. The Equal Pay Act of 1963, Title VII of the Civil Rights Act of 1964, and Title IX of the Education Act Amendments of 1972 created the basic legal framework for feminist advances in the 1970s. Certain benefits from this legislation can be clearly identified. For example, between 1965 and 1975, over 30 million dollars was awarded to women in back-pay settlements when the courts found evidence of violation of the Equal Pay Act, which only covers differences in pay for identical jobs (Berch 1982, 127). Out-of-court settlements account for at least as many millions more (Barrett 1979). Title IX, which covers discrimination in educational programs, expanded women's athletic opportunities and produced other less visible improvements in the treatment of women on campus, such as access to scholarship funds and prohibition of sexual harassment. Although Title IX defines discrimination broadly, actual enforcement has been uneven and rarely energetic, and periodic attempts are made in Congress to amend the law (Gelb and Palley 1982). The substantial changes in athletic programs— in 1973 budgets for men's sports were twenty-two times as great as the budgets for women, while in 1980 they averaged only five times as large (Association of American Colleges 1980)—are particularly at risk now, as the Supreme Court recently decided that Title IX only covers programs directly receiving federal funds. Attempts in Congress to rewrite this law have met strong resistance from the Reagan administration.

Title VII of the Civil Rights Act has had the most sweeping impact of anti-discrimination legislations, but its exact coverage depends on judicial interpretation. For example, in a case where women but not men were required to prove they had made adequate day-care provisions, the Supreme Court held that it is sex discrimination to have different hiring criteria for women with small children than for men with small children. However, a few years later the Court also held that discrimination against "pregnant people" was not discrimination against women. Congress has since passed legislation to correct this loophole. In 1979, the Court also held that, even though government policy almost totally excluded women from the armed forces until 1975, it was not discrimination but "legitimate social policy" to give veterans an absolute priority in Civil Service hiring, so that in some states even the veteran with the lowest score on a civil service exam must be hired before the highest scoring nonveteran can be considered.

There are other limitations to Title VII. The armed forces, Congress, and the courts remain exempt from coverage and can discriminate if they so desire. The military's desire has increased under the Reagan administration, as more jobs are defined as off-limits for women (Holm 1982). The Supreme Court also recently held that a divorced wife of a military man is not entitled to a share of his pension, even though his career typically made it impossible for her to develop a stable work history of her own. These and other arbitrary limits placed on the scope of Title VII are one reason why many feminists believe the Equal Rights Amendment is still necessary.

Affirmative action.   In addition to antidiscrimination legislation, Executive Order 11375, issued in 1967 under President Johnson, requires that companies receiving federal contracts take positive steps to recruit and train women and minority men, set goals and timetables for progress, and demonstrate that they are making good-faith efforts to meet these objectives. Affirmative action policy does *not* require employers to set quotas for the numbers of women or minority men who must be hired or even considered, nor does it demand that unqualified or less qualified candidates be given preference. Public misinformation is partly due to media carelessness with the terms "affirmative action" and "affirmative relief," which is a court judgment that a particular employer has discriminated and that orders a remedy in the form of accelerated hiring or promotion of members of the affected group. Thus, quotas for hiring or for promotions may be set by the judge as "affirmative relief" to repair the wrong done by hiring discrimination, just as back-pay awards may be made when there is a finding of salary discrimination. The Justice Department under Reagan has been attempting to overturn these court-ordered remedies with the claim that they constitute "reverse discrimination" against white male employees.

While there is no legal penalty for simply falling short of affirmative action goals, the fact that records must be kept on hiring and promotion decisions gives rejected candidates better data on which to base legal action. The government also has the power to cancel or suspend a contract if it finds that the contractor has been discriminating. In general, most liberal feminists would agree that affirmative action as a policy helps women, but that vigorous enforcement is crucial, and this depends on government. The commitment in the Reagan administration has been to opposing rather than enforcing affirmative action.

The women's policy network.   Much legislation important to women has been enacted because of the organized efforts of liberal feminists. The women's policy network is an informal collection of feminist organizations, such as NOW and WEAL and the Women's Rights Project of the American Civil Liberties Union, traditional women's organizations such as the League of Women Voters, and influential individuals, including feminist members of Congress and high-ranking administrators, who work together to get women's rights legislation passed and implemented. They have demanded enforcement of existing law and have initiated innovative legislation to secure equal rights for women.

The Equal Credit Opportunity Act of 1974, for example, prohibits discrimination on the basis of sex *or* marital status in any aspect of a credit transaction (such as getting a credit card, a mortgage, a car loan, business credit, etc.). Because of the efforts of the women's policy network, and despite the banks, the Federal Reserve Board has taken a broad view of discrimination, requiring creditors to maintain records in the names of both spouses, to disclose reasons for the denial of credit, and to eliminate questions about childbearing intentions or birth control practices.

Legislative priorities.   Many key issues for liberal feminists are financial. A number of these concerns have been brought together in proposed legislation known as the Women's Economic Equity Act, covering pensions, taxes, alimony and child support, insurance benefits, and Social Security reform. The fact that women continue to be responsible for child care, for example, means that they are disadvantaged by pension systems that penalize interrupted careers, or that exclude part-time employment. Because women are awarded custody of minor children by mutual agreement in most divorce settlements, enforcement of child-support orders is another major financial issue. Since full-time housewives depend on their husbands' income for survival, they may find themselves instantly impoverished when divorced or widowed. Few divorced women receive alimony and typical awards are only for a few years of "transition," although older women who have been out of the labor force have few employment possibilities. "Displaced homemaker" programs are designed to help such women until they are eligible for Social Security (Marano 1980; Crabtree 1980).

The structuring of the Social Security system further contributes to women's poverty. Women who have combined homemaking with paid work typically receive no higher benefits than married women who have been full-time homemakers, even though they have paid additional taxes. A divorced woman is, at best, entitled to a benefit that is half her ex-husband's, collectible only when he retires (Gordon 1979; Burkhauser and Holden 1982). The Social Security Act Amendment of 1983 did little to correct the basic sex inequities of the program (Forman 1983). As a remedy, liberal feminists propose basing benefits on *earnings sharing.* In this plan, the earnings record of husband and wife would be treated as joint property for the duration of the marriage and Social Security benefits would be divided equally. When a marriage ends, the record is split and each individual's later work contributes to raising their own entitlement (Burkhauser and Holden 1982).

The shortage of affordable child care is also a problem that legislation can address. Today, over half of all mothers of children under six are in the labor force, but directly subsidized day care is available only to the very poor, and even this minimal support was drastically cut in the early 1980s. For moderate-income families, the costs of child care are partly subsidized by an income tax credit, helping account for a small rise in the number of day care slots available (Leon 1982; U.S. Bureau of the Census 1982). However, unlike most of Western Europe, the U.S. does not subsidize maternal (or parental) child care leave, nor is private industry obliged to provide benefits beyond medical leave for the actual birth. These policies of non-support limit a woman's ability to have the children she wants (Hofferth and Moore, 1979; Adams and Winston, 1980).

Equality and gender neutrality. Liberal feminists have found it increasingly necessary to insist that equal treatment under the law means more than writing laws in sex-neutral language and more than applying standards based on men's experiences to women. As we have noted, eliminating formal distinctions in the rights of husbands and wives does not eliminate discrimination against the role of "dependent spouse," a role still filled in most instances by women. "Dependent's benefits" are still primarily wives' benefits and "veteran's preference" is still primarily male preference. Military service is more recognized and rewarded as a social contribution than is motherhood. Although the courts will probably continue to see such "gender-neutral" discrimination as a matter of "legitimate social policy," liberal feminists are now calling for specific legislation to extend rights and recognition to roles traditionally filled by women.

There are two different visions of the future that could be secured by such legislation. For some liberal feminists, the ideal situation is one of "androgyny," in which men and women express a similar range of traits (e.g., being both assertive and nurturant), and share breadwinning and homemaking responsibilities equally. Other liberal feminists look to a future in which there would be a free choice between somewhat distinct ways of life, though no longer associated with one's gender. Feminists with the former vision are suspicious of proposals that encourage role specialization, whether in housework or in paid employment, while those who incline toward the latter view are more concerned about policies that penalize people who specialize in housework or other traditionally female roles. For example, the former see alimony at best as a necessary evil, while the latter view it as an entitlement earned by nonfinancial contributions to the career of the employed spouse.

Both models of equality, however, demand changes in social arrange-ments that go beyond mere gender neutrality in the law, as crucial as formal equality must be. The Equal Rights Amendment is the constitutional guar-antee of at least this technical gender neutrality. Most important to liberal feminists is the opportunity to realize individual potential. To reach this sec-ond goal, laws, programs, and policies will have to be revised to give equal protection to those who have chosen nontraditional and traditional roles, or even to directly encourage the combination of the two, without penalizing either those who follow traditional paths or those who have no partner with whom to share parental tasks.

Socialist Feminism: Challenging Capitalism

While socialist feminists agree with the liberal feminist emphasis on chang-ing social policy as a route to equality, they reject a focus on the individual as the object of emancipation efforts. For socialist feminists, it is society as a whole that needs to be emancipated. Because American society is organized on capitalist principles of individual competition and the accumulation of pri-vate wealth, those who are economically, socially, or physically disadvan-taged are in a position to be exploited. Women are both disadvantaged and exploited. Moreover, the capitalist system divided society into "public" and "private" spheres. When production moved out of the home and family con-trol into separate workplaces under the control of capitalists, the status and power of women declined (Tiano 1981), leaving them exploited and op-pressed both in the workplace and at home (Eisenstein 1979; Sokoloff 1981).

From this perspective, many of the rights secured by liberal feminism are hollow, because most women lack the fundamental resources enabling them to make use of these rights. For example, women's freedom to enter a profession or trade is really relevant only to those who have the necessary education. "Bourgeois rights" will not help poor women resist being taken advantage of by capitalists (Fox-Genovese 1980). The debate over legisla-tion protecting women workers in the early part of this century illustrates the difference between formal equality and real opportunities, for example, women's (abstract) right to work is contrasted to the (concrete) necessity for poor women to accept whatever conditions employers set. As govern-ment set some limits for all workers (a minimum wage and shorter work day, for example), protective legislation for some workers came to be seen as less necessary and as a screen for discriminatory practices. Thus, in the 1960s, when the courts began to strike down legislation protecting only women as inconsistent with Title VII, socialist feminists were at first dismayed, but evidence that these "protections" denied women access to better-paying factory jobs dispelled these fears. The belief that social policy should be directed at improving the lives of those who have the least, rather than abstract ideas of equality, remains the guiding force in socialist feminism.

The feminization of poverty. Attempts to balance the budget or increase defense spending at the cost of cutbacks in social welfare programs is an obvious threat to the survival and quality of life of the least advantaged sector of society. This sector is increasingly made up of women and their children, who constitute over three-quarters of the population below the poverty line. Resisting cuts in income support programs has consequently become a priority with feminists groups across the political spectrum (cf. WEAL 1983). But socialist feminists direct particular attention to the structural causes of so many women's poverty.

At the time of the "war on poverty" in the mid-1960s, there were a number of social groups with a disproportionate chance of being poor: old people, rural and urban blacks, and rural whites. Programs designed to meet the needs of these populations were fairly successful. Poverty among the elderly was cut in half, largely as a result of Medicare, cost-of-living adjustments to Social Security, and raising minimum benefits levels for the lowest paid workers (Hess 1983). Black workers and black married couples improved their income positions (U.S. Bureau of the Census 1983a). But the targeting of these programs assumed that only men were breadwinners, even though black families typically rely on two earners, and black and white families that are supported only by women's wages have long been poor.

As poverty was reduced among the elderly, farm couples, and white families between 1965 and 1980, the proportion of the poor who are women rose steadily, especially the nonmarried—single parents, aged widows, and displaced homemakers (U.S. Bureau of the Census 1983b). Even employed women may not earn enough to rise above the poverty level; in 1980, 55 percent of employed women earned less than $150 per week, compared to 22 percent of employed men. The proportion of women among the elderly poor has increased from 60 percent in 1959 to 71 percent in 1982. This trend toward the "feminization of poverty" is one of the most significant developments of recent years (Pearce 1978; Erie, Rein, and Wiget 1983). The priority issue is thus a war on female poverty, which would have to include low-cost child care, affordable housing, better Social Security and pension coverage, and, most importantly, higher wages for women workers (Hess 1983).

Comparable worth. Women's wages are low in part because the occupations in which women are concentrated are systematically undervalued (Treiman and Hartmann 1981). Wage rates are rarely set by simple competition, but instead reflect differences in the social power of various groups. Professionals restrict competition for their jobs by limiting access to the necessary schooling, while craft unions strengthen their relative bargaining position by restricting apprenticeships. Women rarely have the power to control access to schooling or hiring, even for jobs in which women predominate.

Women's relative lack of social power is reflected in their paychecks. Jobs that demand both formal education and specific skills (e.g., librarians, social workers, nurses, elementary school teachers) are poorly paid, but many less skilled "women's" occupations pay too little for women even to support themselves, let alone a family. "One man away from welfare," many women are forced to subsidize their survival through marriage. In contrast, men's wages are based on the assumption they will at least have to support themselves and probably also a family. Thus, jobs that demand similar levels of skill and experience pay very differently depending on whether they are designed to be a man's job or a woman's job. In Connecticut, for example, a statistical typist was found to earn less than a toll collector; in Colorado, senior nurses earned less than groundskeepers at the same hospital.

In order to demand increases in women's pay it is necessary to prove that their jobs do, indeed, call for the same level of skill, responsibility, and effort as men's, and thus can be considered of *comparable worth* to employers (Treiman and Hartmann 1981; Norwood 1982). To prove this is not easy; existing government and corporate skill-rating systems consistently underrate women's skills. For example, the government's 1976 *Dictionary of Occupational Titles* classified a nursery school teacher as no more skilled than a parking lot attendant and a registered nurse as no more skilled than a barber. Therefore, before "equal pay for jobs of comparable worth" can be realized, current methods for job evaluation must be revised. Several unions and state and local governments have done such job studies, but few changes in pay have followed, largely because employers have claimed that it would be too expensive to pay women what the studies say they ought to earn. In some instances, women have had to strike to get what they are owed (McGuire 1982); in other cases, the courts have come to their aid.

Wages for housework? Many women work for no wages at all in the home. The expectation that women will do housework in exchange for financial support is imbedded in common law, although the courts have *never* intervened to assure financial support in an ongoing marriage. Such support varies with the husband's goodwill and his earnings, not with the amount or quality of the housework done. The separation between "public" and "private" divides work, which is done for a paycheck in a discrete workplace, from housework, which is not considered real work at all.

But work it is—varying from a low of about twenty-five hours a week for employed wives with no children to a high of about sixty-seven hours a week for full-time housewives with a child under one year old (Walker and Woods 1976). Whether or not their wives are employed, husbands contribute less than eleven hours a week, typically "helping" rather than holding the primary responsibility (Pleck 1979; Walker and Woods 1976). Planning and carrying out all the tasks required to run a household is a substantial job. If a woman also has a paid job, she has a double workday. Thus, improving employment conditions for women will be only a half-measure as long as housework remains their invisible and "private" burden.

Consequently, socialist feminists attempt to spell out the links between housework and corporate profits, as when consumers do for free what stores once paid clerks to do: bag groceries, pump gas, assemble toys and furniture, deliver milk, etc. (Weinbaum and Bridges 1979; Glazer 1982). Some claim that these links will only be recognized when housework becomes a paid occupation, leading to heated debates on whether private household work should be turned into wage labor, and, if so, who should pay for it (Dalla Costa 1972; Cox 1976; Malos 1978; Sargent 1981). Some argue that husbands should pay, since they benefit most directly from the personal services housework provides; others see the state or individual employers as deriving the ultimate benefit from a motivated labor force and higher total productivity; still others think that wages for housework would be a mistake because it would give further advantages to better-off families, increase the sex-stereotyping of the job, and allow capitalist values to dominate the home (Lopate 1974; Ferree 1983).

In any event, much housework has already left the home. Much food preparation is no longer done in home kitchens but in fast-food restaurants and frozen-food factories by women who are employed at low wages under terrible working conditions (excessive heat, cold, dampness, etc.) (Strasser 1981; Sokoloff 1981). Just as women left their home looms to work in textile mills early in the industrial revolution, women are now preparing meals in factories. Will this move to factories actually make it easier to organize women collectively to resist exploitation? How should women respond to the changing nature of housework—by welcoming these trends or by trying to resist them? How can women who find their own workday lightened by these changes make common cause with the women who now bear these burdens? Would policies that reduce some immediate burdens for working women, such as paid maternity leaves, in the long run define women as undesirable and temporary workers, or make women's dual role more permanent and practical?

International perspectives. One way to evaluate such social policies is to examine trends in other countries, particularly those with a socialist economic system, as in China, the Soviet Union, and Eastern Europe, or a more developed welfare state, such as Sweden (Adams and Winston 1980). Traditional socialist doctrine held that feminists should work for a socialist revolution first, and women's liberation would inevitably follow. Few socialist feminists today would argue that a socialist system is sufficient to liberate women (Weinbaum 1978; Eisenstein 1979; Sargent 1981). In fact, women continue to be treated as second-class citizens in socialist countries, making socialist feminists even more skeptical of the claim that a male-led, male-defined revolution will take women's needs and interests into account (Scott 1976; Eisenstein 1979). Yet there is also considerable evidence that women's opportunities are considerably greater in socialist systems than in capitalist countries. East German women have more equality in education and on the job than do West German women, for example, and income differentials between women and men are lower (Shaffer 1981).

Socialist feminists have paid special attention to the record of socialist governments in the Third World (e.g., China, Cuba) (Andors 1982; Randall 1982). Questions of female literacy, female infanticide, the nutrition of women and children, infant mortality, women's control over their bodies and reproductive decisions, women's access to higher education and to political power are central to evaluating the effects of change. Whether the record of these governments is judged good or poor in feminist terms partially reflects the standard chosen for evaluation. If the comparison is based on either prerevolutionary times or the status of women in neighboring countries, then the women in Third World socialist countries seem fairly well-off. If, however, the standard is in terms of the status of men in the same country at the same time, women remain disadvantaged under socialism (Weinbaum 1978). Despite some progress, structural problems remain, not simply prerevolutionary prejudiced attitudes, which the government often blames (Nazzari 1983). The next step is to identify these structural barriers to women's equality (e.g., inadequate support for child care, excessive priority to military interests, etc.) and to construct a model of socialist transformation that would bring women and men together to make a revolution and keep it faithful to women's interests.

A second task is to identify and correct the processes within economic "development" that have a particularly negative effect on women. These problems often have roots in the worldwide economic system. For example, what are the consequences for the women of both regions when electronics and textile manufacturing is exported from American plants to factories in the Far East? What are the consequences of United States foreign-aid policies that reduce the importance of the noncash subsistence sectors of the economy, where women have traditionally had more power, in favor of enterprises that offer opportunities only to men? Development programs in both socialist and capitalist Third World nations have often ignored women's contributions and needs (Tiano 1981).

Class or sex as first priority?   Situations of shared threat (one's country being bombed, facing starvation, or seeing family members dragged off by death squads) encourage women and men to recognize their common interests and work together. But in addition to these common interests, women and men have separate interests that may conflict. For example, men may prefer to assure their authority in the home and protect their access to better jobs in the workforce by restricting women's options. How can women best deal with these conflicts?

Socialist men typically define their revolution as dealing with "human" problems, and demand that women place their "special interests" on hold until "things improve." Feminists reject this argument, and claim that women's problems are human problems too, and that unless these too are addressed from the start, the resulting social revolution will leave patriarchial assumptions and oppressions untouched—as can be seen in the Soviet Union today. To wait until "after the revolution," or even longer, "until the post-revolutionary problems are worked out," is to wait too long; while women's aspirations are being deferred, men's power is being consolidated (Weinbaum 1978). Therefore, socialist women must organize to fight for their own interests *before* the revolution and maintain feminist organizations afterward.

Socialist feminists find it impossible to decide whether class or sex is the most important oppression because women around the world are the most oppressed and exploited group of workers—and all women work, whether or not they are paid for their labor. In many situations, women's issues *are* the basic survival issues. Throughout the world, women are more often hungry, more often illiterate, more often destitute. The "status of women" thus should never be seen only in terms of opportunities for privileges, but also as involving questions of survival. How best to serve the interests of the plurality of the world's population that is both poor and female remains the challenge of socialist feminism.

Radical Feminism: Expanding Visions of Community

The visionaries and utopians of the New Feminist Movement are the radical feminists, for whom feminist ideas have a transforming force of their own. Radical feminists themselves have typically experienced the power of the movement in personally important ways. For many a woman, the ideas of feminism have been the first step in "saving her own life"—escaping from stifling tradition and the suspicion of madness. The realization that one is not alone, that many of one's problems are socially generated and shared with other women, opens up the possibility of personal liberation by rejecting sexist society and its demands. Women who take that step in isolation may be called insane, and also feel crazy. Women who reject unreasonable social demands collectively might still be labeled mad women by others, but now at least they know themselves to be sane.

Rejecting society's values is personally liberating, permitting the open expression of anger that women too often turn against themselves (in suicide and depression), and freeing the individual from the constraints of social convention. Liberation from the "good girl" image means women can stop oppressing themselves in order to receive social approval. Radical feminists, more than others, are concerned with understanding these social constraints, explaining their oppressive force to other women, and finding ways of living outside the boundaries of "acceptable female behavior." The individual liberation provided by radical feminism carries admitted social costs. Women who live without the protection of a man may be considered "fair game" for sexual attack, and without a male income the risk of poverty is substantial. Radical feminists are also ridiculed and attacked for defying patriarchal conventions by refusing to "dress nicely" and "talk softly." Those who have chosen the lesbian alternative are subjected to additional penalties in this homophobic society.

The power of consciousness to transform personal lives thus does not lie solely in the individual, but demands the creation of a feminist community. All people need and seek validation for their vision of the world. Radical feminists, in rejecting the sexism of everyday life, need social support for their perceptions of reality as well as acceptance as individuals. Creating a feminist community with an alternate value system, a community that will affirm the strength and anger in women that patriarchy suppresses, is one of the highest priorities for radical feminists. They hope that such a community will be a model in miniature of a world without patriarchy, and that experiencing it will encourage other women to defy the existing system. In this sense, radical feminism makes all feminist politics personal, demanding that feminism be relevant to how women live their lives at this moment.

Language and consciousness. It is not surprising to find women artists, poets, and novelists in the forefront of radical feminist activities, since individual consciousness, and its power to transform one's life, are central to any creative person. Moreover, women who are creative and innovative are especially likely to chafe under the constraint of "proper" behavior. By evoking experiences that others have self-protectively repressed, and expressing them in terms that make them recognizable and shared, creative artists can turn personal experiences into political grievances. Artists affirm the power of language to transform social arrangements by bringing the invisible to consciousness. Many leading radical feminists are themselves poets as well as political essayists (e.g., Adrienne Rich, Marge Piercy, Robin Morgan).

Even when artists create imagery that mobilizes and unites, their work can seem bizarre to those who do not share its symbolic vocabulary. Radical feminists describe themselves as "Amazons," "furies," and "witches," images of female anger and power that arouse fear in our society, but are valued by feminists for the strength and defiance they convey. Radical feminists also use language to symbolize their break with maleness, for example, spelling women "wimmin" or taking a new name, such as Kathy Sarachild, Judy Chicago, or Starhawk. They also link images of women and nature, treating the link between environmental degradation and violence against women (the rape of the sea, the violation of "Mother Nature") as more than metaphor (Griffin 1979). Symbols such as spinning and witchcraft may be difficult to interpret without the literary-historical framework that has come to be taken for granted in feminist communities, and by strengthening the in-group feeling of those in the relatively small radical feminist community, this shared language might also foster exclusivity. Yet much of the best creative work by radical feminists has had strong popular appeal and has spread feminist ideas to many women who have never directly experienced feminist communities and consciousness-raising.

Separatism as strategy or goal? The extent to which supportive communities for women should also be communities *of* women has always been a matter of controversy. For some radical feminists, the primary value of separatism is temporary and strategic, a way for women to learn to trust and value other women. In this model, men are a distraction and a waste of time since they have been socialized to expect to be the center of attention. Keeping men away thus frees women to discover themselves on their own time and in their own way (Morgan 1980).

Most radical feminists see separatism as a valuable goal in itself. In this view, women relating to women is the core social relationship, allowing an equality and openness impossible for men, who are more competitive and emotionally shallow. For some, the ultimate form of feminist community envisioned for the future is one solely of women (Gearhardt 1980). Since sexuality is positively valued, but only within the caring relationships of the community, lesbianism is an essential part of their feminism. Heterosexuality is defined as a social institution that breaks women's initial attachment to women (their mothers) and channels it into an attachment to men, from which men profit (Rich 1980).

But separatism as a goal holds relatively little attraction for women who do not see all their problems as stemming from sexism. Those with experience of race or class oppression feel a common bond with men also facing these problems, but they are excluded or marginalized by definitions of feminism that make separatism a goal. Black women in particular have stressed that this goal must necessarily limit diversity and force women to choose which of their oppressions is worst (Hooks 1981). Moreover, separatism as a goal considers men incapable of change and irredeemably oppressive (Daly 1978). Although movements and revolutions led by men have always ended up dehumanizing and scapegoating "the enemy," perhaps feminist revolutionaries could break this cycle of oppression and recognize some of the ways in which men also are victimized by systems of race, class, and sexuality, and develop a vision of the future for the whole human race.

The men's movement.   Recent years have also seen the formation of men's groups somewhat allied to the New Feminist Movement, but organized separately to fight sexism as it affects men. Most of these groups share the radical feminist emphasis on personal transformation, focusing on the cultural restraints on male emotionality and deep friendships. Members support one another in exploring the "soft" side of their personalities. These groups are usually organized on local level, with a relatively small membership, so that close personal ties can be encouraged.

Contrary to stereotype, members of these groups are typically heterosexual males concerned about their relationships with women and children as well as with men. Gay men more often gravitate to explicitly gay groups. Both types of groups typically recognize homophobia as a key element in confining people within the limits of sex-stereotyped behavior, forcing straight men continually to "prove" their masculinity by aggression and coldness. By supporting men who try to be different, these groups facilitate changes in the social relationships of men and women, and men with each other. There have now been at least seven national conferences of men's movement groups, and a 1981 source listed thirty local men's centers. Sev-

eral groups have sponsored projects to reform rapists and batterers by raising their consciousness about the roots of their violent behavior (Gross,
Smith, and Wallston 1983).

There are also a few men's backlash organizations that claim to be part of
the men's movement, such as Free Men, which presents men as being oppressed by feminism. These groups emphasize supporting fathers in custody
battles even when fathers have not been actively involved in child care before the divorce. In their eyes, men and women are engaged in a power
struggle in which feminists appear very powerful and men their victims.
(Haddad 1979; Gross, Smith, and Wallston 1983).

Antiviolence organizing. Radical feminists have been at the
forefront of efforts to combat violence against women. There have been numerous local protests, for example, against sentences for rapists that fail to
reflect the gravity of the offense. In some recent rape cases bystanders
failed to intervene or actually cheered; in others, authorities trivialize the
crime or blame the victim. But there are also indications that public awareness of the seriousness of this crime has risen. By taking their protests to
the street, radical feminists mobilize public opinion and encourage vigorous
prosecution.

Popular pornographic magazines provide models of sexual violence and
lend an air of social approval to violence against women (Smith 1976; Lederer 1980). In Indianapolis, in 1984, feminists spearheaded a successful drive
for a city ordinance banning pornography as a violation of women's civil rights
(e.g., to walk freely) rather than as offensive sexuality. Antiviolence groups
have also addressed the problems of woman-battering, incest, and crimes
against prostitutes, a particularly degraded and defenseless class of women.
Internationally, antiviolence groups press for an end to practices such as
genital mutilation in North Africa; female infanticide in India and China; sut-
tee (widow-burning) in India; the murder of women who have "dishonored
the family" all over the world; and selling women into sexual slavery as prostitutes (Daly 1978; Barry 1979; Morgan 1982).

For radical feminists, the definition of antiviolence organizing also encom-
passes environmental and antiwar activities (Lord 1982). Around the world,
women, especially feminists, have taken a highly visible role protesting the
arms race (Tiffany 1982). Popular belief links women's roles as mothers and
moral guardians with pacifism, and some radical feminists have incorporated
this sentiment in a broad ideology that reasserts the nineteenth-century
feminist claim to female moral superiority (McAllister 1982). This approach
views women as having special qualities of nurturance, compassion, and un-

derstanding that bring women closer to nature and generate special concern for the fate of the earth. Women, nature, and peace form a harmonious triad threatened by men's essential drive to dominate and exploit (Griffin 1979; Johnson 1982). Of course, this equation of masculinity with waging war and femininity with disarmament is one that many conservatives share, but with a reversal of the values placed on these "masculine" and "feminine" poles of behavior. It is important to describe how women's experiences, rather than essential nature, give rise to the pacifist and environmental values women express, as some feminists are beginning to do (Ruddick 1980; Gilligan 1982).

Racism and feminist identity. The emphasis on essential differences between women and men can be seen as part of a tendency in radical feminism to draw sharp boundaries between oppressors (men) and innocent victims of oppression (women). This view fails to consider how women themselves oppress other women and men, particularly in terms of class and race. Instead, victimization and powerlessness are seen as the common experience of all women, just as violence and power are seen as the common attributes of all men. Women are urged to *sisterhood,* "generally understood as a nurturant, supportive feeling of attachment and loyalty to other women which grows out of a shared experience of oppression" (Dill; 1983, 132). Images of victimization and of sisterhood as an egalitarian community of women have been challenged by black and other minority women in the movement (Hooks 1981; Dill 1983). Black women note the benefits white women obtain by supporting or accepting racist practices, and remember the history of white women sacrificing the needs of black women when their own security is threatened (Davis 1981; Palmer 1983; Murray 1984).

Because of their concern with identity and self-definition, this challenge has been taken very seriously by white radical feminists. They are actively struggling to eliminate the racism in their own consciousness, to develop genuinely egalitarian relationships with black women, and to make the struggle against racism a priority for the movement as a whole. However, this struggle is defined primarily in terms of individual transformation, rather than as conventionally political. Since few radical feminists are involved in mainstream politics, they can do relatively little about issues such as housing and nutrition that black women see as vital. Moreover, the demand that black women define themselves as sisters of white feminists continues to be experienced as coercive and insensitive by women who are aware of the power differentials this terminology disguises (Dill 1983).

The present struggle over recognizing and eliminating racism in the movement is an important one, both because racism anywhere is a serious issue, and because it cannot be resolved without radical feminism itself undergoing a profound transformation. Self-purification by breaking connections to patriarchal institutions can be liberating but it can also lead to a sense of self-righteousness. Victimization can become an excuse for inaction and an evasion of responsibility for one's own contributions to oppressive social relationships. Separatism creates the groundwork for building intense and supportive communities, but women who refuse to cut their ties to men can feel excluded from the community, as many black (and white) women have experienced. The isolation of separatist communities makes ideological purity and mutual interdependence easier to maintain, but at the cost of limiting access to immediate sources of power. The boundaries between women and men come to be seen in increasingly polarized and absolute terms; the hope of ever changing men is replaced by despair. Black women, who have still not despaired of changing white women despite centuries of racism, find this attitude of hopelessness unrealistic and counterproductive (Hooks 1981).

Radical feminists' confrontation with racism as a reality in the movement, as well as in society at large, could provoke change, but adding racism (and classism, anti-Semitism, and heterosexism) to a laundry list of "isms" the movement opposes is not the same thing as developing a strategy for actively opposing them. It is still too early to tell whether radical feminists will be successful in reconstructing their images of self, sisterhood, and society in response to these critical viewpoints, or in developing a strategy for change sensitive to the diversity of women's experiences.

Conclusions

Each of the four different directions taken by contemporary feminism has achieved some praiseworthy success, and each points to further struggle for still unmet goals. Sometimes feminists engaged in activities of only one sort see this as "the" movement and interpret their strategy as "the" direction the movement is taking. We consider this an unfortunate tendency because it encourages narrow and defensive definitions of what a good feminist should be and want. Instead, we see the New Feminist Movement as spreading in many directions simultaneously, engaging activists with quite different ideas of what is ultimately desirable, a not uncommon aspect of social movements. As Gerlach and Hine (1970) argue, there is an important difference between the general goals of a movement, where broad agreement obtains, and specific objectives, where disagreement is the rule. While some social movements have been torn apart trying to achieve consensus on objectives and a single ideal strategy, the New Feminist Movement, for the moment, appears to be proceeding in diverse but complementary directions.

Despite defeats in some areas, such as the failure of the ERA, the movement is neither dead nor dying. Yet also, despite the many successes, its major goals remain to be achieved. New challenges and controversies emerge faster than the old issues can be resolved, so the feminist agenda continues to grow. What then is the next step? No one strategy will achieve the heterogeneous and often contradictory objectives of all feminists, nor will any one strategy satisfy the contradictory values of all participants in the movement. Neither will a single approach be ideal from the standpoint of gaining support from various constituencies and potentially co-optable publics. It is probably fortunate, therefore, that the New Feminist Movement will continue to be as diverse as the many women who have made it their own.

The future of the New Feminist Movement is inclusive and open-ended. Some of these directions are illustrated above. Top left, a black woman expresses a new political awareness that is reshaping voting patterns. Top right, organizing among women workers may revitalize the union movement, increase pay equity, and transform gender relations in the workplace. Bottom right, as minority women join the struggle for reproductive freedom, concern over sterilization abuse increasingly accompanies the demand for the right to choose abortion. Bottom left, Barbara Love, Ti-Grace Atkinson, and Kate Millett confer at the recent Forum on the Future conference. Radical feminists are in the process of redefining women's traditional values and nature as essential to world peace and a nonhierarchical society. *Photographs courtesy of Joan E. Biren.*

CHAPTER EIGHT

Visions and Revisions

In the preceding chapters, we have traced the development of the New Feminist Movement from its roots in postwar demographic trends, through its flowering in the 1970s, to its current maturity as a broad-based social movement. In this chapter, we briefly consider the nature of this feminist transformation and its implications for future generations of women. We begin with a broad overview of where we have been, look at where we are now, and finally venture some thoughts about the future.

Twenty Years of Feminism

Increases in the education and labor-force participation of women combined with continuing discrimination and changing family relationships in the period between 1945 and 1963 set the stage for the rebirth of feminist activity in the United States. Women's own political experience, the example of black civil rights activists, and liberating cultural currents provided material resources and ways of viewing the situation that encouraged mobilization. By the mid-1960s all the essential elements of a social movement were in place: widespread grievances, the rudiments of an organizational structure, and an ideological framework with strong historical roots. Three major traditions of thought and action—moral reformism, liberalism, and socialism—fed into the emerging feminist critique centered on issues of sex stereotyping, self-determination in sexuality and reproduction, and equal rights.

But troubles and ideas alone do not create social movements. The emergence of the New Feminist Movement hinged upon other events of the 1960s. President Kennedy's Commission on the Status of Women led to the construction of a network of activist women that in turn gave birth to NOW and other bureaucratic organizations. The black civil rights movement and the New Left brought younger women to feminist consciousness, mobilizing students and housewives, through the technique of consciousness-raising, into egalitarian organizations at the grass-roots level.

The rapid growth of awareness and support for the movement in the 1970s strained its fragile organizational structure. Changes in public awareness and opinion were dramatic, even for people with no direct contact with the movement. Among the problems faced by the emergent movement were those of organizing supporters for effective action, reaching out to minority and working-class women, and incorporating their concerns in the movement's ideological framework.

By the mid-1970s, the bureaucratic and collectivist strands were woven together into a tapestry of feminist organizational life. Links were forged between grass-roots groups and national organizations, giving the movement a unique vitality and scope. National organizations began to develop mass-memberships, although internal conflicts threatened the growing solidarity of the movement. Debates over lesbianism, pornography, abortion, political endorsements, racism, and anti-Semitism created serious strains, yet dealing with these issues probably strengthened rather than weakened the movement by forcing feminists to set priorities and to recognize the value of diversity.

In the late 1970s and early 1980s, despite the continuing proliferation of groups with special concerns, a consolidating trend emerged around the struggles for an Equal Rights Amendment and to preserve reproductive rights. In the process, a significant part of the organized movement was transformed into a political interest group, operating at state and national levels. These efforts both increased the dangers of co-optation and incited a powerful backlash movement, locking pro- and antifeminist groups in battle on a number of fronts.

Despite the symbolic unifying importance of the ERA and reproductive rights, many feminist accomplishments and aims reflect a more diverse set of priorities. Career, liberal, radical, and socialist feminists have worked separately, as well as together, on issues particularly important to them. Some of these goals and priorities (such as attaining equal pay for jobs of comparable worth, equity in education, and safety from sexual assault) are widely shared, but no single, unique feminist agenda has yet emerged, nor does it seem likely to do so. Each of the directions also poses important questions and problems for the movement now and in the future.

In this chapter, we bring the four distinct types of contemporary feminism back together to provide an overview of the diverse and dynamic reality that is the New Feminist Movement today, and explore some of the implications of this diversity for the future growth of the movement. And, finally, we assess the extent to which the changes of the last twenty years are likely to prove enduring.

The Depth of the Feminist Transformation

How fundamental are the changes that feminists seek? This is an important question both for students of social movements and for those who support or oppose certain feminist aims. As we look at the diversity of groups and goals clustered under the heading of the New Feminist Movement, what we find defies easy categorization as a reform or revolutionary movement. To some extent, this lack of fit to prevailing models reflects the special character of contemporary feminism. Few, if any, other social movements even attempt to speak on as many different levels or to as wide a range of concerns. Still, the movement is in many ways similar to other social movements, and so the inability to apply these common categories suggests a flaw in the categories themselves.

Reform or revolution? The sociological distinction between reform and revolutionary movements is based on the extent to which existing arrangements are challenged, despite debate about what constitutes the core challenge. Some theorists focus on the challenge to existing ideas of how society ought to be organized (e.g., Smelser 1963). In this view, movements that seek to change rules about how things should be done are called reform movements, while those that challenge values about what things should be done at all are called revolutionary. Other theorists focus on the challenge posed to the persons and institutions holding power in a society (Gamson 1975; Tilly 1978). Movements that change the balance of power among those already integrated in the system are called reform movements, while movements that attempt to dislodge the existing power elites in favor of new contenders are seen as revolutionary. Neither of these distinctions should be confused with the popular notion that movements that use violent tactics are revolutionary and those that are nonviolent are reformist.

Where, then, should we classify the New Feminist Movement? Those who are concerned with creating a new form of community seek fundamental value changes. Both socialist and radical feminists engage in deep analysis of the basic structures that support patriarchal values, believing that effective strategies for change need to be grounded in a proper understanding of the dynamics of the existing system. Career and liberal feminists do not address such values directly, but rather focus on the disjunction between values of equality, self-development, individual achievement, and freedom from restraint, on the one hand, and the actual norms of male preference, discriminatory treatment, and restriction of women's development, self-expression, and activity, on the other. Does this mean that there are two revolutionary and two reform strands?

If we consider the challenge posed to existing institutions and controlling elites, the revolutionary step is the struggle to redirect social institutions to meet the collective needs and interests of women. Career feminists and radical feminists, however, look first and foremost to a transformation of individual women, who, alone or with their sisters, will replace male authority with female. Women's potential, women's values, women's experience will thus find expression and thereby create the new society. It is the liberal and socialist feminists who want immediate institutional change. They consider it important for women as a group to contend for power and they see feminist activists as representatives of women collectively. Access to the system for individuals (career model) and building alternative institutions (radical model) are only helpful insofar as they bring women into confrontation with existing power structures. Because only the liberal and socialist strands see women collectively as contenders for control over existing social institutions, and therefore engage in political battles, should we see these two strands as revolutionary, and career and radical feminists as reformist?

Each of these two classifying schemes dividing revolutionary from reform movements is apparently incompatible with the other, because both lack any model of how norms and values relate to the control exercised by power elites. A more adequate account would recognize how those who control the institutions of society use this power not only to compel obedience and repress dissent but also to create definitions of reality that serve their interests. Such definitions tell people who they "really" are and what they can expect in life (expectations that can be kept low), while major social problems are defined as natural and inevitable rather than unfair and intolerable.

Recognizing that there are two levels of social control—one over the realm of ideas (ideological hegemony) and the other over physical activity (coercive force)—suggests that fundamental challenges exist on *both* levels. The career and radical strands of feminism provide a new set of higher expectations to women, so that treatment that was once taken for granted is now perceived as unjust. The liberal and socialist strands do not contradict, but rather complement, this approach. The higher expectations of women are taken as given, and action is directed toward effective ways of realizing a social order that offers justice and freedom to women. From this perspective, then, no single strand of feminism can be seen as revolutionary in its implications, for no one strand alone both redefines and restructures the world in which women now live. Instead, the complementary goals of the various strands combine to pose a challenge to the social order that is potentially revolutionary.

Extremists and moderates. Feminists who feel that a complete, revolutionary transformation of society is necessary take offense at the term "reformist," but "revolutionary" carries equally negative connotations for feminists who seek more discrete and limited goals. Both, however, contribute to each other's goals in the process of deliberate social change. "Revolutionary" activists see connections among different issues and emphasize the system-wide nature of social problems. Theirs is a *pro-active* view of social change, centering on a vision of a society dramatically different from the present. In contrast, a *reactive* view of social change assesses the costs and benefits of any particular institution or policy with "all other things being equal," that is, essentially unchanged. One might say that some take the offensive and some the defensive positions. For example, pay for housework and unrestricted abortion are both reactive demands, for they assume a society in which childbearing and child rearing continue to be very costly for women. Since a total transformation of society cannot take place overnight, any given change needs to be evaluated from both the pro-active and the reactive standpoints: how well does it serve to advance the movement's ultimate goals, and what does it do to help and protect those currently disadvantaged? The revolutionary's commitment to ultimate goals and the reformer's sensitivity to present realities can help to keep the pro-active and the reactive standards of evaluation in balance.

In addition, extremists serve an important function in any social movement by legitimizing the strivings and demands of the moderates (Killian 1972). This is true because the "respectable" moderates are not inherently respectable, but only in contrast with those in the movement who persist in "going too far." Without the pressure generated by "extremists," they would appear to be "far out" and their demands would become harder to attain, producing an overall shift to the right, even if "mainstream" feminists did not move at all rightward. Thus, even those feminists who are committed to a modest agenda have a stake in the continuing activity and visibility of feminists with a much more sweeping plan of action. Extremist groups themselves, however, have little credibility or legitimacy. Without the sympathy and support of more moderate, respectable groups, those who advocate drastic changes can be portrayed as insane and dangerous, and safely re-pressed. In this sense, extremists depend on moderates for protection. Be-cause of these relationships of reciprocal support, the permanence of the movement as a whole and the preservation of its gains depend on the soli-darity between extreme and moderate groups.

The Breadth of the Feminist Transformation

Although we have discussed each of the four directions currently taken by feminists as if each were almost a separate movement, they jointly account for the growth and influence of feminism in society at large, and each has made essential contributions to the movement as a whole.

Consciousness-raising. Pioneered among feminists of the collec-tivist strand of the early 1970s, consciousness-raising remains an important element of feminist thinking, even though the small group discussion format has become less significant. Radical feminists, in particular, continue to stress transforming individual values and ways of seeing. A "conversion ex-perience," along with allegiance to a community of like-minded others, have typically been associated with religious rather than political movements (Wil-son 1973). But religion and politics are not so easily separated. Within its political framework, radical feminism increasingly incorporates religious ele-ments (Spretnak 1982). The radical feminist vision of an egalitarian society based on female values often emphasizes a mother figure as emblem and source of power, sometimes representing the earth, sometimes a matriar-chial deity. There are rituals for expressing communion with nature and/or the Goddess, invoking identification with neolithic Goddess cults and vari-eties of real and imagined forms of historical witchcraft (Adler 1979).

Although some liberal and socialist feminists are highly critical of such spir-itual concerns, the relationship between religion and politics among radical feminists should alert us to the important role that religion plays in creating a sense of community and supporting an alternate identity. As the present social order does not validate women's sense of worth or power, such confir-mation is sought in prehistory and theology. Religion thus appears as a form of social criticism, a model of dignity and justice that can, to some extent, be realized here and now.

Consciousness-raising as a technique has a great deal more in common with religious conversion than it does with individual psychotherapy, to which it has often and inaccurately been compared. Unlike therapy, which attempts to increase individual happiness through adjustment to the social order, both consciousness-raising and religious conversion depict individual pain as the inevitable cost of bringing a new world into existence and both create personal commitments that will make accommodation to the status quo virtually impossible. Consciousness-raising and conversion provide frameworks for criticizing existing reality and for reinterpreting both one's own past and all history. Both generate confidence in the ultimate truth of their alternative reality, creating an internally consistent view of the world that can be transmitted across generations.

This type of alternative vision, whether or not expressed in religious terms, is essential in combatting the ideological hegemony of male supremacy. Consciousness-raising as a specific political practice is directed toward challenging these dominant ideas. New words are created to describe what had previously been hidden from consciousness, unnamed and invisible. New words, such as sexism, male chauvinism, and homophobia, imply new ways of thinking; in turn, changes in how one looks at reality make new words essential. The term "wife-battering" rather than "domestic violence," for example, puts women's experience in the center.

Most feminists have gone through a consciousness-raising experience of some sort, thereby making a more or less thorough and dramatic break with the invisible ideology of male supremacy. Because feminists declare the validity of relationships different from those assumed to be "natural" in patriarchy, they are often perceived as deviant—perhaps more than a little odd, and possibly dangerous. Such deviance is necessary to challenge ideological hegemony, just as political struggle is necessary to challenge institutional control.

Radical feminism forces us to become aware of both these dimensions of social change. By stressing the power and importance of consciousness (who one thinks oneself to be and how one relates to other people), radical feminists have made an important and underestimated contribution to the New Feminist Movement. Imagining a new world and committing oneself to someday living in it may be the first crucial steps in bringing that imagined world into being.

Visible gains on the occupational front. Career feminists have made occupational advances that, though limited, contribute to the construction of a secure base for future feminist actions. These advantages are often falsely taken as evidence that the movement has accomplished its goals and is no longer necessary. Still, the legacy of nineteenth-century feminism was access to higher education and, in more limited numbers, to certain professions, as well as the right of women to keep their own earnings and their own children. Feminists of the early part of this century built upon these gains to win the vote and the right to hold political office. Feminists of the last two decades have also secured new rights and opportunities.

The demand for "equal pay for equal work" has reached a level of support where it has become self-evident, despite widespread inequality in jobs and standards of evaluation. Many gains in the professions now seem secure as well; for example, the appointment of a woman, however conservative, to the Supreme Court, effectively settles the question whether women should practice law, even though acceptance in the "legal fraternity" still may be halfhearted. Inroads into medicine, engineering, and political office, as well as women-owned businesses, provide additional resources for women as a group. Although collective efforts were essential in producing these gains, individual women, feminist or not, secure the benefits. These resources may or may not be used immediately to advance other women, but they enhance women's collective power base and hence the potential for long-term effective action. Mueller (1983) argues that the most successful outcomes for movements historically have been those that provided generalized resources for future mobilizations. For example, access to education provided a pool of educated women who could use their knowledge and skills to advance women's interests, and every later feminist mobilization has drawn heavily upon this pool.

One danger is that such accomplishments will soon appear so natural and normal that they will no longer be seen as the result of feminist action. It is easy to forget that, until quite recently, women were not appointed as judges, could not lead most religious congregations, were not permitted to fight fires, drive trucks, or serve in the diplomatic corps, and were denied essential financial support for college athletics, professional and graduate education, and campaigns for public office. Such systematic discrimination could never have been reversed simply by individual requests for special exceptions; the rules themselves had to be changed. While Sandra Day O'Connor and Sally Ride are certainly exceptional women, they are not nearly as exceptional as they appear. Many superbly qualified women of past generations were denied the opportunities that the movement has secured for women today (Tobin 1983).

Yet some feminists with a broader agenda claim that such accomplishments are not relevant to their real concerns. Insufficient as these changes are, they are the bedrock for future gains. As these once-radical changes become part of the taken-for-granted world, people assume that this is how things must always have been, and cease to see any particular social force as responsible. This is a problem that is not peculiar to feminism: most people find it hard to imagine a time when the police shot strikers, or when black people were refused service at lunch counters.

The failure-through-success when once-radical demands become assimilated into the mainstream may tempt social movement leaders to increasingly extreme positions, as their hopes for ultimate success seem as remote as ever (Miller 1983). Unlike co-optation by partial success, movement goals are not abandoned or moderated; instead, public attitudes shift to encompass them. In the end, the movement is identified, not with the changes that have occurred, but with the tasks left undone. Thus the most secure accomplishments of the last twenty years are no longer seen as particularly feminist, while the remaining goals are still vulnerable to attack.

Career feminists in particular have transformed portions of taken-for-granted reality in ways that have empowered individual women, created new aspirations for the coming generation, and provided footholds for institutional change. While these changes are still too limited, they are nonetheless valuable contributions to the movement as a whole.

Movement organizations. The variety of organizations arising as a coherent political force, phoenixlike, from the ashes of the suffrage movement, are a significant contribution of feminist efforts and an important force for continued change. Liberal feminists in particular, as active contenders for political power, have constructed mass-based and elite organizations that can effectively lobby, mobilize women voters, and sponsor legislation to advance women's interests. More important than any specific policy outcome is the fact that these organizations have come to represent women collectively, with a legitimate role in shaping public policy. Enforcement is also crucial, and no piece of legislation, not even the ERA, is a magic wand that can itself convey equality. While some antidiscrimination legislation is on the books, these gains are hollow without continued pressure for their enforcement from women as an organized interest group.

The campaign for the ERA solidified these groups and produced a new generation of politically experienced and committed women prepared to use their organizational strength on a wide range of issues. Some have taken an "insider" stance, and work on government policy on a routine basis; others adopt an "outsider" position, taking highly visible stands and struggling for influence among many other institutionalized interest groups. Both rely on the continued activity of feminist organizations for their credibility as spokespersons for women.

Some analysts see the organizational achievements of social movements as especially significant. Tarrow (1982), for example, suggests that "reforms producing institutionalized participation are both more durable and more productive of further reforms than substantive rights." Feminist organizations have achieved access to the time, money, and votes of individual feminists, the attention of the mass media, and the ear of policymakers at all levels of government. These resources can be used either to accomplish a particular goal or to increase the movement's generalized control over resources that can in turn be put to use in future struggles. Such institutionalized participation means that feminist organizations can exercise some leverage in pushing for new gains and protecting old ones. But such pressure group tactics depend on sustaining a high level of organizational commitment and stirring supporters to action when the situation demands.

The importance of such continuing feminist organizations can be seen in the collapse of feminism in the 1920s and 1930s. Individual feminists did not reduce their commitment to women, nor did they cease to be active in a variety of roles in politics and government. But feminist organizations became fragmented and wasted their energies fighting one another. Feminism as a collective political position was thus undermined, some substantive gains were lost, and the struggles and accomplishments of the feminist movement were erased from collective memory. Individual feminists remained in some influential positions but were largely isolated until the 1960s when, as we have seen, they became an important resource for the remobilization of a feminist movement.

Thus, the institutionalized political participation that feminists, especially liberal feminists, have achieved in the past two decades can be seen as both fragile and durable. Its fragility arises from its dependence on the continued mobilization of feminist resources in ongoing organizations. Should the organizations fragment or falter, women's ability to contend for power in this society will be seriously impaired, regardless of individual commitment to feminist goals. At the same time, the institutionalized participation of feminists in the political process—as judges, elected officials, lobbyists, or simply voters—is a durable resource that provides protection for gains already won, sustains commitments to enforcement, and facilitates continued efforts for change.

A shift from equal rights to real equality. Emphasis on achieving equality rather than merely gender neutrality as the central goal of the New Feminist Movement is now apparent. Feminist literature of the 1960s typically ignored issues of class and race; today the relationships among different types of inequality are recognized, and the movement is committed to changing more than the status of women. To some extent this shift in focus reflects a change in economic realities. While the 1960s were relatively prosperous, and women's anger could focus on the extent to which they were excluded from this prosperity, the hard times of the late 1970s and early 1980s have focused attention on the impoverishment of women. The social and economic arrangements that create and maintain a poverty population must themselves be challenged. A study conducted in the mid-1970s found that feminist leaders were, with black leaders, among the most radical in their support for greater equality of income (Verba, Orren, and Ferree 1985).

Socialist feminists have contributed significantly to this shift in focus, in part by developing persuasive political arguments based on comprehensive analyses of social and economic institutions. The ideology of unrestrained competition and an uncontrolled marketplace is neither an accurate description of the American economic system, nor a desirable goal. Women historically not only find themselves on the bottom of the ladders of power and wealth, but are also charged with responsibility for others—children, the ill, the handicapped, and the elderly—who are in no position to compete. Feminists are increasingly seeing their own interests and the interests of these other groups as complementary rather than competing. The idea of community as requiring social responsibility for all its members has increasingly replaced the demand for the right to compete as the central focus of feminist thinking.

Second, this shift in focus can be partially attributed to the efforts and successes of the movement in incorporating the concerns of poor, working-class, black, and other minority women. The middle-class definition of feminism as equality of rights and opportunities for individual achievement has always rung hollow for women who know the costs of race and class. Their definition of feminism begins from the demand that mothers should not have to put their children to bed hungry. As white, middle-class feminists have sought out and listened to this point of view, they have increasingly come to recognize its validity. Opportunities created in the movement to work across the lines of class and race continue to encourage awareness about all forms of oppression.

Third, parallels drawn between sexism and racism in early years of the movement continue to bear fruit today, as feminist and black leaders work with one another and adopt a broadened perspective on social and economic issues. Seeing how all women and black men bear the brunt of economic "dislocations" has made it more difficult for white feminists to pursue their own interests without regard for those of black people. Whether defending affirmative action from right-wing assault, or trying to prevent or restore cuts in social welfare programs, feminists have increasingly come to realize that their interests are inseparable from those of other disadvantaged groups. Consequently, coalitions between feminists and nonfeminists have become increasingly popular and feasible (Carden 1981).

For all these reasons, the movement today is wider and broader than it was in the 1960s. The movement's growth in the 1980s has been substantial, reflecting a maturity and depth of purpose that could only be hoped for in those early years.

Prospects for the Future

While it is impossible to predict specifically how the New Feminist Movement will develop through the year 2000, there are certain issues that will obviously have to be faced. Will changes brought about by feminism take root and grow, or will there be a period of reaction and retrenchment, in which women lose what once seemed securely won? This question reflects an increasing concern among feminists for the next generation: will those who are now only children ever understand what feminism is all about?

The feminism of the early part of this century provides a historical lesson about the development of social movements. Although feminism was expressed in a strong and well-organized social movement in 1920, its organizational forms withered in the following decades. Most young women growing up in the twenties and thirties were not exposed to feminism as a coherent perspective. Observers soon noted that the average age of feminists was relatively high, and rising. Feminism was seen as "old-fashioned" and feminists as "out of touch" with modern, "emancipated" women and the "realities" of expanded opportunity and egalitarian relationships.

Alice Rossi (1982), looking at this pattern, suggests that the permanence of feminist accomplishments is achieved through a two-step, two-generation process. The first generation, angered by the limits imposed on them as women, struggles to achieve certain crucial structural changes. The second generation lives in the new set of social relationships and explores the opportunities thus created, experiencing the freedom as well as the limits of this restructured world. The third generation takes the freedom for granted and experiences the limits most acutely, thus becoming again the first generation, struggling to remove these restraints. Rossi argues that it is not enough for changes to be made on a structural level, that they must be assimilated into women's everyday life before the demand for further changes can be known. Her argument is based both on the empirical historical record and on the theoretical premise that feminist demands arise from women's experience. Without that resonance in experience, feminist claims will fail to evoke a significant response.

Gloria Steinem argues, on the other hand, that the apparent conservatism of young women is merely a stage in the individual's life cycle. Unlike men, for whom youth is a period of radicalism, tempered by the increasing responsibilities and rewards of career and fatherhood, women may become radicalized by aging. Extrapolating from the male model is misleading, because it is women's experiences in getting married, employed, divorced, fired, and simply older that convey the difficulty of being female in this society, and turn women into feminists (Steinem 1983). But the real difficulties facing women now are not the same as they were even twenty years ago.

How successfully will feminism in the 1980s address the concerns felt by young women today? This is the core problem of generational change in social movements. If the movement were not successful in accomplishing any of its goals, then the issues would remain identical from generation to generation, and the need for the movement to change would be minimized. The demands could become ritualized, the organizations stagnant, and yet they would still be relevant. But when the movement achieves some substantial successes, the necessity for change becomes apparent to all.

There is no doubt that young women today face different choices and problems than young women did in 1960, partly because of the successes of the New Feminist Movement. Few young women expect to spend their lives as full-time housewives; few accept discrimination against women as justified and inevitable; few consider battering and sexual assault something women want or deserve. Most are aware that opportunities for women in politics and the professions have increased substantially over the past decade; most expect their husbands to share housework and child care. There are organized, active feminist groups at all levels, dealing with issues that were invisible two decades ago, defending gains that were then unimaginable, and offering opportunities for community with other women that did not then exist.

Measured against an ideal of equality or against the full feminist agenda, these changes seem trifling. But the sense of changeless repression, of constant pressure for women to become kitchen-bound domestic servants that animated young feminists in the late 1960s, is not reflected in the experience of younger women today, who blithely expect to "have it all." The blatant discrimination and contempt that women experienced in the job market, in professional schools, and in politics that angered the older feminists has been replaced by more subtle, though equally serious, obstacles. To experienced feminists it seems that young women today simply expect to encounter no problems, which is highly improbable. The new issues and concerns that have emerged within the movement have expanded the agenda of women already aware of their status as women and committed to change, but what of the younger women?

One possibility is that they are being socialized to take a feminist perspective as part of their natural view of the world. Their expectations are relatively high, so that their frustration at encountering the many remaining obstacles may lead them to support the movement as a matter of simple justice or self-interest. This model assumes that the ties across generations, between mother and daughter, teacher and student, are adequate to the task of transmitting a feminist perspective. When combined with young women's own experiences as they leave the relative egalitarianism of school and entry-level jobs, and lose the temporary power of youthful sexual desirability, committed feminists will gradually emerge. In this view, there is no reason to fear that the next generation will be nonfeminist to any significant degree.

Another possibility is that young women are a population isolated by historical circumstance from the main currents of contemporary feminism. Because they do not share the same experiences and have not participated in the gradual evolution of feminist thought, they find today's movement difficult to understand. In this view, feminists today have a specific responsibility to ensure that feminist history is not again obliterated. Thus feminism may grow, or fail to grow, among young women in proportion to the time and effort invested in reaching them, teaching them how these ideas have developed, and encouraging them to care about all women, not just themselves. At the same time, this model concedes that this generation may not find feminism personally relevant.

There is a third possibility. As generations change, we see a need to recognize that feminism is not simply a form of received wisdom. The agenda of any specific branch of the movement cannot be taught as a fixed and orthodox position without doing violence to a deeper premise and goal of feminism. Feminism demands that women speak for themselves, articulate their own needs and concerns, define their own identity. From this perspective, the challenge the movement faces is to allow young women today the room in which to shape their own feminism, and to encourage and support their search. If the New Feminist Movement rises to this challenge, its agenda will probably shift in terms of priorities, if not general direction. Thus, the younger generation will define the movement, rather than being merely recruits to older women's campaigns.

In sum, the New Feminist Movement has changed American society in significant ways, but once accomplished these changes no longer seem so significant. The movement's gains are rarely credited to it, and when they are, they are seen as the result of effective actions by "moderates." The role of the "extremists" in legitimating the rest of the movement is typically ignored. The new reality created by feminism on a structural level has become assimilated into women's lives, but at the same time the aspirations and expectations that women form through their experiences make structual limits and patriarchal control seem ever more confining and in need of change. And so feminism is, and will continue to be, reborn and redefined in every generation.

REFERENCES

Adams, C., and K. Winston. 1980. *Mothers at work: Public policies in the U.S., China, and Sweden.* New York: Longman.

Adler, M. 1979. *Drawing down the moon.* Boston: Beacon Press.

Ahrens, L. 1980. Battered women's refuges: Feminist co-operatives or social service institutions? *Radical America,* May–June, 41–47.

Altbach, E. H., ed. 1971. *From feminism to liberation.* Cambridge, Mass.: Schenkman.

American Council on Life Insurance. 1981. *MAP '81.* Washington, D.C.: ACLI.

Andors, P. 1982. Cuban women twenty years later. *Guardian: Independent Radical Newsweekly* 34, no. 36:21.

Arms, S. 1975. *Immaculate deception: A new look at women and childbirth in America.* Boston: Houghton Mifflin.

Association of American Colleges. 1980. On campus with women. *Project on the Status of Education of Women* 28 (Fall):4.

————. 1982. On campus with women. *Project on the Status of Education of Women* 12, no. 1:5, 9.

Auzaldua, G., and C. Moraga, eds. 1981. *This bridge called my back: Writings by radical women of color.* Watertown, Mass.: Persephone Press.

Banks, O. 1981. *Three faces of feminism.* New York: St. Martin's Press.

Barrett, N. 1979. Women in the job market. In *The subtle revolution,* ed. R. Smith. Washington, D.C.: Urban Institute.

Barry, K. 1979. *Female sexual slavery.* New York: Prentice-Hall.

Bart, P. 1970. Portnoy's mother's complaint. *Transaction* 8, no. 12:69–74.

Beckwith, B. 1984. He-man, she-woman: *Playboy* and *Cosmo* groove on genes. *Columbia Journalism Review,* January–February, 46–47.

Bennetts, L. 1980. How women took charge at the Democratic convention. *Ms.,* November, 58–66.

Benson, D. J., and G. Thomson. 1982. Sexual harassment on a university campus: The confluence of authority relations, sexual interest, and gender stratification.

Social Problems 29, no. 3:236–51.

Berch, B. 1982. *The endless day: The political economy of women and work.* New York: Harcourt, Brace, Jovanovich.

Berger, B. 1968. *Working-class suburb: A study of auto-workers in suburbia.* Berkeley: Univ. of California Press.

Berkin, C. R. 1979. Not separate, not equal. In *Women of America: A History,* ed. C. R. Berkin and M. B. Norton, 273–88. Boston: Houghton Mifflin.

Bers, T. H., and S. G. Mezey. 1981. Support for feminist goals among leaders of women's community groups. *Signs* 6:737–48.

Bessmer, S. 1982. Anti-obscenity: A comparison of the legal and feminist approaches. In *Women, power, and policy,* ed. E. Boneparth. Elmsford, N.Y.: Pergamon.

Blau, F. 1979. Women in the labor force: An overview. In *Women: A feminist perspective,* ed. J. Freeman, 265–89. Palo Alto, Calif.: Mayfield.

Blumberg, R. L. 1984. *Civil rights: The 1960s freedom struggle.* Boston: Twayne.

Boles, J. 1979. *The politics of the ERA: Conflict and the decision process.* New York: Longman.

Boston Women's Health Book Collective. 1976. *Our bodies, ourselves.* New York: Simon & Schuster.

Breines, W. 1979. A review essay. *Feminist Studies* 5:496–506.

———, M. Cerullo, and J. Stacey. 1978. Social biology, family studies, and the antifeminist backlash. *Feminist Studies* 4:43–67.

Bronfenbrenner, U. 1958. Socialization and social class through time and space. In *Readings in social psychology,* ed. E. E. Maccoby, T. M. Newcomb, and E. H. Harley, 400–425. New York: Holt.

Broverman, I., D. Broverman, F. Clarkson, P. Rosenkrantz, and S. Vogel. 1970. Sex role stereotypes and clinical judgment of mental health. *Journal of Consulting and Clinical Psychology* 34:1–7.

Brown, R. M. 1984. In defense of traditional values: The antifeminist movement. In *Women and the family: Two decades of change,* ed. B. B. Hess and M. B. Sussman. *Marriage and Family Review,* 7, no. 3/4 (Fall/Winter, 1984).

Brownmiller, S. 1975. *Against our will: Men, women, and rape.* New York: Simon & Schuster.

Bunch, C. 1980. What not to expect from the U.N.'s women's conference in Copenhagen. *Ms.,* July, 80–83.

Bunch–Weeks, C. 1970. A broom of one's own: Notes on the women's liberation program. In *The new woman: An anthology of women's liberation,* ed. J. Cooke, C. Bunch-Weeks, and R. Morgan, 185–210. Greenwich, Conn.: Fawcett.

Burkhauser, R., and K. Holden. 1980. *A challenge to Social Security: The changing roles of women and men in American society.* New York: Academic Press.

Burris, V. 1983. Who opposed the ERA? The social bases of antifeminism. *Social Science Quarterly* 64, no. 2:305–17.

Caballero, C., P. Giles, and P. Shaver. 1975. Sex role traditionalism and fear of success. *Sex Roles* 1, no. 4:319–26.

Cancian, F., and B. Ross. 1981. Mass media and the women's movement: 1900–1977. *Journal of Applied Behavioral Science* 17:9–26.

Carden, M. L. 1974. *The new feminist movement.* New York: Russell Sage.

———. 1978. The proliferation of a social movement: Ideology and individual incentives in the contemporary women's movement. In *Research in social movements: Conflict and change,* vol. 1, ed. L. Kriesberg, 179–96. Greenwich, Conn.: JAI Press.

———. 1981. The evolution of movement activity: Causes and effects. Paper presented at the annual meeting of the American Sociological Association.

Carr, I. C. 1984. Second feminist conference of Latin America and the Caribbean: Two reports. *Women's Studies International,* no. 3, April:26–29.

Carroll, J. W., B. Hargrove, and A. T. Lummis. 1983. *Women of the cloth: A new opportunity for the churches.* New York: Harper & Row.

Cassell, J. 1977. *A group called women: Sisterhood and symbolism in the feminist movement.* New York: McKay.

Chafe, W. 1972. *The American woman: Her changing social, economic and political roles, 1920–1970.* New York: Oxford Univ. Press.

———. 1977. *Women and equality: Changing patterns in American culture.* New York: Oxford Univ. Press.

Cherlin, A. 1982. The interrelationship of feminist values and demographic trends. Paper presented at the annual meeting of the Eastern Sociological Society.

———, and P. Walters. 1981. Trends in U.S. men's and women's sex role attitudes: 1972–78. *American Sociological Review* 46:453–60.

Chesler, P. 1972. *Women and madness.* New York: Avon.

Chodorow, N. 1975. *The reproduction of mothering: Psychoanalysis and the sociology of gender.* Berkeley: Univ. of California Press.

Clymer, A. 1984. Poll sees gain equalling loss if Democrats pick a woman. *New York Times,* 30 April.

Coleman, J. S. 1957. *Community conflict.* Glencoe, Ill.: Free Press.

Collins E. G., and T. B. Blodgett. 1981. Sexual harassment: Some see it, some won't. *Harvard Business Review* 2:76–95.

Combs, M. W., and S. Welch. 1982. Blacks, whites, and attitudes toward abortion. *Public Opinion Quarterly* 46:510–20.

Conover, P. J., and V. Gray. 1983. *Feminism and the New Right: Conflict over the American family.* New York: Praeger.

Conscience. 1983. Newsletter of Catholics for Free Choice. October–November. Washington, D.C.

Corcoran, M., and G. Duncan. 1983. Why do women earn less? *Institute for Social Research Newsletter.*

Costain, A. 1981. Representing women: The transition from social movement to interest group. *Western Political Quarterly* 34:100–113.

———. 1982. Femininity v. feminism: The battle of the 80s. *Second Century Rad-*

cliffe News, January, 9.

Cox, N. 1976. *Counter-planning from the kitchen: Wages for housework.* New York: New York Wages for Housework Committee.

Crabtree, J. 1980. The displaced homemaker: Middle-aged, alone, broke. *Aging,* January–February, 17–20.

Dalla Costa, M. 1972. Women and the subversion of the community. *Radical America* 6, no. 1:67–102.

Daly, M. 1978. *Gyn/ecology: The metaethics of radical feminism.* Boston: Beacon Press.

Davis, A. 1981. *Women, race, and class.* New York: Random House.

Davis, J., and D. G. Taylor. 1977. Short-term trends in American society: The NORC General Social Survey, 1972–77. Paper presented at the annual meeting of the American Sociological Association.

Deaux, K., and J. Ullman. 1983. *Women of steel.* New York: Praeger.

De Beauvoir, S. 1953. *The second sex.* New York: Knopf.

Degler, C. 1980. *At odds: Women and the family in America from the Revolution to the present.* New York: Oxford Univ. Press.

Deitch, C. 1982. The New Right, feminism, and abortion: Patterns of public opinion: 1972–80. Paper presented at the annual meeting of the American Sociological Association.

Densmore, D. 1968. *On celibacy.* Boston: No More Fun and Games. Mimeo.

Diamond, I. 1980. Pornography and repression: A reconsideration. *Signs* 5, no. 4:686–701.

Dinnerstein, D. 1976. *The mermaid and the minotaur.* New York: Harper & Row.

Dill, B. T. 1983. Race, class and gender: Prospects for an all-inclusive sisterhood. *Feminist Studies* 9, no. 1:131–50.

Donnerstein, E. 1980. Aggressive erotica and violence against women. *Journal of Personality and Social Psychology* 39:269–77.

Dunbar, R. 1970. Female liberation as the basis of social revolution. In *Sisterhood is powerful,* ed. R. Morgan. New York: Random House.

Dworkin, A. 1978. Safety, shelter, rules, and love: The promise of the ultra-right. *Ms.,* June, 62ff.

Easton, B. 1979. Feminism and the contemporary family. In *A heritage of her own: Toward a new social history of American women,* ed. N. F. Cott and E. H. Pleck. New York: Simon & Schuster.

Ehrenreich, B., and D. English. 1978. *For her own good: 150 years of experts' advice to women.* New York: Doubleday.

Eisenstein, Z. 1979. *Capitalist patriarchy and the case for socialist feminism.* New York: Monthly Review Press.

Elshtain, J. B. 1981. Mr. Right is dead. *Nation,* 14 November, 496–97.

———. 1982. Feminism, family and community. *Dissent,* Fall, 442–49.

Erie, S. P., M. Rein, and B. Wiget. 1983. Women and the Reagan revolution. In

Families, Politics and Public Policy, ed. I. Diamond. New York: Longman.

Evans, S. 1979. *Personal politics: The roots of women's liberation in the civil rights movement and the New Left.* New York: Vintage.

Ferree, M. M. 1974. A woman for president? Changing responses, 1958–1972. *Public Opinion Quarterly* 38:390–99.

———. 1976. The emerging constituency: Feminism, employment and the working class. Ph. D. diss., Harvard University.

———. 1980. Working class feminism: A consideration of the consequences of employment. *Sociological Quarterly* 21:173–84.

———. 1983a. The women's movement in the working class. *Sex Roles* 9:493–505.

———. 1983b. Housework: Reconsidering the costs and benefits. In *Women, families and public policy,* ed. I. Diamond. New York: Longman.

———, and F. D. Miller. 1984. Mobilization and meaning: Some social psychological contributions to the resource mobilization perspective. *Sociological Inquiry,* in press.

Firestone, S. 1970. *The dialectic of sex.* New York: Morrow.

Flacks, R. 1971. *Youth and social change.* Chicago: Markham.

Flexner, E. 1959. *Century of struggle: The women's rights movement in the United States.* Cambridge: Harvard Univ. Press.

Forman, M. 1983. Social Security is a woman's issue. *Social Policy* 14, no. 7:35–38.

Fox-Genovese, E. 1980. The personal is not political enough. *Marxist Perspectives,* Winter, 94–113.

Freedman, E. 1979. Separatism as strategy: Female institution-building and American feminism. *Feminist Studies* 5:512–29.

Freeman, J. 1973. The origins of the women's liberation movement. *American Journal of Sociology* 78:792–811.

———. 1975. *The politics of women's liberation.* New York: David McKay.

———. [Joreen] 1976a. Trashing: The dark side of feminism. *Ms.,* April, 49ff.

———. 1976b. Something did happen at the Democratic national convention. *Ms.,* October, 74ff.

Friedan, B. 1963. *The feminine mystique.* New York: Dell.

———. 1981. *The second stage.* New York: Summit.

Fritz, L. 1979. *Dreamers and dealers: An intimate appraisal of the women's movement.* Boston: Beacon.

Fruchter, R., N. Fatt, P. Booth, and D. Seidel. 1977. The women's health movement: Where are we now? In *Seizing our bodies,* ed. C. Dreifus, 271–87. New York: Random House.

Gabin, N. 1982. They have placed a penalty on womankind: The protest actions of women auto workers in Detroit area UAW locals, 1945–47. *Feminist Studies* 8:372–98.

Gamson, W. 1968. *Power and discontent.* Homewood, Ill.: Dorsey.

———. 1975. *The strategy of social protest.* Homewood, Ill.: Dorsey.

Gearhart, S. 1979. *The wanderground.* Watertown, Mass: Persephone Press.

Gelb, J., and M. Palley. 1982. *Women and public policies.* Princeton: Princeton Univ. Press.

Gerlach, L., and V. Hine. 1970. *People, power and change.* Indianapolis: Bobbs-Merrill.

Giele, J. Z. n.d. *The first feminist movement.* Boston: Twayne. In press.

Gilder, G. 1973. *Sexual suicide.* New York: Time.

———. 1980. *Wealth and poverty.* New York: Basic Books.

Gilligan, C. 1982. *In a different voice.* Cambridge: Harvard Univ. Press.

Gittell, M., and N. Naples. 1982. Activist women: Conflicting ideologies. *Social Policy,* Summer, 25–27.

Glazer, N. 1982. The invisible intersection: Involuntary unpaid labor outside the home and women's work. Paper presented at the annual meeting of the Eastern Sociological Society.

Goldberg, R. 1983. *Organizing women workers: Dissatisfaction, consciousness, and action.* New York: Praeger.

Gordon, L. 1977. *Woman's body, woman's right.* New York: Penguin.

Gordon, N. 1979. Institutional responses: The Social Security system. In *The subtle revolution,* ed. R. Smith, 223–56. Washington, D.C.: Urban Institute.

Gornick, V., and B. Moran, eds. 1971. *Women in sexist society.* New York: Basic Books.

Graham, P. A. 1978. Expansion and exclusion: A history of women in American higher education. *Signs* 3:759–73.

Granovetter, M. 1973. The strength of weak ties. *American Journal of Sociology* 78:1360–80.

Greer, G. 1970. *The female eunuch.* New York: McGraw-Hill.

Grier, W., and P. M. Cobbs. 1968. *Black rage.* New York: Basic Books.

Griffin, S. 1971. Rape: The all-American crime. *Ramparts* 10:26–35.

———. 1979. *Woman and nature: The roaring inside her.* New York: Harper & Row.

Grimstad, K., and S. Rennie, eds. 1975. *The new woman's survival sourcebook.* New York: Knopf.

Gross, A., R. Smith, and B. Wallston. 1983. The men's movement: Personal vs. political. In *Social movements of the sixties and seventies,* ed. J. Freeman, 71–81. New York: Longman.

Gurin, P. 1982. Group consciousness. *ISR Newsletter* (Institute for Social Research, University of Michigan), Spring–Summer, 4–5.

Gutek, B., and B. Morash. 1982. Sex-ratios, sex role spillover and sexual harassment of women at work. *Journal of Social Issues* 38, no. 4:55–74.

Hacker, H. 1951. Women as a minority group. *Social Forces* 30 (October):60–69.

Haddad, R. 1979. The men's liberation movement: A perspective. Columbia, Md.: Free Men.

Haignere, L. 1981. Admission of women to medical schools: A study of organizational response to social movement and public policy pressures. Ph. D. diss., University of Connecticut, Storrs.

Harding, S. 1981. Family reform movements: Recent feminism and its opposition. *Feminist Studies* 7:57–75.

Hayden, C., and M. King. 1966. A kind of memo. *Liberation* 11:35–36.

Hess, B. 1983a. New faces of poverty. *American Demographics,* May, 26–31.

———. 1983b. Protecting the American family: Public policy and the New Right. In *Families and change: Social needs and public policy,* ed. R. G. Genovese. South Hadley, Mass.: J. F. Bergin.

Hewitt, E., and S. Hiatt. 1973. *Women priests: Yes or no.* New York: Seabury.

Heywoode, T. 1977. Working class feminism. Paper presented at the annual meeting of the Society for the Study of Social Problems.

Hole, J., and E. Levine. 1971. *Rebirth of feminism.* New York: Quadrangle.

Holm, J. 1982. *Women in the military: An unfinished revolution.* Ignacio, Calif.: Presidio Press.

Hooks, B. 1981. *Ain't I a woman: Black women and feminism.* Boston: South End Press.

Horner, M. 1969. Why bright women fail. *Psychology Today* 36, no. 6:36ff.

Howe, F., and C. Ahlum. 1973. Women's studies and social change. In *Academic women on the move,* ed. A. Rossi and A. Calderwood. New York: Russell Sage.

Huber, J. 1976. Toward a sociotechnological theory of the women's movement. *Social Problems* 23:371–88.

Hull, G., P. Scott, and B. Smith. 1982. *All the women are white, all the blacks are men, but some of us are brave: Black women's studies.* Old Westbury, N.Y.: Feminist Press.

Inglehardt, R. 1977. *The silent revolution: Changing values and political styles among Western publics.* Princeton: Princeton Univ. Press.

Jaffe, F., B. Lindheim, and P. R. Lee. 1981. *Abortion politics: Private morality and public policy.* New York: McGraw-Hill.

Jensen, I., and B. Gutek. 1982. Attributions and assignment of responsibility for sexual harassment. *Journal of Social Issues* 38, no. 4:121–36.

Johnson, J. 1981. Program enterprise and official co-optation in the battered women's shelter movement. *American Behavioral Scientist* 24:827–42.

Johnson, L. 1982. Weaving a web of life: Women's Pentagon Action, 1981. *Win* 18, no. 2:16–20.

Johnson, M. 1980. Women and elective office. *Society* 17, no. 4:63–69.

Joseph, G., and J. Lewis. 1981. *Common differences: Conflicts in black and white feminist perspectives.* Garden City, N.Y.: Doubleday.

Kanter, R. M. 1977. *Men and women of the corporation.* New York: Basic Books.

Kessler-Harris, A. 1976. Women, work and the social order. In *Liberating women's history,* ed. B. A. Carroll. Urbana: Univ. of Illinois Press.

Killian, L. 1972. The significance of extremism in the black revolution. *Social Problems* 20:41–49.

Klotzberger, N. 1973. Political action by academic women. In *Academic women on the move*, ed. A. Rossi and A. Calderwood. New York: Russell Sage.

Kluegel, J., and E. Smith. 1982. Whites' beliefs about blacks' opportunities. *American Sociological Review* 47, no. 4:518–31.

Koedt, A. 1970. The myth of the vaginal orgasm. In *Notes from the second year*, ed. S. Firestone and A. Koedt. New York: New York Radical Feminists.

Komarovsky, M. 1962. *Blue collar marriage*. New York: Random House.

Koziara, K. S., and P. J. Insley. 1982. Organizations of working women can pave the way for unions. *Monthly Labor Review*, June, 53–55.

Kramer, J. 1970. The founding cadre. *New Yorker*, 28 November, 52–140.

Langer, E. 1973. Notes for the next time: A memoir of the 1960s. *Working Papers*, Fall, 48–83.

———. 1976. Why big business is trying to defeat the ERA: The economic implications of inequality. *Ms.*, May, 64ff.

Lasch, C. 1977. *Haven in a heartless world: The family besieged*. New York: Basic Books.

Laws, J. L. 1975. The psychology of tokenism: An analysis. *Sex Roles* 1, no. 1:51–67.

Lederer, L. 1980. *Take back the night*. New York: Wm. Morrow.

LeGrande, L. 1978. Women in labor organizations: Their ranks are increasing. *Monthly Labor Review*, August, 8–14.

Leon, C. B. 1982. Occupational winners and losers, 1972–80. *Monthly Labor Review*, June, 18–28.

Lewis, D. 1977. A response to inequality? Black women, racism and sexism. *Signs* 3:339–61.

Lindsey, K. 1980. Women's commissions in exile. *Ms.*, February, 23–25.

Livingston, J. 1982. Responses to sexual harassment on the job. *Journal of Social Issues* 38, no. 4:5–22.

Lopate, C. 1974. Pay for housework? *Social Policy* 5 (September–October):27–31.

Lord, L. 1982. Pornography and militarism. *Women Against Violence in Pornography and Media Newspage* 6, no. 10:1–3.

Lowell, L. 1980. Abortion: A question of survival. *Win*, 1 August, 15–28.

Lundberg, F., and M. F. Farnham. 1947. *Modern woman: The lost sex*. New York: Universal Library.

Luttrell, W. 1984. Beyond the politics of victimization. *Socialist Review* 14, no. 1:42–47.

McAllister, P. 1982. *Reweaving the web of life: Feminism and nonviolence*. Philadelphia: New Society Publishers.

McCarthy, J. D., and M. Zald. 1977. Resource mobilization and social movements: A partial theory. *American Journal of Sociology* 82 (May):1212–41.

McGuire, M. 1982. Feminist strike in San Jose. *Win* 18, no. 9:4–7.

McIntosh, M., A. Wong, N. Cagatay, U. Funk, H. Safa, L. Ahmed, D. Izraeli, K. Ahooja-Patel, and C. Bunch. 1981. Comments on Tinker's "A feminist view of Copenhagen." *Signs* 6, no. 4:771–89.

Macke, A. S. 1982. Using the National Longitudinal Surveys to examine changes in women's role behavior. *Journal of Social Issues* 38, no. 1:39–51.

Maitland, S. 1982. *A map of the new country: Women and Christianity.* Boston: Routledge, Kegan Paul.

Malos, E. 1978. Housework and the politics of women's liberation. *Socialist Revolution* 37:41–72.

———. 1980. *The politics of housework.* London: Allison & Busby.

Marano, C. 1980. Displaced homemakers: Critical needs and trends. Paper presented at Agricultural Outlook Conference, U.S. Department of Agriculture, Washington, D.C.

Martin, D. 1976. *Battered wives.* San Francisco: Glide; New York: Pocket Books, 1977.

Martin, S. E. 1980. *Breaking and entering: Policewomen on patrol.* Berkeley: Univ. of California Press.

Mason, K. O., and L. L. Bumpass. 1975. U.S. women's sex role ideology, 1970. *American Sociological Review* 40:1212–19.

Mason, K. O., J. Czajka, and S. Arber. 1976. Change in U.S. sex role attitudes, 1964–74. *American Sociological Review* 41:537–96.

Mead, M. 1935. *Sex and temperament in three savage societies.* New York: Wm. Morrow; New York: Dell, 1963.

Mies, M., and K. Jayawardena. 1981 *Feminism in Europe.* The Hague: Institute of Social Studies.

Miller, F. 1983. The end of SDS and the emergence of Weathermen: Demise through success. In *Social movements of the sixties and seventies,* ed. Jo Freeman, 279–300. New York: Longman.

Millett, K. 1970. *Sexual politics.* Garden City, N.Y.: Doubleday.

Milkman, R. 1979. Women's work and economic crises. In *A heritage of her own,* eds. N. F. Cott and E. H. Pleck. New York: Simon & Schuster.

———. 1982. Redefining "women's work": The sexual division of labor in the auto industry during World War II. *Feminist Studies* 8:336–71.

Molm, L. 1978 Sex role attitudes and the employment of married women: The direction of causality. *Sociological Quarterly* 19, no. 4:522–33.

Morgan, M. 1973. *The total woman.* New York: Pocket Books.

Morgan, R., ed. 1970. *Sisterhood is powerful: An anthology of writings from the women's liberation movement.* New York: Vintage.

Morgan, R. 1973. Lesbianism and feminism: Synonyms or contradictions. In *The lesbian tide.* Reprinted in Morgan, *Going too far.*

———. 1980. *Going too far.* New York: Random House.

———. 1982. *The anatomy of freedom.* New York: Doubleday.

Morris, M. 1973. Newspapers and the new feminists: Blackout as social control.

Journalism Quarterly 50:37–42.

Mottl, T. 1978. The analysis of countermovements. *Social Problems* 27:620–35.

Moynihan, D. P. 1965. *The Negro family: The case for national action.* Washington, D.C.: USGPO.

MS. 1982. No comment: The supposed death of feminism, July, 112.

Mueller, C. 1980. Feminism and the new woman in public office. Paper presented at the annual meeting of the Eastern Sociological Society.

———. 1983a. In search of a constituency for the new religious right. *Public Opinion Quarterly* 47, no. 2:213–28.

———. 1983. Women's movement success and the success of social movement theory. Paper presented at the conference on the Women's Movement in Comparative Perspective, Cornell University.

———, and T. Dimieri. 1982. The structure of belief systems among contending ERA activists. *Social Forces* 60:657–75.

Murray, P. 1984. Minority women and feminist spirituality. *Witness* 67, no. 2:5–9.

Myrdal, G. 1944. *An American dilemma.* New York: Harper & Row.

Nazzari, M. 1983. The woman question in Cuba: Some structural constraints on its solution. *Signs* 9, no. 2:246–63.

O'Brien, D. J. 1975. *Neighborhood organizations and interest groups.* Princeton: Princeton Univ. Press.

Ochs, C. 1977. *Behind the sex of God.* Boston: Beacon Press.

O'Connell, M. 1980. Women in the state police. Unpublished.

O'Farrell, B., and S. Harlan. 1982. Craftworkers and clerks: The effect of male co-worker hostility on women's satisfaction with non-traditional jobs. *Social Problems* 29, no. 3:252–64.

Olson, M. 1968. *The logic of collective action.* New York: Schocken.

O'Neill, W. 1969. *Everyone was brave: The rise and fall of feminism in America.* Chicago: Quadrangle Books.

O'Reilly, J. 1982. Phyllis Schlafly's last fling. *Ms.,* September, 46ff.

Paige, J. 1971. Political orientation and riot participation. *American Sociological Review* 36 (October):810–20.

Palmer, P. M. 1983. White women/black women: The dualism of female identity and experience in the U.S. *Feminist Studies* 9, no. 1:151–70.

Pearce, D. 1979. The feminization of poverty: Women, work and welfare. In *Working women and families,* ed. K. F. Feinstein, 103–24. Beverly Hills: Sage.

Petchesky, R. 1980. Reproductive freedom: Beyond a woman's right to choose. *Signs* 5, no. 4:661–85.

———. 1981. Antiabortion, antifeminism, and the rise of the New Right. *Feminist Studies* 7:206–46.

Pettigrew, T. F. 1979. The ultimate attribution error: Extending Allport's cognitive analysis of prejudice. *Personality and Social Psychology Bulletin* 5:461–71.

Piercy, M. 1970. The Grand Coolie Damn. In *Sisterhood is powerful,* ed. R. Morgan. New York: Vintage.

Pinard, M. 1968. Mass society and political movements: A new formulation. *Ameri-*

can Journal of Sociology 73 (May):682–90.

Pleck, J. 1979. Men's family roles: Three perspectives and some new data. *Family Co-ordinator,* October, 481–88.

Pogrebin, L. C. 1982. Anti-Semitism in the women's movement. *Ms.,* June, 45ff.

Randall, M. 1982. Nicaragua: A struggle for dignity. *Guardian: Independent Radical Newsweekly* 34, no. 2:510–11.

Reid, E. 1975. Between the official lines. *Ms.,* November, 88ff.

Rich, A. 1976. *Of woman born: Motherhood as experience and institution.* New York: Norton.

———. 1980. Compulsory heterosexuality and lesbian existence. *Signs* 5, no. 4:631–60.

Robinson, D. A. 1979. Two movements in pursuit of equal employment opportunity. *Signs* 4:413–33.

Roper Organization, Inc. 1980. *The 1980 Virginia Slims American women's opinion poll.* Storrs, Conn.: Roper Center.

Rossi, A., ed. 1973. *The feminist papers: From Adams to deBeauvoir.* New York: Columbia Univ. Press.

———. 1977. A biosocial perspective on parenting. *Daedalus* 106:1–31.

———. 1982. *Feminists in politics: A panel analysis of the first National Women's Conference.* New York: Academic Press.

Rothman, B. K. 1982. *In labor: Women and power in the birthplace.* New York: W. W. Norton.

Rothschild-Whitt, J. 1979. The collectivist organization: An alternative to rational-bureaucratic models. *American Sociological Review* 44:509–27.

Rubin, L. 1977. *Worlds of pain: Life in the working class family.* New York: Basic Books.

Ruddick, S. 1980. Maternal thinking. *Feminist Studies* 6, no. 3:343–67.

Ruether, R. 1983. *Sexism and God-talk: Toward a feminist theology.* Boston: Beacon Press.

Runciman, W. G. 1966. *Relative deprivation and social justice.* London: Routledge & Kegan Paul.

Rupp, L. 1979. Women's place is in the war: Propaganda and public opinion in the U.S. and Germany, 1939–1945. In *Women of America: A history,* ed. C. R. Berkin and M. B. Norton. Boston: Houghton Mifflin.

Russell, D. 1975. *The politics of rape: The victim's perspective.* New York: Stein & Day.

Ryan, M. P. 1979. *Womanhood in America.* 2d ed. New York: New Viewpoints.

———. 1981. *The Cradle of the middle class.* New York: Cambridge Univ. Press.

Rytina, N. 1981. Occupational segregation and earning differences by sex. *Monthly Labor Review,* January, 49–52.

Sargent, L. 1981. *Women and revolution.* Boston: South End Press.

Sayers, J. 1982. *Biological Politics: Feminist and antifeminist perspectives.* London: Tavistock.

Scharf, L. 1980. *To work and to wed: Female employment, feminism and the Great*

Depression. Westport, Conn.: Greenwood Press.

Scheppele, K. 1977. Feminism as a response to sociological ambivalence. Paper presented at the annual meeting of the American Sociological Association.

Schlesinger, M., and P. Bart. 1981. Collective work and self-identity: The effect of working in a feminist illegal abortion collective. In *Workplace democracy and social change,* ed. F. Lindenfeld and J. Rothschild-Whitt. Boston: Porter-Sargent.

Schneider, B. 1982. Consciousness about sexual harassment among heterosexual and lesbian women workers. *Journal of Social Issues* 38, no. 4:75–94.

Schrieber, E. M. 1978. Education and change in American opinions on a woman for president. *Public Opinion Quarterly* 42:171–82.

Scott, H. 1974. *Does socialism liberate women? Experiences from Eastern Europe.* Boston: Beacon Press.

Shaffer, H. 1981. *Women in the two Germanies.* Elmsford, N.Y.: Pergamon.

Shipp, E. R. 1984. A feminist offensive against exploitation. *New York Times,* 10 June.

Showalter, E. 1979. Feminism's awkward age: The deflated rebels of the 1920s. *Ms.,* January, 64–79.

Shulman, A. K. 1980. Sex and power: Sexual bases of radical feminism. *Signs* 5, no. 4:590–604.

Sidel, R. 1978. *Urban survival: The world of working class women.* Boston: Beacon Press.

Simons, M. 1979. Racism and feminism: A schism in the sisterhood. *Feminist Studies* 5:384–401.

Smelser, N. 1963. *A Theory of Collective Behavior.* New York: Free Press.

Smith, D. 1976. Sexual aggression in American pornography: The stereotype of rape. Paper presented at the American Sociological Association.

Smith, E. R., and J. R. Kluegel. 1984. Beliefs and attitudes about women's opportunity: Comparisons with beliefs about blacks and a general model. *Social Psychology Quarterly* 47, no. 1:81–94.

Sokoloff, N. 1981. *Between money and love: The dialectics of women's home and market work.* New York: Praeger.

Spitze, G., and J. Huber. 1982. Effects of anticipated consequences on ERA opinion. *Social Science Quarterly* 63:323–32.

Spock, B. 1945. *The common sense book of baby and child care.* New York: Duell, Sloan & Pearce; New York: Pocket Books, 1957.

Spretnak, C., ed. 1982. *The politics of women's spirituality: Essays on the rise of spiritual power within the feminist movement.* New York: Doubleday.

Stacey, J. 1983. The new conservative feminism. *Feminist Studies* 9:559–83.

Stiehm, J. 1982. Women, men, and military service: Is protection necessarily a racket? In *Women, power, and policy,* ed. E. Boneparth, 282–93. New York: Pergamon.

Stember, C. H. 1976. *Sexual racism.* New York: Harper & Row.

Steinem, G. 1983. An appeal to young women: Address to NWPC annual meeting, San Antonio, Spring 1983. Cited in *Comment* 14, no. 2.

Stimpson, C. 1971. *Thy neighbor's wife, thy neighbor's servants: Women's liberation and black civil rights.* In *Woman in sexist society,* ed. V. Gornick and B. K. Moran. New York: Basic Books.

Strasser, S. 1982. *Never done: A history of American housework.* New York: Pantheon.

Stricker, F. 1979. Cookbooks and lawbooks. In *A heritage of her own,* ed. N. F. Cott and E. H. Pleck. New York: Simon & Schuster.

Tangri, S., M. Burt, and L. Johnson. 1982. Sexual harassment at work: Three explanatory models. *Journal of Social Issues* 38, no. 4:33–54.

Tarrow, S. 1983. Struggling to reform: Social movements and policy change during cycles of protest. Western Societies Occasional Papers, no. 15, Center for International Studies, Cornell University.

Tax, M. 1981. *The rising of the women: Feminist solidarity and class consciousness, 1880–1917.* New York: Monthly Review Press.

Thom, M. 1984. The all-time definitive map of the gender gap. *Ms.,* July, 55–61.

Thornton, A., and D. Freedman, 1979. Changes in the sex role attitudes of women, 1962–1977: Evidence from a panel study. *American Sociological Review* 44:832–42.

Thornton, A., D. Alwin, and D. Camburn. 1983. Causes and consequences of sex role attitudes and attitude change. *American Sociological Review* 48:211–27.

Tiano, S. 1981. The separation of women's remunerated and household work. Paper given at the annual meeting of the American Sociological Association.

Tierney, K. 1982. The battered women's movement and the creation of the wife-beating problem. *Social Problems* 29:207–20.

Tiffany, J. 1982. Militant women for peace: International actions by women against militarism and nuclear technology. *New Women's Times* 8, no. 6:12–14.

Tilly, C. 1978. *From mobilization to revolution.* Reading, Mass.: Addison Wesley.

Tinker, I. 1981. A feminist view of Copenhagen. *Signs* 6:531–37.

Tobin, S. 1983. Why not a feminist? *Feminist Special,* Spring, 6–9.

Treiman, D., and H. Hartmann. 1981. *Women, work and wages: Equal pay for jobs of equal value.* Washington, D. C.: National Academy Press.

Trimberger, M. K. 1979. Women in the Old and New Left: The evolution of a politics of personal life. *Feminist Studies* 5:432–50.

Tuchman, G. 1978. *Making news: A study in the construction of reality.* New York: Free Press.

U.S. Bureau of the Census. 1975. *Historical statistics of the United States: Colonial times to 1970.* Washington D.C.: USGPO.

———. 1981. *Statistical abstract of the United States: 1981.* Washington, D.C.: USGPO.

———. 1983a. Money income and poverty status of families and persons in the U.S., 1982. *Current Population Reports* P-60, no. 140 (July).

———. 1983b. *Statistical abstract of the United States, 1982–3.* Washington, D.C.: USGPO.

———. 1983c. Child support and alimony, 1981. *Current Population Reports* P-23, no. 124 (Advance Report, May).

———. 1983d. Household and family characteristics, March, 1982. *Current Population Reports* P-20, no. 381 (May).

———. 1983e. Childcare arrangements of working mothers: June 1982. *Current Population Reports* P-23, no. 129 (November).

———. 1984. *Fertility of American women: June, 1983. Current Population Reports* P-20, no. 386 (Advance Report, April).

U.S. Department of Education. 1982. *Digest of educational statistics.* National Center for Educational Statistics. Washington, D.C.: USGPO.

U.S. Department of Labor. 1980. Earnings and other characteristics of organized workers, May 1980. *Bureau of Labor Statistics, Bulletin 2105.* Washington, D.C.: USGPO.

U.S. Department of Labor. 1982. The female-male earnings gap: A review of employment and earnings issues. *Bureau of Labor Statistics Report 673.* Washington, D.C.: USGPO.

U.S. Merit Systems Protection Board. 1981. *Sexual harassment in the workplace: Is it a problem?* Washington, D.C.: USGPO.

Vandepol, A. 1982. Dependent children, child custody, and mothers' pensions: The transformation of state-family relationships in the early 20th century. *Social Problems* 29:221–35.

Vanek, J. 1974. Time spent in housework. *Scientific American,* November, 116–20.

VanGelder, L. 1970. The trials of Lois Lane. In *Sisterhood is powerful,* ed. R. Morgan. New York: Vintage.

———. 1978. Four days that changed the world: Behind the scenes at Houston. *Ms.,* March, 54ff.

Vanneman, R., and T. F. Pettigrew. 1972. Race and relative deprivation in the U.S. *Race* 13, no. 4:461–86.

Verba, S., and N. Nie. 1972. *Participation in America.* New York: Harper & Row.

Verba, S., G. Orren, and G. D. Ferree. 1985. *Equality in America.* Cambridge: Harvard Univ. Press.

Viguerie, R. 1980. *The New Right: We're ready to lead.* Falls Church, Va.: Viguerie.

Walker, K., and M. Woods. 1976. Time use: A measure of household production of family goods and services. Paper presented at the annual meeting of the American Home Economics Association.

Wallace, M. 1982. A black feminist's search for sisterhood. In *But some of us are brave,* ed. G. Hull, P. Scott, and B. Smith, 5–12. Old Westbury, N.Y.: Feminist Press.

Walshok, M. L. 1981. *Blue collar women: Pioneers on the male frontier.* Garden City, N.Y.: Anchor Books.

Ware, S. 1981. *Beyond suffrage: Women in the New Deal.* Cambridge: Harvard Univ. Press.

WEAL, 1983. *Washington Report,* June–July, 3.

Weber, M. 1922. *Wirtschaft und gesellschaft.* Tübingen: Mohr. English edition: 1947. *The Theory of Social and Economic Organization,* trans. A. M. Henderson and T. Parsons. New York: Oxford Univ. Press.

Weinbaum, B. 1978. *The curious courtship of women's liberation and socialism.* Boston: South End Press.

Weinbaum, B., and A. Bridges. 1979. The other side of the paycheck: Monopoly capital and the structure of consumption. In *Capitalist patriarchy and the case for socialist feminism,* ed. Z. Eisenstein, 190–205. New York: Monthly Review Press.

Weisstein, N. 1968. *Kinder, kirche* and *kuche* as scientific law: Psychology constructs the female. In *Sisterhood is powerful,* ed. R. Morgan. Boston: New England Free Press; New York: Vintage, 1970.

Welch, S. 1975. Support among women for the issues of the women's movement. *Sociological Quarterly* 16:216–27.

Wells, R. V. 1979. Women's lives transformed: Demographic and family patterns in America, 1600–1970. In *Women of America: A history,* ed. C. R. Berkin and M. B. Norton. Boston: Houghton Mifflin.

Willis, E. 1970. Women and the left. In *Notes from the second year,* ed. Anne Koedt and S. Firestone. New York: New York Radical Feminists.

Wilson, J. 1973. *Introduction to social movements.* New York: Basic Books.

Withorn, B. 1980. Helping ourselves. *Radical America,* May–June, 25–38.

Women's Action Almanac, 1980. New York: Wm. Morrow.

Yankelovich, D. 1981. *New rules: Searching for self-fulfillment in a world turned upside down.* New York: Random House.

Zinn, H. 1964. *SNCC: The new abolitionists.* Boston: Beacon Press.

SELECTED BIBLIOGRAPHY

Banks, Olive. *Faces of Feminism.* New York: St. Martin's Press, 1981. A historical account of the development of modern feminism in both Britain and the United States, emphasizing the three different traditions—moral reform, liberalism, socialism—that have nurtured feminist thought and activities. The differing importance of these three traditions in the United States and Britain accounts for differences in the direction of recent feminist ideas in the two countries.

Boles, Janet. *The Politics of the ERA.* New York: Longman, 1979. An analysis of why the ratification of the Equal Rights Amendment was able to get off to a quick start, but eventually stalled in the state legislatures. The case studies of early, late, and nonratifying states also provide insights into the dynamics of feminist organizing in the state capitols.

Boneparth, Ellen. *Women, Power, and Policy.* New York: Pergamon, 1981. A collection of diverse essays covering a range of important policy questions facing feminists, from pornography to the draft. The institutionalization of the women's movement as an interest group provides a central focus, and the essay by Costain on this topic is especially noteworthy.

Carden, Maren Lockwood. *The New Feminist Movement.* New York: Russell Sage, 1974. One of the earliest accounts of the reemergence of feminism, this book remains a valuable description of the diverse activities of the early years. Identifies incipient problems and strains that developed in later years, such as the role of lesbians in the movement and the feminist ambivalence about power.

Cassell, Joan. *A Group Called Women.* New York: David McKay, 1977. An anthropologist's view of the small groups of the collectivist strand in the early years. The discussions of the symbols used to create feelings of sisterhood and of the processes of collective decision making convey the flavor of the interactions of those times.

Conover, Pamela, and Gray, Virginia. *Feminism and the New Right.* New York: Praeger, 1983. An analysis of the struggle between feminists and antifeminists over the ERA and abortion, and the relation of both of these activist groups to the opinions of the nonactivist public. They examine the obstacles both groups face, the resources they draw on, and the successes they have had. On the basis of considerable and diverse data, they conclude that the strength and success of the New Right have been usually overestimated, but that this counter-mobilization by antifeminists changes the nature of the problems feminists confront.

Davis, Angela. *Women, Race, and Class.* New York: Random House, 1981. A fascinating history of the usually invisible struggles of poor women and black women against sexism, relating that history to struggles going on today. Davis makes the connections between basic feminism and fighting for an education or a decent wage, and thus provides a useful introduction to socialist feminist analysis.

Evans, Sara. *Personal Politics: The Roots of the Women's Movement in Civil Rights and the New Left.* New York: Vintage, 1979. Evans's compelling account of the position and contributions of women in the social movements of the sixties tells how these women rediscovered feminism, and how this eventually led to the formation of a separate women's movement. Based on interviews with nearly all the principals involved, this oral history of the emergence of the collectivist strand clarifies important concepts such as sexism and consciousness-raising.

Flexner, Eleanor. *A Century of Struggle.* Cambridge: Harvard University Press, 1959. This is the classic history of feminism from the earliest stirrings in America to the passage of the suffrage amendment. While later scholarship has supplemented this story, it has not supplanted this book as an informative and inspiring view of what feminists have done.

Freeman, Jo. *The Politics of Women's Liberation.* New York: David McKay, 1975. The definitive analysis of the two branches of feminism in the early 1970s, including consideration of the strengths and weaknesses of each, and of the networks from which they drew their adherents. Freeman relates the internal dynamics of each branch to its goals and to the outcomes it can expect to obtain, and views the older branch as successfully influencing public policy.

Friedan, Betty. *The Feminine Mystique.* New York: Dell, 1963. An important view of where we were twenty years ago, and therefore an invaluable reference point for how far we have come—as well as how far we have yet to go. Friedan's picture of what it meant to be a housewife in the 1950s is still compelling, even though she unfortunately restricts her analysis to college-educated women and ends up suggesting reforms that institutionalize a double day of housework and paid work for women.

Fritz, Leah. *Dreamers and Dealers.* Boston: Beacon Press, 1979. Fritz conveys the excitement of the early days with a close-up view of the action in this personal chronicle of her involvement in the emerging movement in New York City. The pictures of the strains between the "respectable" women and the "radicals," the surfacing of lesbianism as an issue, and the overall political climate of the times are especially vivid and insightful.

Gelb, Joyce, and Palley, Marion. *Women and Public Policies.* Princeton: Princeton University Press, 1982. A scholarly analysis of the transformation of part of the movement into an organized and effective interest group. The authors describe in detail the role of this interest group in achieving certain key policy victories for women. By following the struggles over policy on a few select issues, Gelb and Palley are able to make clear what feminist organizations do in Washington and why implementation is even more important than legislation in securing women's rights.

Hooks, Bell. *Ain't I a Woman: Black Women and Feminism.* Boston: South End Press, 1981. An effective description of the ways white women's and middle-class women's perspectives have been taken for granted by the movement as a whole, despite the participation of individual black women and their efforts to challenge these assumptions. Hooks also offers constructive alternatives that focus on restructuring the economic system to serve the needs of the poor.

Joseph, Gloria, and Lewis, Jill. *Common Differences.* Garden City, N.Y.: Doubleday, 1981. An unusual and self-revealing dialogue between a black feminist and a white feminist about the issues that unite and divide them. While the authors can scarcely be seen as representatives of all women of their race, each has the opportunity to comment on the assumptions the other takes for granted and to make her own priorities clear, which may provide an example of constructive debate for other feminists to follow.

McGlen, Nancy, and O'Connor, Karen. *Women's Rights: The Struggle for Equality in the 19th and 20th Centuries.* New York: Praeger, 1983. A history of feminism that presents connections between the struggles of feminists in the ninteenth century and those of present days, focusing on issues of attaining political, educational, employment, and family rights. By presenting the historical dimension of existing rights for women, as well as the continuing limits on these rights, the authors make clear that women's rights have not evolved, but have been painstakingly achieved.

Rossi, Alice. *The Feminist Papers.* New York: Columbia University Press, 1973. This volume presents an essential historical overview of feminist writings by combining long excerpts from the writings themselves with extensive commentary on the biography of the writer and the nature of the times in which she wrote.

————. *Feminists in Politics.* New York: Academic Press, 1982. An analysis of the current feminist struggles based on a survey of delegates in the IWY convention in Houston, both feminist and antifeminist. By surveying delegates both before and after the convention, Rossi examines the effects of the convention as a political event and as a meeting place for feminists of very different backgrounds. The priorities revealed in this survey give direction to current feminist efforts and indicate likely conflicts and changes in future years.

INDEX

DATE DUE			
JUN 9 '90			
MAR 1 4 '94			
OCT 17 '94			
MAR 1 4 '95			
JUN 05 '95			
AUG 1 0 1999			
OCT 2 3 1999			
DEC 0 3 2001			